The
Pirenne Thesis

Analysis, Criticism and Revision

PROBLEMS IN
EUROPEAN CIVILIZATION

Under the editorial direction of
John Ratté
Amherst College

The Pirenne Thesis

Analysis, Criticism, and Revision

Third Edition

Edited and with an introduction by

Alfred F. Havighurst
Amherst College

D.C. HEATH AND COMPANY
Lexington, Massachusetts   Toronto   London

PREFACE TO THE THIRD EDITION

In this edition the selections that appeared in the second edition remain almost intact. There are, however, significant additions. One is an excerpt from Howard L. Adelson's important article "Early Medieval Trade Routes," and the selection from Philip Grierson's well-known "Commerce in the Dark Ages: A Critique of the Evidence" has been expanded, thus giving more space to actual analysis of evidence. Lynn White Jr.'s examination of medieval technology, which was represented in the first edition, is restored, this time from a later publication. The two final selections, entirely new to this collection, underline the continuing controversy—an effective challenge to Pirenne from William C. Bark, written in 1958, and still one of the finest discussions we have; and a well-informed, clearly stated summary of the "present status" of the Pirenne thesis, emphasizing those aspects that have withstood attack, from Bryce Lyon's authoritative biography of Pirenne published in 1974.

I wish to thank the scholars, represented in this collection, for their interest, assistance, and good will.

Amherst, Massachusetts
February 1975   A. F. H.

CONTENTS

INTRODUCTION

The "Pirenne Thesis" is a set of ideas developed by the celebrated Belgian historian, Henri Pirenne (1862–1935) concerning the transition from classical antiquity to medieval civilization—a problem which, from about 1930, dominated the study of the early Middle Ages for two generations, transforming a static period into one marked by dynamic research and reinterpretation. To subject the Pirenne thesis to analysis, criticism, and revision was to pose problems in historical method (how one arrives at historical "truth"); in historical interpretation (the relation of ideas to evidence); in historiography (the nature of historical narrative); and in the philosophy of history (what *is* history after all?).

So accepted today is the idea that the early Middle Ages, in the eyes of historians, is a fluid period, that it is with astonishment we read the pronouncement made in 1906 by Professor George Burton Adams of Yale, then a prominent medievalist:

> We may, I think, say with truth that there is no other considerable portion of history . . . that has been as yet investigated with such minuteness as that which embraces the history of Europe from the beginning of the fifth century to the end of the ninth, and we may add that . . . regarding all questions of importance in this field, there is now a nearly or quite general consensus of opinion among scholars. . . . I wish to be distinctly understood to raise [the] question . . . whether we ought not now to expect and encourage as the next proper advance of our work attempts at a final constructive history of this age.[1]

The historical interpretation of the early Middle Ages of Professor Adams's day became, if not "final," something of a dogma, resisting

[1] "The Present Problems of Medieval History," *Congress of Arts and Sciences,* ed. Howard J. Rogers, II (New York, 1906), pp. 126–29.

change. It was a view that gave isolated and perfunctory treatment to Byzantium and Islam, and then turned wholeheartedly to the West: the Merovingians and Clovis, the Carolingians and Charlemagne, then the stem duchies in Germany and the Capetians in France, and the rest. Even the *Cambridge Medieval History* (8 vols.; 1911–1936), which brought together the scholarship of distinguished medievalists from many countries, still treated the Byzantine and Arab worlds as quite apart from the West, and the emphasis throughout remained narrowly political and religious; encyclopedic in character, no interpretation or philosophy integrated its various sections. The abridged version was out-of-date at publication, and it was then observed that the appearance of this *Shorter Cambridge Medieval History* (1952) probably marked the end of medieval history written as past politics organized around dynastic periods. For, under quite different controlling assumptions, the story of the early Middle Ages had for some years been in the process of revision, and many of the very historians who had contributed to the *Cambridge History* were participating in this revision. As new questions were asked, the evidence of the past was brought into sharper focus, yielding greater knowledge and new understanding.

Powerful and original minds have, in the course of the twentieth century, recast the historical image of the early Middle Ages, as comparison of standard works before 1914 with those of sixty years later readily reveals. Thus Charles Diehl (French) and Norman H. Baynes (British) have debated, to the delight and instruction of their readers, the nature of Byzantine civilization—Was it essentially Greco-Roman, or was it something quite alien, that is, Oriental? Thus Philip Hitti (Lebanese-American) on the Arabs and Islam; thus Marc Bloch (hero of the French Resistance in World War II) on French rural history. But if there was any individual in particular who upset the tranquility of the historian's world it was Henri Pirenne, national historian of Belgium and long associated with the University of Ghent. One encounters him wherever one turns in the historiography on the Middle Ages of the past fifty years.

His most enduring achievement, no doubt, was his seven-volume *Histoire de Belgique,* published from 1899 to 1932,[2] together with a collection of source materials, *Bibliographie de l'Histoire de Belgique,* first published in 1893, with a third edition in 1931. But his

---

[2] The fine 1952 edition, in four volumes, is illustrated and includes *La Belgique et la Guerre Mondiale.*

international fame as a medievalist springs from two revolutionary ideas. The first of these was his explanation of the origin of medieval towns in the tenth and eleventh centuries, which was developed when he was still comparatively young—just before and just after the turn of the century. He found the answer not, as did others, in the transfer of political authority from feudal lords to communities, but rather in economic and social forces creating a new order. In time his interpretations received wide acceptance, and some would say these conclusions constitute his most definitive contribution to historical scholarship.[3]

But as his life and study progressed, Pirenne became concerned with even larger problems, and he framed wider hypotheses for dealing with them. Put in the most general terms, the question he faced and which, as a consequence of his influence, the whole of early medieval scholarship has confronted since, is that of the relation of Roman antiquity to the First Europe. Some historians at least had been aware of what they were doing when they divided the story of Western civilization into the Ancient World, the Middle Ages, and Modern Times. They realized of course that such periodization is arbitrary. But repetition of language tends to influence thought. It came to be taken for granted that the "Ancient World" and the "Middle Ages" were easily distinguished the one from the other, and that a distinct break came in the fifth century with the disappearance of "Roman" emperors in the West, the emergence of "Germanic" kingdoms, and the triumph of Christianity. These developments, with slight accommodation, could be treated as simultaneous and dramatized in a comparatively brief span of years, and thus regarded as heralding a new epoch. Such certainly was the textbook point of view; with some qualifications, it was a controlling assumption of scholars as well.

A quite radically different concept came out of the investigations of Pirenne. He concluded that the Roman world—economically, culturally, and even, in essence, politically—continued in all important particulars through the centuries of the German invasions. It was rather the impact of Islam in the seventh and eighth centuries which, by destroying the unity of the Mediterranean, ended the Roman world and led to a strikingly different civilization in the Carolingian era.

---

[3] Pirenne developed his interpretation in a series of articles from 1893 to 1905. See Bryce Lyon, *Henri Pirenne: A Biographical and Intellectual Study* (Ghent, 1974), pp. 96–97, 117, 122–27, 161–62.

"Without Islam the Frankish Empire would probably never have existed and Charlemagne, without Mahomet, would be inconceivable," he wrote in a famous sentence.

These ideas of the Pirenne thesis took shape over a period of years. It was during World War I, when Pirenne was held prisoner by the Germans, that his mind began to turn and to return to the problem of the end of the ancient world. During the early twenties research developed and refined his ideas to which he soon gave currency. "Mahomet et Charlemagne" in 1922 was followed by "Un contraste économique: Mérovingiens et Carolingiens" in 1923, both articles in the *Revue Belge de Philologie et d'Histoire*. In 1922 he was in America, lecturing in a more popular manner before university audiences on his ideas about both the beginning of the Middle Ages and his earlier construct, the medieval town. These lectures were published by Princeton University Press in 1925 as *Medieval Cities*. At the Sixth International Congress of Historical Sciences at Oslo in 1928, Pirenne read a paper, "L'expansion d'Islam et le commencement du moyen âge," to the opening plenary session. Animated discussion ensued—French, German, Polish, Italian, Dutch and Hungarian scholars participating, with Pirenne stoutly adhering to this position in the face of criticism. Reflection and research continued, tested in articles and public lectures, especially in 1933–1934. His hypothesis and the supporting evidence was so well established in his mind that when he began, on January 14, 1935, the manuscript of *Mahomet et Charlemagne,* the first draft was completed in less than four months. But soon beset with illness he did not live to put his manuscript in final form.[4] He died in October 1935. *Mahomet et Charlemagne* was published in 1937, with an English edition in 1939. But *Medieval Cities* had long since given wide circulation to the Pirenne thesis. "No volume of similar size," wrote Professor Gray C. Boyce in 1941, "has so affected medieval historical scholarship in many generations."[5]

Pirenne's argument rests, in the main, upon the nature and extent of trade in the Mediterranean and in Western Europe from the fifth to the ninth centuries; consequently, economic historians especially are drawn into the debate. But his impact has also been very considerable in Byzantine studies, for Pirenne lengthened the unity of the Mediterranean world and the control of Roman ideas; upon German

---

[4] For more details concerning Pirenne's research, see *ibid.*, pp. 324–28, 374–75, 387.
[5] *Byzantion* 15 (1940–41): 460, n. 25.

historians, for he tended to minimize the Germanic contribution to Western civilization; upon historians of Islam, whose story now became a central theme in European history; and upon philosophers of history concerned with theories of change.

The issues raised by Pirenne may be summarized by the following four categories of consideration.

1. What developments in human experience distinguish the Roman world from the Middle Ages? When do we begin to think in terms of the First Europe? This is the central question, and, as W. C. Bark suggests,[6] to answer it we must define such terms as Middle Ages and First Europe; and in talking about when they came into being, we must decide how they began.

2. In considering such matters we confront other questions: What was the impact of the Germans on Rome and Western Europe, and what was that of the Arabs? Is either closely associated with the "fall" of Rome and the advent of a new civilization?

3. Geographically we are concerned mainly with the land of the Franks. What, then, was the character of the Merovingian era (roughly the fifth to the eighth centuries), and what that of the Carolingian era (the eighth and ninth centuries), and further, what is their relation one to the other? Are they in sharp contrast or do they present essential continuity?

4. Since Pirenne's arguments derive chiefly from trade and industry, what can historians conclude about commerce in the Mediterranean and in Western Europe from 400–1000? This is a difficult and controversial question indeed, since the evidence is so limited, "little more than occasional chronicle references and some archaeological data in the form of coin finds," as one historian recently summarized this problem.[7]

It is to Pirenne's research and conclusions on these matters, to the controversy his thesis generated, and to the new vitality of early medieval studies to which it so powerfully contributed that the attention of the student is directed in this problem.

We first study Pirenne's exposition in the attractive *Medieval Cities*. Then from more detailed treatment in *Mohammed and Charlemagne* we have his conclusions, in summary form, on the significance of the Germanic invasions of the Roman Empire, a brief statement of the nature of Islamic expansion into the Mediterra-

---

[6] *Origins of the Medieval World* (Stanford, 1958), p. 3.
[7] Gerald A. J. Hodgett, *A Social and Economic History of Medieval Europe* (London, 1972), p. 47.

nean and the West, and then a more elaborate presentation, comparing "Political Organization" and "Intellectual Civilization" in the Merovingian and Carolingian periods. The text in *Mohammed and Charlemagne* has two limitations. The first, and the more important, is that we cannot be absolutely sure that in all respects the published text represents Pirenne's views, for he left the manuscript in rough form; considerable editing was necessary. The second limitation is the English translation, as published, which is often infelicitous, occasionally misleading, and sometimes inaccurate. The translation used in our selection attempts to remedy these defects.

To provide discussion and criticism of the Pirenne thesis, from a vast body of commentary available have been chosen articles and books on the basis of their scholarly qualities and their usefulness to students encountering the early Middle Ages in depth for the first time. The selections have also been chosen and arranged so as to indicate something of the trend over the years of the response to Pirenne. Initially, much of the reaction, though admiring, was skeptical. Professor Norman H. Baynes, writing in 1929, finds little support for Pirenne in contemporary sources from the Merovingian period and suggests that the unity of the Mediterranean was actually broken by Vandal pirates in the sixth century. An associate of Baynes, H. St. L. B. Moss, writing some eight years later, declared that "the onus of proof . . . lies on those who would seek to show that industry and trade suffered no vital and permanent setback when the fall of the Empire had removed the unified framework of civil and military defense."

Thereafter, the evidence is more thoroughly examined and reexamined. In a well-known article published in 1943 Professor Robert S. Lopez held untenable Pirenne's position that trade between East and West all but disappeared in the Carolingian era. A few years later an Arabic specialist, Dr. Daniel C. Dennett, tells us that "there is no evidence to prove that the Arabs either desired to close, or actually did close the Mediterranean to the commerce of the West either in the seventh or eighth centuries."

In the fifties a bolder position was developed by certain scholars who maintained that Pirenne was strangely parochial, even naive, in limiting his analysis to the south and west. This group is represented in our discussion by Professor Sture Bolin, a Swedish scholar, who studied the Baltic and North Sea areas and concluded on the basis of literary sources supported by evidence from numismatics that the

Carolingian Franks were the commercial links between the Arabs and the Varangians. A distinguished French scholar, Professor Robert Latouche, explains his rejection of the Pirenne theory of the "Grand Commerce" of the Merovingian period. The appeal to numismatics is further presented in interesting fashion by Professor Howard L. Adelson. But this is a highly controversial matter, as at once evident in the forceful selection by Professor Philip Grierson.

These excerpts provide ample evidence of the truism that the study of the past provides no answers unless questions are first asked. But Dennett, in the selection included in this book, found the question of trade, which so occupied Pirenne, too narrow and too dogmatic. "Economic factors," he declared, "play a subsidiary role and present merely aspects in the great causative process." And Anne Riising, in an article written in 1952 (not included in our selections) expressed doubt that the proper questions had been asked. She declared that "much vagueness and many possibilities of conflict have been caused by lack of clear definitions," and that "more than anything else a revision of the very formulation of the problem is needed." Such a restatement is included below. It is from an American scholar, Paul Craig Roberts, who observes that the validity of the Pirenne thesis rests not on the volume of trade in the Merovingian period but on the quality of that trade. On the other hand, a fellow American, Professor Lynn White, concludes that the essential problem posed by Pirenne was how to explain "the transfer of Europe's center of gravity from the Mediterranean to the great northern plains." He finds the answer in an agricultural revolution in the early Middle Ages.

The analysis concludes with two selections that summarize the problem as it now stands and which provide some perspective. William Carroll Bark's challenge to Pirenne is no less effective today than when written in 1958. We are also fortunate in having an up-to-date (1974) summary of the problem from a long-time student of Pirenne, Bryce Lyon, who has just capped his Pirenne studies with a definitive examination of Pirenne's life and thought.

The catastrophic role in the transition from Rome to the First Europe attributed by Pirenne to the Arabs has been generally rejected as contrary to the evidence. On the other hand, most historians do now accept his larger concept that a new civilization, radically different from antiquity, did not emerge in Western Europe until the eighth century. We may go further and say that Pirenne has left a permanent imprint, at least for our time, upon medieval studies; nearly every historian thinks differently because of him. Put in context his central contribution would appear to be this: to emancipate medieval historians from interests too exclusively political, legal, and religious in nature; to gain recognition of the importance of Islam and of Byzantium in the story of Western civilization; and to make historians more aware of the limits of understanding and the errors in interpretation which follow from facile periodization of European history.

But Pirenne's stature is even larger when one considers his conception of the nature of historical truth. Any subsequent research demonstrating that he overstated some of his conclusions would not have disturbed him. This was well understood by one of his most learned and articulate critics, Robert Latouche. Pirenne, wrote Latouche,

> *had too keen a sense of reality to wish to see his own ideas and even his most fruitful hypotheses interpreted too rigidly. In order to throw his ideas into bolder relief, he liked to strike hard and often, leaving to those who followed him the more thankless task of refining and elaborating them.*[8]

But Pirenne's own language was even more refined. Midway in his career he observed:

> *All those engaged in searching for the truth know that the glimpses they have of it are necessarily fugitive. The images glitter for an instant to make way for new and always more dazzling transparencies. Quite different from that of the artist, the work of the scholar is inevitably provisional. He knows this and rejoices in it, for the rapid obsoleteness of his books is the very proof of the progress of his science.*[9]

Analysis, criticism and revision would likely have had Pirenne's blessing.

[8] Robert Latouche, *The Birth of the Western Economy* (London, 1961), p. 143.
[9] As quoted in Georges Gérardy, *Henri Pirenne, sa vie et son oeuvre* (Brussels, 1962), p. 4 (editor's translation).

Chronological Table

Roman Empire

A.D. 284–305	Diocletian, *Roman Emperor*
306–337	Constantine I (The Great), *Roman Emperor*
330	*Byzantium rebuilt as Constantinople*
379–395	Theodosius I (The Great), *Roman Emperor*
395	*Permanent division of Empire, East and West*
474–491	Zeno, *East Roman Emperor*
476	*Deposition of the last Roman Emperor in the West* (Romulus Augustus); *replaced by the German,* Odoacer.
527–565	Justinian, *East Roman Emperor*
610–641	Heraclius I, *East Roman Emperor*
717–741	Leo III (The Isaurian), *East Roman Emperor*

Germania

ca. 370	*Pressure of Huns on Goths in Eastern Europe*
378	*Battle of Adrianople; Visigoths defeat Romans*
395	*Huns* (Attila) *on the Danube*
451	*Final Defeat of Huns at Châlons* (Champagne)
395–408	*Visigothic Revolt* (Alaric) *against Eastern Empire*
410	*Visigothic "Sack of Rome"*
ca. 400–600	*Visigothic Kingdom in Southern Gaul and Spain (Continues in Spain until 711)*
ca. 420	*Beginnings of Anglo-Saxon Invasions of Britain*
ca. 400–430	*Franks, Burgundians, Vandals cross the Rhine into Gaul*
ca. 400–600	*Burgundian Kingdom in Rhone Valley (Absorbed by Franks, end of 6th century)*
ca. 429–534	*Vandal Kingdom in North Africa (Reconquered by Justinian)*
455	*Vandals* (Gaiseric) *plunder Rome*
ca. 400–751	*Merovingian Kingdom of the Franks in Gaul*
481–511	Clovis, *Merovingian King of the Franks*
538–594	Gregory, *Bishop of Tours (History of the Franks)*
639–751	*Rois Fainéants, Merovingian Kingdom of Franks in Gaul*

Romania

476	*Deposition of* Romulus Augustus, *last Roman-born Emperor of West*

476–493	Odoacer, *King of the Romans*
489	Theodoric *leads Ostrogoths from Eastern Empire into Italy*
493–526	Theodoric, *Ostrogothic King of Italy (Ravenna)*
ca. 480–575	Cassiodorus, *Roman statesman and scholar*
480–525	Boethius, *Roman statesman and philosopher*
535–553	Justinian's *Reconquest (under* Belisarius) *of Africa, Italy, Sicily, and portions of Spain*
539–751	*Byzantine Exarchy in Ravenna*
552	*First appearance of Lombards (federated with Eastern Empire against the Ostrogoths)*
568	*Lombards conquer Po Valley*

Christianity

313	*Edict of Milan, Toleration of Christianity*
325	*Council of Nicaea*
354–430	St. Augustine of Hippo
379	*Death of* St. Basil
440–461	Leo I (The Great), *Bishop of Rome ("Pope")*
ca. 480–550	St. Benedict
ca. 590	St. Columban (Irish) *comes to Gaul*
590–604	Pope Gregory I (The Great)
597	St. Augustine (Benedictine) *lands in Britain*
ca. 673–735	The Venerable Bede
ca. 675–754	St. Boniface

Islam

ca. 570–632	Mohammed
632	*Beginning of Caliphate* (Abu Bakr)
634–644	Omar Caliph *and Conquest of Syria, Persia, and Egypt*
661–750	Omayyad *Caliphate at Damascus*
661–680	Muawiya, *first Omayyad Caliph*
685–705	Abdu-l-Malik, *Caliph*
711	*Islam reaches Spain*
732	*Battle of Tours; defeat of the Arabs by Charles Martel*
750–1258	Abbasid *Caliphate at Bagdad*
786–809	Harun-al-Raschid, *Caliph at Bagdad*

Carolingian Frankish Kingdom

| 687–714 | Pepin of Heristal, *Mayor of the Palace* |
| 714–741 | Charles Martel, *Mayor of the Palace* |

741–768	Pepin the Short, *Mayor of the Palace and (751) King of the Franks*
751	*Lombards take Ravenna*
768–814	Charlemagne, *King of the Franks, King of the Lombards, Emperor of the Romans*
782	Alcuin of York *comes to Palace School at Aachen*
800	*Coronation of* Charlemagne *at Rome as Emperor*
814–840	Louis the Pious, *Emperor*
843	*Peace of Verdun, beginning of breakup of Carolingian Empire*

Conflict of Opinion

I. What was the origin of the "First Europe"? How was the world of antiquity which we call Roman transformed into the medieval society we call European? From the eighteenth century of Edward Gibbon until well into the twentieth century such questions gave historians little trouble.

> If we must select any year as the dividing line between ancient history and the Middle Ages, it is impossible to choose a better date than 476 [the year in which the last Roman emperor, Romulus Augustus, was deposed by the German, Odoacer]. . . . It is . . . in every way correct, as well as convenient to style him [Odoacer] as the first German king of Italy and to treat his reign as the commencement of a new era.
>
> —Charles Oman (1898)

However, historical scholarship of the past half-century has submitted the role of the Germans and the whole story of the transition to medieval society to reappraisal.

> Few historians today can still pretend that the Germanic invasions of the fourth and fifth centuries were catastrophic for Western Europe, destroying ancient civilization and launching centuries of "Gothic barbarism."
>
> —Bryce Lyon (1960)

II. A brilliant contribution was made by Henri Pirenne, who put forth the view that it was the Moslems in the seventh and eighth centuries, and not the Germans in the fifth, who destroyed the Roman world.

The sources for the statements in this Conflict of Opinion are as follows: Charles Oman, *The Dark Ages, 476–918* (1898), pp. 3, 5; Bryce Lyon, "L'Oeuvre de Henri Pirenne après vingt-cinq ans," *Le Moyen Age*, 66 (1960); 474; Henri Pirenne, *Mohammed and Charlemagne* (1939), pp. 164, 234, and *Medieval Cities* (1948), p. 29; H. St. L. B. Moss, "The Economic Consequences of the Barbarian Invasions," *Economic History Review* 7 (1936–1937): 215; Daniel C. Dennett, Jr., "Pirenne and Muhammad," *Speculum* 23 (April 1948): 189; Archibald R. Lewis, *Naval Power and Trade in the Mediterranean: A.D. 500–1100* (1951), pp. 97, 130; Robert Latouche, *The Birth of Western Economy* (1961), p. 125; Sture Bolin, "Mohammed, Charlemagne and Ruric," *Scandinavian Economic History Review* 1 (1953): 9, 27; Karl F. Morrison, "Numismatics and Carolingian Trade: A Critique of the Evidence," *Speculum* 38 (July 1963): 409; Gerald A. J. Hodgett, *A Social and Economic History of Medieval Europe* (London, 1972), p. 46; William Carroll Bark, *Origins of the Medieval World* (1958), p. 6; Lynn White, Jr., *The Transformation of the Roman World* (1966), pp. 301, 308; Bryce Lyon, *Henri Pirenne: A Biographical and Intellectual Study* (1974), p. 456; Paul Craig Roberts, "The Pirenne Thesis: Economies or Civilizations? Towards Reformulation," *Classica et Mediaevalia* 25 (1964): 314.

Islam had shattered the Mediterranean unity which the Germanic invasions had left intact. This was the most essential event of European history which had occurred since the Punic Wars. It was the end of the classic tradition. It was the beginning of the Middle Ages.

Without Mohammed Charlemagne would have been inconceivable.
—Henri Pirenne (1937)

Pirenne opened up the larger question of the nature of historical change from the fifth century to the tenth. Did Roman civilization survive as the basis for western civilization, or was there a break—perhaps a catastrophic break—in the fifth century or in the eighth? Pirenne found the answer in an analysis of trade.

In the days of the Merovingians, Gaul was still a maritime country, and trade and traffic flourished because of that fact. The Empire of Charlemagne, on the contrary, was essentially an inland one; . . . it was a closed State, a State without foreign markets, living in a condition of almost complete isolation.
—Henri Pirenne (1925)

III. This matter of trade became the focal point in the debate over the "Pirenne thesis."

The onus of proof . . . lies on those who would seek to show that industry and trade suffered no vital and permanent setback when the fall of the Empire in the West had removed the unified framework of civil and military defence.
—H. St. L. B. Moss (1937)

There is no evidence to prove that the Arabs either desired to close, or actually did close the Mediterranean to the commerce of the West either in the seventh or the eighth centuries.
—Daniel C. Dennett, Jr. (1948)

Pirenne obviously saw an important fact, but picked the wrong villain. It was not the Arabs but Byzantium who destroyed the ancient unity of the Mediterranean. . . . Byzantium used her naval power to channel trade as suited her interests.
—Archibald R. Lewis (1951)

. . . this so-called Merovingian economic activity which, so the theory runs, was inherited from the ancient world, continued to flourish until it was blocked by the Norman conquest, went into rapid decline from the middle of the seventh century and finally petered out under the Carolingians. We believe the opposite to be the case.

—Robert Latouche (1956)

If the basic problem which confronts us . . . can be solved at all, then it is through a study of the coins which have been discovered. . . . The Frankish empire was a country of transit between the fur- and slave-producing territory in northern, central and eastern Europe and the Mohammedan world. This conclusion may be somewhat startling but it is incontestable.

—Sture Bolin (1953)

In the last analysis, one can draw no firm conclusions regarding trade routes from the numismatic remains.

—Karl F. Morrison (1963)

What emerges from the most modern and informed scholarship is that trade over the years from the beginning of the fourth century to the end of the ninth fluctuated. In the Mediterranean basin it declined in the fourth and early fifth centuries, revived in the sixth and early seventh, was reduced again at the end of the seventh and in the early eighth centuries and probably continued at a low level throughout the ninth century.

—Gerald A. J. Hodgett (1972)

IV. Continued research has clarified the problem though it has hardly resolved the controversy. But attacks upon the Pirenne Thesis have in no way diminished admiration for Pirenne himself.

The Pirenne Thesis, which twenty years ago was widely accepted by medieval historians, is now accepted by virtually none without important qualifications.

—William Carroll Bark (1958)

The scholarship of the past quarter century has virtually destroyed Pirenne's fertile hypothesis, but it has no more dimmed esteem for him than criticism of the *Decline and Fall* has altered admiration for Gibbon.

—Lynn White, Jr. (1966)

As yet Pirenne's theory, though revised, has not been replaced by any other more credible or convincing on the enigma of the end of the ancient world and the beginning of the Middle Ages.

—Bryce Lyon (1974)

V. The larger problem of the emergence of European civilization distinct from antiquity—the question posed by Pirenne—remains. It has been a central issue of scholarly research for the past two generations.

I suggest Pirenne can be vindicated by showing that what is now western Europe of what was the Western Empire had no independent social, economic, political or cultural foundations. Its life-line was its economic orientation to Rome. . . . When the West was cut off from the Empire by the Moslems and infested with the Germans, Roman civilization simply died.

—Paul Craig Roberts (1964)

Pirenne observed that the most significant fact in European history is the transfer of Europe's center of gravity from the Mediterranean to the great northern plains where it remains. . . . Its essential cause, although Pirenne held other views, . . . was the emergence north of the Alps of a larger and more stable agricultural surplus than could be achieved in the Mediterranean area. The hand of the peasant on the plow was guiding the course of history.

—Lynn White, Jr. (1966)

MAPS

MAP 1
Europe and the Mediterranean World, About 814.

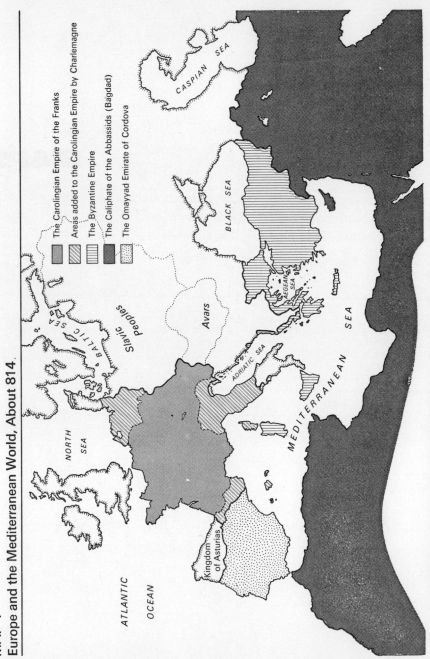

MAP 2
Europe in the Ninth Century: Trade Routes

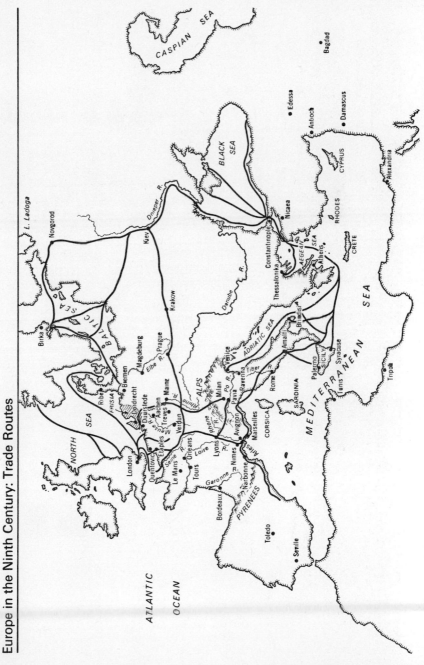

Henri Pirenne

MEDIEVAL CITIES

The Mediterranean

The Roman Empire, at the end of the third century, had one outstanding general characteristic: it was an essentially Mediterranean
commonwealth. Virtually all of its territory lay within the watershed of
that great land-locked sea; the distant frontiers of the Rhine, the
Danube, the Euphrates and the Sahara, may be regarded merely as
an advanced circle of outer defenses protecting the approaches.

The Mediterranean was, without question, the bulwark of both its
political and economic unity. Its very existence depended on mastery
of the sea. Without that great trade route, neither the government,
nor the defense, nor the administration of the *orbis romanus* would
have been possible.

As the Empire grew old this fundamentally maritime character
was, interestingly enough, not only preserved but was still more
sharply defined. When the former inland capital, Rome, was abandoned, its place was taken by a city which not only served as a
capital but which was at the same time an admirable seaport—
Constantinople.

The Empire's cultural development, to be sure, had clearly passed
its peak. Population decreased, the spirit of enterprise waned, barbarian hordes commenced to threaten the frontiers, and the increasing
expenses of the government, fighting for its very life, brought in their
train a fiscal system which more and more enslaved men to the State.
Nevertheless this general deterioration does not seem to have appreciably affected the maritime commerce of the Mediterranean. It
continued to be active and well sustained, in marked contrast with
the growing apathy that characterized the inland provinces. Trade
continued to keep the East and the West in close contact with each
other. There was no interruption to the intimate commercial relations
between those diverse climes bathed by one and the same sea. Both

From Henri Pirenne, *Medieval Cities: Their Origins and the Revival of Trade*, trans. by
Frank D. Halsey (copyright 1925 © 1952 by Princeton University Press; Princeton
Paperback, 1969), pp. 3–55. Omission of footnotes. Reprinted by permission of Princeton
University Press. Acknowledgment is also made of corrections in the English version
suggested by Professor John Benton of the California Institute of Technology.

manufactured and natural products were still extensively dealt in: textiles from Constantinople, Edessa, Antioch, and Alexandria; wines, oils, and spices from Syria; papyrus from Egypt; wheat from Egypt, Africa, and Spain; and wines from Gaul and Italy. There was even a reform of the monetary system based on the gold *solidus,* which served materially to encourage commercial operations by giving them the benefit of an excellent currency, universally adopted as an instrument of exchange and as a means of quoting prices.

Of the two great regions of the Empire, the East and the West, the first far surpassed the second, both in superiority of civilization and in a much higher level of economic development. At the beginning of the fourth century there were no longer any really great cities save in the East. The center of the export trade was in Syria and in Asia Minor, and here also was concentrated, in particular, the textile industry for which the whole Roman world was the market and for which Syrian ships were the carriers.

The commercial prominence of the Syrians is one of the most interesting facts in the history of the Lower Empire. It undoubtedly contributed largely to that progressive orientalization of society which was due eventually to end in Byzantinism. And this orientalization, of which the sea was the vehicle, is clear proof of the increasing importance which the Mediterranean acquired as the aging Empire grew weak, gave way in the North beneath the pressure of the barbarians, and contracted more and more about the shores of this inland sea.

The persistence of the Germanic tribes in striving, from the very beginning of the period of the invasions, to reach these same shores and to settle there is worth special notice. When, in the course of the fourth century, the frontiers gave way for the first time under their blows, they poured southward in a living flood. The Quadi and the Marcomanni invaded Italy; the Goths marched on the Bosporus; the Franks, the Suevi, and the Vandals, who by now had crossed the Rhine, pushed on unhesitatingly towards Aquitaine and Spain. They had no thought of merely colonizing the provinces they coveted. Their dream was rather to settle down, themselves, in those happy regions where the mildness of the climiate and the fertility of the soil were matched by the charms and the wealth of civilization.

This initial attempt produced nothing more permanent than the devastation which it had caused. Rome was still strong enough to drive the invaders back beyond the Rhine and the Danube. For a century and a half she succeeded in restraining them, but at the cost of exhausting her armies and her finances.

More and more unequal became the balance of power. The incursions of the barbarians grew more relentless as their increasing numbers made the acquisition of new territory more imperative, while the decreasing population of the Empire made a successful resistance constantly less possible. Despite the extraordinary skill and determination with which the Empire sought to stave off disaster, the outcome was inevitable.

At the beginning of the fifth century, all was over. The whole West was invaded. Roman provinces were transformed into Germanic kingdoms. The Vandals were installed in Africa, the Visigoths in Aquitaine and in Spain, the Burgundians in the Valley of the Rhône, the Ostrogoths in Italy.

This nomenclature is significant. It includes only Mediterranean countries, and little more is needed to show that the objective of the conquerors, free at last to settle down where they pleased, was the sea—that sea which for so long a time the Romans had called, with as much affection as pride, *mare nostrum*. Towards the sea, as of one accord, they all turned their steps, impatient to settle along its shores and to enjoy its beauty.

If the Franks did not reach the Mediterranean at their first attempt, it is because, having come too late, they found the ground already occupied. But they too persisted in striving for a foothold there. One of Clovis's earliest ambitions was to conquer Provence, and only the intervention of Theodoric kept him from extending the frontiers of his kingdom as far as the Côte d'Azur. Yet this first lack of success was not due to discourage his successors. A quarter of a century later, in 536, the Franks made good use of Justinian's offensive against the Ostrogoths and wrung from their hard-pressed rivals the grant of the coveted territory. It is interesting to see how consistently the Merovingian dynasty tended, from that date on, to become in its turn a Mediterranean power.

Childebert and Clotaire, for example, ventured upon an expedition beyond the Pyrenees in 542, which, however, proved to be ill-starred. But it was Italy in particular that aroused the cupidity of the Frankish kings. They formed an alliance, first with the Byzantines and then with the Lombards, in the hope of setting foot south of the Alps. Repeatedly thwarted, they persisted in fresh attempts. By 539, Theudebert had crossed the Alps, and the territories which he had occupied were reconquered by Narses in 553. Numerous efforts were made in 584–585 and from 588 to 590 to get possession anew.

The appearance of the Germanic tribes on the shore of the Mediterranean was by no means a critical point marking the advent of a new era in the history of Europe. Great as were the consequences which it entailed, it did not sweep the boards clean nor even break the tradition. The aim of the invaders was not to destroy the Roman Empire but to occupy and enjoy it. By and large, what they preserved far exceeded what they destroyed or what they brought that was new. It is true that the kingdoms they established on the soil of the Empire made an end of the latter in so far as being a *State* in Western Europe. From a political point of view the *orbis romanus,* now strictly localized in the East, lost that ecumenical character which had made its frontiers coincide with the frontiers of Christianity. The Empire, however, was far from becoming a stranger to the lost provinces. Its civilization there outlived its authority. By the Church, by language, by the superiority of its institutions and law, it prevailed over the conquerors. In the midst of the troubles, the insecurity, the misery and the anarchy which accompanied the invasions there was naturally a certain decline, but even in that decline there was preserved a physiognomy still distinctly Roman. The Germanic tribes were unable, and in fact did not want, to do without it. They barbarized it, but they did not consciously germanize it.

Nothing is better proof of this assertion than the persistence in the last days of the Empire—from the fifth to the eighth century—of that maritime character pointed out above. The importance of the Mediterranean did not grow less after the period of the invasions. The sea remained for the Germanic tribes what it had been before their arrival—the very center of Europe, the *mare nostrum*. The sea had had such great importance in the political order that the deposing of the last Roman Emperor in the West (476) was not enough in itself to turn historical evolution from its time-honored direction. It continued, on the contrary, to develop in the same theater and under the same influences. No indication yet gave warning of the end of that commonwealth of civilization created by the Empire from the Pillars of Hercules to the Aegean Sea, from the coasts of Egypt and Africa to the shores of Gaul, Italy and Spain. In spite of the invasion of the barbarians the new world conserved, in all essential characteristics, the physiognomy of the old. To follow the course of events from Romulus Augustulus to Charlemagne it is necessary to keep the Mediterranean constantly in view.

All the great events in political history are unfolded on its shores. From 493 to 526 Italy, governed by Theodoric, maintained a hegemony over all the Germanic kingdoms, a hegemony through which the power of the Roman tradition was perpetuated and assured. After Theodoric, this power was still more clearly shown. Justinian failed by but little of restoring imperial unity (527–565). Africa, Spain, and Italy were reconquered. The Mediterranean became again a Roman lake. Byzantium, it is true, weakened by the immense effort she had just put forth, could neither finish nor even preserve intact the astonishing work which she had accomplished. The Lombards took Northern Italy away from her (568); the Visigoths freed themselves from her yoke. Nevertheless she did not abandon her ambitions. She retained, for a long time to come, Africa, Sicily, Southern Italy. Nor did she loose her grip on the West—thanks to the sea, the mastery of which her fleets so securely held that the fate of Europe rested at that moment, more than ever, on the waves of the Mediterranean.

What was true of the political situation held equally well for the cultural. It seems hardly necessary to recall that Boëthius (480–525) and Cassiodorus (477–c. 562) were Italians as were St. Benedict (480–534) and Gregory the Great (590–604), and that Isidorus of Seville (570–636) was a Spaniard. It was Italy that maintained the last schools at the same time that she was fostering the spread of monachism north of the Alps. It was in Italy, also, that what was left of the ancient culture flourished side by side with what was brought forth anew in the bosom of the Church. All the strength and vigor that the Church possessed was concentrated in the region of the Mediterranean. There alone she gave evidence of an organization and spirit capable of initiating great enterprises. An interesting example of this is the fact that Christianity was brought to the Anglo-Saxons (596) from the distant shores of Italy, not from the neighboring shores of Gaul. The mission of St. Augustine is therefore an illuminating sidelight on the historic influence retained by the Mediterranean. And it seems more significant still when we recall that the evangelization of Ireland was due to missionaries sent out from Marseilles, and that the apostles of Belgium, St. Amand (689–693) and St. Remade (c. 668), were Aquitanians.

A brief survey of the economic development of Europe will give the crowning touch to the substantiation of the theory which has here been put forward. That development is, obviously, a clear-cut, direct continuation of the economy of the Roman Empire. In it are rediscovered all the latter's principal traits and, above all, that Mediterranean character which here is unmistakable. To be sure, a general decline in social activity was apparent in this region as in all others. By the last days of the Empire there was a clearly marked decline which the catastrophe of the invasions naturally helped accentuate. But it would be a decided mistake to imagine that the arrival of the Germanic tribes had as a result the substitution of a purely agricultural economy and a general stagnation in trade for urban life and commercial activity.

The supposed dislike of the barbarians for towns is an admitted fable to which reality has given the lie. If, on the extreme frontiers of the Empire, certain towns were put to the torch, destroyed and pillaged, it is nonetheless true that the immense majority survived the invasions. A statistical survey of cities in existence at the present day in France, in Italy and even on the banks of the Rhine and the Danube, gives proof that, for the most part, these cities now stand on the sites where rose the Roman cities, and that their very names are often but a transformation of Roman names.

The Church had of course closely patterned the religious districts after the administrative districts of the Empire. As a general rule, each diocese corresponded to a *civitas*. Since the ecclesiastical organization suffered no change during the era of the Germanic invasions, the result was that in the new kingdoms founded by the conquerors it preserved intact this characteristic feature. In fact, from the beginning of the sixth century the word *civitas* took the special meaning of "episcopal city," the center of the diocese. In surviving the Empire on which it was based, the Church therefore contributed very largely to the safeguarding of the existence of the Roman cities.

But it must not be overlooked, on the other hand, that these cities in themselves long retained a considerable importance. Their municipal institutions did not suddenly disappear upon the arrival of the Germanic tribes. Not only in Italy, but also in Spain and even in Gaul, they kept their *decuriones*—a corps of magistrates provided with a judicial and administrative authority, the details of which are not clear but whose existence and Roman origin is a matter of record. There is to be noticed, moreover, the presence of the *defensor civitatis,* and the practice of inscribing notarized deeds in the *gesta municipalia.*

It is also well established that these cities were the centers of an economic activity which itself was a survival of the preceding civilization. Each city was the market for the surrounding countryside, the winter home of the great landed proprietors of the neighborhood and, if favorably situated, the center of a commerce the more highly developed in proportion to its nearness to the shores of the Mediterranean. A perusal of Gregory of Tours gives ample proof that in the Gaul of his time there was still a professional merchant class residing in the towns. He cites, in some thoroughly characteristic passages, those of Verdun, Paris, Orléans, Clermont-Ferrand, Marseilles, Nîmes, and Bordeaux, and the information which he supplies concerning them is all the more significant in that it is brought into his narrative only incidentally. Care should of course be taken not to exaggerate its value. An equally great fault would be to undervalue it. Certainly the economic order of Merovingian Gaul was founded on agriculture rather than on any other form of activity. More certainly still this had already been the case under the Roman Empire.

But this does not preclude the fact that inland traffic, the import and export of goods and merchandise, was carried on to a considerable extent. It was an important factor in the maintenance of society. An indirect proof of this is furnished by the institution of market-tolls. Thus were called the tolls set up by the Roman administration along the roads, in the ports, at bridges and fords, and elsewhere. The Frankish kings let them all stay in force and drew from them such copious revenues that the collectors of this class of taxes figured among their most useful functionaries.

The continued commercial activity after the disappearance of the Empire, and, likewise, the survival of the towns that were the centers thereof and the merchants who were its instruments, is explained by the continuation of Mediterranean trade. In all the chief characteristics it was the same, from the fifth to the eighth centuries, as it had been just after Constantine. If, as is probable, the decline was the more rapid after the Germanic invasions, it remains nonetheless true that there is presented a picture of uninterrupted intercourse between the Byzantine East and the West dominated by the barbarians. By means of the shipping which was carried on from the coasts of Spain and Gaul to those of Syria and Asia Minor, the basin of the Mediterranean did not cease, despite the political subdivisions which it had seen take place, to consolidate the economic unity which it had shaped for centuries under the imperial commonwealth. Because of this fact, the economic organization of the world lived on after the political transformation.

In lack of other proofs, the monetary system of the Frankish kings would alone establish this truth convincingly. This system, as is too well known to make necessary any lengthy consideration here, was purely Roman or, strictly speaking, Romano-Byzantine. This is shown by the coins that were minted: the *solidus,* the *triens,* and the *denarius*—that is to say, the *sou,* the *third-sou* and the *denier.* It is shown further by the metal which was employed: gold, used for the coinage of the *solidus* and the *triens.* It is also shown by the weight which was given to specie. It is shown, finally, by the effigies which were minted on the coins. In this connection it is worth noting that the mints continued for a long time, under the Merovingian kings, the custom of representing the bust of the Emperor on the coins and of showing on the reverse of the pieces the *Victoria Augusti* and that, carrying this imitation to the extreme, when the Byzantines substituted the cross for the symbol of that victory they did the same. Such extreme servility can be explained only by the continuing influence of the Empire. The obvious reason was the necessity of preserving, between the local currency and the imperial currency, a conformity which would be purposeless if the most intimate relations had not existed between Merovingian commerce and the general commerce of the Mediterranean. In other words, this commerce continued to be closely bound up with the commerce of the Byzantine Empire. Of such ties, moreover, there are abundant proofs and it will suffice to mention merely a few of the most significant.

It should be borne in mind, first of all, that at the start of the eighth century Marseilles was still the great port of Gaul. The terms employed by Gregory of Tours, in the numerous anecdotes in which he happens to speak of that city, make it seem a singularly animated economic center. A very active shipping bound it to Constantinople, to Syria, Africa, Egypt, Spain and Italy. The products of the East— papyrus, spices, costly textiles, wine and oil—were the basis of a regular import trade. Foreign merchants, Jews and Syrians for the most part, had their residence there, and their nationality is itself an indication of the close relations kept up by Marseilles with Byzantium. Finally, the extraordinary quantity of coins which were struck there during the Merovingian era gives material proof of the activity of its commerce. The population of the city must have comprised, aside from the merchants, a rather numerous class of artisans. In every respect it seems, then, to have accurately preserved, under the government of the Frankish kings, the clearly municipal character of Roman cities.

The economic development of Marseilles naturally made itself felt in the hinterland of the port. Under its attraction, all the commerce of Gaul was oriented toward the Mediterranean. The most important market-tolls of the Frankish kingdom were situated in the neighborhood of the town at Fos, at Arles, at Toulon, at Sorgues, at Valence, at Vienne, and at Avignon. Here is clear proof that merchandise landed in the city was expedited to the interior. By the course of the Rhone and of the Saone, as well as by the Roman roads, it reached the north of the country. The charters are still in existence by which the Abbey of Corbie (Department of Pas-de-Calais) obtained from the kings an exemption from tolls at Fos on a number of commodities, among which may be remarked a surprising variety of spices of eastern origin, as well as papyrus. In these circumstances it does not seem unwarranted to assume that the commercial activity of the ports of Rouen and Nantes, on the shores of the Atlantic Ocean, as well as of Quentovic and Duurstede, on the shores of the North Sea, was sustained by the ramifications of the export traffic from far-off Marseilles.

But it was in the south of the country that this effect was the most appreciable. All the largest cities of Merovingian Gaul were still to be found, as in the days of the Roman Empire, south of the Loire. The details which Gregory of Tours supplies concerning Clermont-Ferrand and Orléans show that they had within their walls veritable colonies of Jews and Syrians, and if it was so with those towns which there is no reason for believing enjoyed a privileged status, it must have been so also with the much more important centers such as Bordeaux or Lyons. It is an established fact, moreover, that Lyons still had at the Carolingian era a quite numerous Jewish population.

Here, then, is quite enough to support the conclusion that Merovingian times knew, thanks to the continuance of Mediterranean shipping and the intermediary of Marseilles, what we may safely call a great commerce. It would certainly be an error to assume that the dealings of the oriental merchants of Gaul were restricted solely to articles of luxury. Probably the sale of jewelry, enamels and silk stuffs resulted in handsome profits, but this would not be enough to explain their number and their extraordinary diffusion throughout all the country. The traffic of Marseilles was, above all else, supported by goods for general consumption such as wine and oil, spices and papyrus. These commodities, as has already been pointed out, were regularly exported to the north.

The oriental merchants of the Frankish Empire were virtually engaged in wholesale trade. Their boats, after being discharged on the quays of Marseilles, certainly carried back, on leaving the shores of Provence, not only passengers but return freight. Our sources of information, to be sure, do not tell much about the nature of this freight. Among the possible conjectures, one of the most likely is that it probably consisted, at least in good part, in human chattels—that is to say, in slaves. Traffic in slaves did not cease to be carried on in the Frankish Empire until the end of the ninth century. The wars waged against the barbarians of Saxony, Thuringia and the Slavic regions provided a source of supply which seems to have been abundant enough. Gregory of Tours speaks of Saxon slaves belonging to a merchant of Orléans, and it is a good guess that this Samo, who departed in the first half of the seventh century with a band of companions for the country of Wends, whose king he eventually became, was very probably nothing more than an adventurer trafficking in slaves. And it is of course obvious that the slave trade, to which the Jews still assiduously applied themselves in the ninth century, must have had its origin in an earlier era.

If the bulk of the commerce in Merovingian Gaul was to be found in the hands of oriental merchants, their influence, however, should not be exaggerated. Side by side with them, and according to all indications in constant relations with them, are mentioned indigenous merchants. Gregory of Tours does not fail to supply information concerning them, which would undoubtedly have been more voluminous if his narrative had had more than a merely incidental interest in them. He shows the king consenting to a loan to the merchants of Verdun, whose business prospers so well that they soon find themselves in a position to reimburse him. He mentions the existence in Paris of a *domus negociantum*—that is to say, apparently, of a sort of market or bazaar. He speaks of a merchant profiteering during the great famine of 585 and getting rich. And in all these anecdotes he is dealing, without the least doubt, with professionals and not with merely casual buyers or sellers.

The picture which the commerce of Merovingian Gaul presents is repeated, naturally, in the other maritime Germanic kingdoms of the Mediterranean—among the Ostrogoths of Italy, among the Vandals of Africa, among the Visigoths of Spain. The Edict of Theodoric contained a quantity of stipulations relative to merchants. Carthage continued to be an important port in close relations with Spain, and her ships, apparently, went up the coast as far as Bordeaux. The laws of the Visigoths mentioned merchants from overseas.

In all of this is clearly manifest the vigorous continuity of the commercial development of the Roman Empire after the Germanic invasions. They did not put an end to the economic unity of antiquity. By means of the Mediterranean and the relations kept up thereby between the West and the East, this unity, on the contrary, was preserved with a remarkable distinctiveness. The great inland sea of Europe no longer belonged, as before, to a single State. But nothing yet gave reason to predict that it would soon cease to have its time-honored importance. Despite the transformations which it had undergone, the new world had not lost the Mediterranean character of the old. On the shores of the sea was still concentrated the better part of its activities. No indication yet gave warning of the end of the commonwealth of civilization, created by the Roman Empire from the Pillars of Hercules to the Aegean Sea. At the beginning of the seventh century, anyone who sought to look into the future would have been unable to discern any reason for not believing in the continuance of the old tradition.

Yet what was then natural and reasonable to predict was not to be realized. The world-order which had survived the Germanic invasions was not able to survive the invasion of Islam.

It is thrown across the path of history with the elemental force of a cosmic cataclysm. Even in the lifetime of Mahomet (571–632) no one could have imagined the consequences or have prepared for them. Yet the movement took no more than fifty years to spread from the China Sea to the Atlantic Ocean. Nothing was able to withstand it. At the first blow, it overthrew the Persian Empire (637–644). It took from the Byzantine Empire, in quick succession, Syria (634–636), Egypt (640–642), Africa (698). It reached into Spain (711). The resistless advance was not to slow down until the start of the eighth century, when the walls of Constantinople on the one side (713) and the soldiers of Charles Martel on the other (732) broke that great enveloping offensive against the two flanks of Christianity.

But if its force of expansion was exhausted, it had nonetheless changed the face of the world. Its sudden thrust had destroyed ancient Europe. It had put an end to the Mediterranean commonwealth in which it had gathered its strength.

The familiar and almost "family" sea which once united all the parts of this commonwealth was to become a barrier between them. On all its shores, for centuries, social life, in its fundamental characteristics, had been the same; religion, the same; customs and ideas, the same or very nearly so. The invasion of the barbarians from the North had modified nothing essential in that situation.

But now, all of a sudden, the very lands where civilization had been born were torn away; the Cult of the Prophet was substituted for the Christian Faith, Moslem law for Roman law, the Arab tongue for the Greek and the Latin tongue.

The Mediterranean had been a Roman lake; it now became, for the most part, a Moslem lake. From this time on it separated, instead of uniting, the East and the West of Europe. The tie which was still binding the Byzantine Empire to the Germanic kingdoms of the West was broken.

The Ninth Century

The tremendous effect the invasion of Islam had upon Western Europe has not, perhaps, been fully appreciated.

Out of it arose a new and unparalleled situation, unlike anything that had gone before. Through the Phoenicians, the Greeks, and finally the Romans, Western Europe had always received the cultural stamp of the East. It had lived, as it were, by virtue of the Mediterranean; now for the first time it was forced to live by its own resources. The center of gravity, heretofore on the shore of the Mediterranean, was shifted to the north. As a result the Frankish Empire, which had so far been playing only a minor role in the history of Europe, was to become the arbiter of Europe's destinies.

There is obviously more than mere coincidence in the simultaneity of the closing of the Mediterranean by Islam and the entry of the Carolingians on the scene. There is the distinct relation of cause and effect between the two. The Frankish Empire was fated to lay the foundations of the Europe of the Middle Ages. But the mission which it fulfilled had as an essential prior condition the overthrow of the traditional world-order. The Carolingians would never have been called upon to play the part they did if historical evolution had not been turned aside from its course and, so to speak, "de-Saxoned" by the Moslem invasion. Without Islam, the Frankish Empire would probably never have existed and Charlemagne, without Mahomet, would be inconceivable.

This is made plain enough by the many contrasts between the Merovingian era, during which the Mediterranean retained its time-honored historical importance, and the Carolingian era, when that influence ceased to make itself felt. These contrasts were in evidence everywhere: in religious sentiment, in political and social institutions, in literature, in language and even in handwriting. From whatever standpoint it is studied, the civilization of the ninth century shows a distinct break with the civilization of antiquity. Nothing would be more fallacious than to see therein a simple continuation of the preceding centuries. The coup d'état of Pepin the Short was considerably more than the substitution of one dynasty for another. It marked a new orientation of the course hitherto followed by history. At first glance there seems reason to believe that Charlemagne, in assuming the title of Roman Emperor and of Augustus, wished to restore the ancient tradition. In reality, in setting himself up against the Emperor of Constantinople, he broke that tradition. His Empire was Roman only insofar as the Catholic Church was Roman. For it was from the Church, and the Church alone, that came its inspiration. The forces which he placed at her service were, moreover, forces of the north. His principal collaborators, in religious and cultural matters, were no longer, as they had previously been, Italians, Aquitanians, or Spaniards; they were Anglo-Saxons—a St. Boniface or an Alcuin—or they were Swabians, like Einhard. In the affairs of the State, which was not cut off from the Mediterranean, southerners played scarcely any role. The Germanic influence commenced to dominate at the very moment when the Frankish Empire, forced to turn away from the Mediterranean, spread over Northern Europe and pushed its frontiers as far as the Elbe and the mountains of Bohemia.[1]

In the field of economics the contrast, which the Carolingian period shows to Merovingian times, is especially striking. In the days

---

[1] The objection may be raised that Charlemagne conquered in Italy the kingdom of the Lombards and in Spain the region included between the Pyrenees and the Ebro. But these thrusts towards the south are by no means to be explained by a desire to dominate the shores of the Mediterranean. The expeditions against the Lombards were provoked by political causes and especially by the alliance with the Papacy. The expedition in Spain had no other aim than the establishing of a solid frontier against the Moslems.

of the Merovingians, Gaul was still a maritime country and trade and traffic flourished because of that fact. The Empire of Charlemagne, on the contrary, was essentially an inland one. No longer was there any communication with the exterior; it was a closed State, a State without foreign markets, living in a condition of almost complete isolation.

To be sure, the transition from one era to the other was not clear-cut. The trade of Marseilles did not suddenly cease but, from the middle of the seventh century, waned gradually as the Moslems advanced in the Mediterranean. Syria, conquered by them in 633–638, no longer kept it thriving with her ships and her merchandise. Shortly afterwards, Egypt passed in her turn under the yoke of Islam (638–640), and papyrus no longer came to Gaul. A characteristic consequence is that, after 677, the royal chancellery stopped using papyrus. The importation of spices kept up for a while, for the monks of Corbie, in 716, believed it useful to have ratified for the last time their privileges of the *tonlieu* of Fos. A half century later, solitude reigned in the port of Marseilles. Her foster-mother, the sea, was shut off from her and the economic life of the inland regions which had been nourished through her intermediary was definitely extinguished. By the ninth century Provence, once the richest country of Gaul, had become the poorest.

More and more, the Moslems consolidated their domination over the sea. In the course of the ninth century they seized the Balearic Isles, Corsica, Sardinia, Sicily. On the coasts of Africa they founded new ports: Tunis (698–703); later on, Mehdia to the south of this city; then Cairo, in 973. Palermo, where stood a great arsenal, became their principal base in the Tyrrhenian Sea. Their fleets sailed it in complete mastery; commercial flotillas transported the products of the West to Cairo, whence they were redispatched to Bagdad, or pirate fleets devastated the coasts of Provence and Italy and put towns to the torch after they had been pillaged and their inhabitants captured to be sold as slaves. In 889 a band of these plunderers even laid hold of Fraxinetum (the present Garde-Frainet, in the Department of the Var not far from Nice) the garrison of which, for nearly a century thereafter, subjected the neighboring populace to continual raids and menaced the roads which led across the Alps from France to Italy.

The efforts of Charlemagne and his successors to protect the coasts from Saracen raiders were as impotent as their attempts to oppose the invasions of the Norsemen in the north and west. The hardihood and seamanship of the Danes and Norwegians made it easy for them to plunder the coasts of the Carolingian Empire during the whole of the ninth century. They conducted their raids not only from the North Sea, the Channel, and the Gulf of Gascony, but at times even from the Mediterranean. Every river which emptied into these seas was, at one time or another, ascended by their skillfully constructed barks, splendid specimens whereof, brought to light by recent excavations, are now preserved at Oslo. Periodically the valleys of the Rhine, the Meuse, the Scheldt, the Seine, the Loire, the Garonne and the Rhone were the scene of systematic and persistent pillaging. The devastation was so complete that, in many cases indeed, the population itself disappeared. And nothing is a better illustration of the essentially inland character of the Frankish Empire than its inability to organize the defense of its coasts, against either Saracens or Norsemen. For that defense, to be effective, should have been a naval defense, and the Empire had no fleets, or hastily improvised ones at best.

Such conditions were incompatible with the existence of a commerce of first-rate importance. The historical literature of the ninth century contains, it is true, certain references to merchants (*mercatores, negociatores*), but no illusion should be cherished as to their importance. Compared to the number of texts which have been preserved from that era, these references are extremely rare. The capitularies, those regulations touching upon every phase of social life, are remarkably meager insofar as applies to commerce. From this it may be assumed that the latter played a role of only secondary, negligible importance. It was only in the north of Gaul that, during the first half of the ninth century, trade showed any signs of activity.

The ports of Quentovic (a place now vanished, near Etaples in the Department of Pas-de-Calais) and Duurstede (on the Rhine, southwest of Utrecht) which under the Merovingian monarchy were already trading with England and Denmark, seem to have been centers of a widely extended shipping. It is a safe conjecture that because of them the river transport of the Friesians along the Rhine, the Scheldt and the Meuse enjoyed an importance that was matched by no other region during the reigns of Charlemagne and his successors. The cloths woven by the peasants of Flanders, and which contemporary texts designate by the name of Friesian cloaks, together with the wines of Rhenish Germany, supplied to that river traffic the substance of an export trade which seems to have been fairly regular up to the day when the Norsemen took possession of the ports in question. It is known, moreover, that the *deniers* coined at Duurstede had a very extensive circulation. They served as prototypes for the oldest coins of Sweden and Poland, evident proof that they early penetrated, no doubt at the hands of the Norsemen, as far as the Baltic Sea. Attention may also be called, as having been the substance of a rather extensive trade, to the salt industry of Noirmoutier, where Irish ships were to be seen. Salzburg salt, on the other hand, was shipped along the Danube and its affluents to the interior of the Empire. The sale of slaves, despite the prohibitions that were laid down by the sovereigns, was carried on along the eastern frontiers, where the prisoners of war taken from among the pagan Slavs found numerous purchasers.

The Jews seem to have applied themselves particularly to this sort of traffic. They were still numerous, and were found in every part of Francia. Those in the south of Gaul were in close relations with their co-religionists of Moslem Spain, to whom they are accused of having sold Christian children.

It was probably from Spain, or perhaps also from Venice, that these Jews obtained the spices and the valuable textiles in which they dealt. However, the obligation to which they were subjected of having their children baptized must have caused a great number of them to emigrate south of the Pyrenees at an early date, and their commercial importance steadily declined in the course of the ninth century. As for the Syrians, they were no longer of importance at this era.

It is, then, most likely that the commerce of Carolingian times was very much reduced. Except in the neighborhood of Quentovic and Duurstede, it consisted only in the transport of indispensable commodities, such as wine and salt, in the prohibited traffic of a few slaves, and in the barter, through the intermediary of the Jews, of a small number of products from the East.

Of a regular and normal commercial activity, of steady trading carried on by a class of professional merchants, in short, of all that constitutes the very essence of an economy of exchange worthy of the name, no traces are to be found after the closing off of the Mediterranean by the Islamic invasion. The great number of markets, which were to be found in the ninth century, in no way contradicts this assertion. They were, as a matter of fact, only small local marketplaces, instituted for the weekly provisioning of the populace by means of the retail sale of foodstuffs from the country. As a proof of the commercial activity of the Carolingian era, it would be equally beside the point to speak of the existence of the street occupied by merchants at Aix-la-Chapelle near the palace of Charlemagne, or of similar streets near certain great abbeys such as, for example, that of St. Riquier. The merchants with whom we have to do here were not, in fact, professional merchants but servitors charged with the duty of supplying the Court or the monks. They were, so to speak, employees of the seignorial household staff and were in no respect merchants.

There is, moreover, material proof of the economic decline which affected Western Europe from the day when she ceased to belong to the Mediterranean commonwealth. It is furnished by the reform of the monetary system, initiated by Pepin the Short and completed by Charlemagne. That reform abandoned gold coinage and substituted silver in its place. The *solidus* which had heretofore, conforming to the Roman tradition, constituted the basic monetary unit, was now only nominal money. The only real coins from this time on were the silver *deniers,* weighing about two grams, the metallic value of which, compared to that of the dollar, was approximately eight and one-half cents. The metallic value of the Merovingian gold *solidus* being nearly three dollars, the importance of the reform can be readily appreciated. Undoubtedly it is to be explained only by a prodigious falling off of both trading and wealth.

If it is admitted, and it must be admitted, that the reappearance of gold coinage, with the florins of Florence and the ducats of Venice in the thirteenth century, characterized the economic renaissance of Europe, the inverse is also true: the abandoning of gold coinage in the eighth century was the manifestation of a profound decline. It is not enough to say that Pepin and Charlemagne wished to remedy the monetary disorder of the last days of the Merovingian era. It would have been quite possible for them to find a remedy without giving up the gold standard. They gave up the standard, obviously, from necessity—that is to say, as a result of the disappearance of the yellow metal in Gaul. And this disappearance had no other cause than the interruption of the commerce of the Mediterranean. The proof of this is given by the fact that Southern Italy, remaining in contact with Constantinople, retained like the latter a gold standard, for which the Carolingian sovereigns were forced to substitute a silver standard. The very light weight of their *deniers,* moreover, testifies to the economic isolation of their Empire. It is inconceivable that they would have reduced the monetary unit to a thirtieth of its former value if there had been preserved the slightest bond between their States and the Mediterranean regions where the gold *solidus* continued to circulate.

But this is not all. The monetary reform of the ninth century not only was in keeping with the general impoverishment of the era in which it took place, but with the circulation of money which was noteworthy for both lightness and inadequacy. In the absence of centers of attraction sufficiently powerful to draw money from afar, it remained, so to speak, stagnant. Charlemagne and his successors in vain ordered that *deniers* should be coined only in the royal mints. Under the reign of Louis the Pious, it was necessary to give to certain churches authorization to coin money, in view of the difficulties, under which they labored, of obtaining cash. From the second half of the ninth century on, the authorization to establish a market was almost always accompanied by the authorization to establish a mint in the same place. The State could not retain the monopoly of minting coins. It was consistently frittered away. And that is again a manifestation, by no means equivocal, of the economic decline. History shows that the better commerce is sustained, the more the monetary system is centralized and simplified. The dispersion, the variety, and in fact the anarchy which it manifests as we follow the course of the ninth century, ends by giving striking confirmation to the general theory here put forward.

There have been some attempts to attribute to Charlemagne a far-seeing political economy. This is to lend him ideas which, however great we suppose his genius to have been, it is impossible for him to have had. No one can submit with any likelihood of truth that the projects which he commenced in 793, to join the Rednitz to the Altmühl and so establish communication between the Rhine and the Danube, could have had any other purpose than the transport of troops, or that the wars against the Avars were provoked by the desire to open up a commercial route to Constantinople. The stipulations, in other respects inoperative, of the capitularies regarding coinages, weights and measures, the market-tolls and the markets, were intimately bound up with the general system of regulation and control which was typical of Carolingian legislation. The same is true regarding the measures taken against usury and the prohibition enjoining members of the clergy from engaging in business. Their purpose was to

combat fraud, disorder and indiscipline and to impose a Christian morality on the people. Only a prejudiced point of view can see in them an
attempt to stimulate the economic development of the Empire.

We are so accustomed to consider the reign of Charlemagne as an
era of revival that we are unconsciously led to imagine an identical
progress in all fields. Unfortunately, what is true of literary culture, of
religion, of customs, institutions, and statecraft is not true of communications and commerce. Every great thing that Charlemagne accomplished was accomplished either by his military strength or by
his alliance with the Church. For that matter, neither the Church nor
arms could overcome the circumstances in virtue of which the Frankish Empire found itself deprived of foreign markets. It was forced, in
fact, to accommodate itself to a situation which was inevitably pre-
scribed. History is obliged to recognize that, however brilliant it
seems in other respects, the era of Charlemagne, considered from an
economic viewpoint, is an age of regression.

The financial organization of the Frankish Empire makes this
plain. It was, indeed, as rudimentary as could be. The public taxes,
which the Merovingians had preserved in imitation of Rome, no
longer existed. The resources of the sovereign consisted only in the
revenue from his demesnes, in the tributes levied on conquered
tribes and in the booty got by war. The market-tolls no longer contributed to the replenishment of the treasury, thus attesting to the
commercial decline of the period. They were nothing more than a
simple extortion brutally levied in kind on the infrequent merchandise
transported by the rivers or along the roads. The sorry proceeds,
which should have served to keep up the bridges, the docks and the
highways, were swallowed up by the functionaries who collected
them. The *missi dominici,* created to supervise their administration,
were impotent in abolishing the abuses which they proved to exist
because the State, unable to pay its agents, was likewise unable to
impose its authority on them. It was obliged to call on the aristocracy
which, thanks to their social status, alone could give free services.
But in so doing it was constrained, for lack of money, to choose the
instruments of power from among the midst of a group of men
whose most evident interest was to diminish that power. The recruit-
ing of the functionaries from among the aristocracy was the fundamental vice of the Frankish Empire and the essential cause of its
dissolution, which became so rapid after the death of Charlemagne.
Surely, nothing is more fragile than that State the sovereign of which,

all-powerful in theory, is dependent in fact upon the fidelity of his independent agents.

The feudal system was in embryo in this contradictory situation. The Carolingian Empire would have been able to keep going only if it had possessed, like the Byzantine Empire or the Empire of the Caliphs, a tax system, a financial control, a fiscal centralization and a treasury providing for the salary of functionaries, for public works, and for the maintenance of the army and the navy. The financial impotence which caused its downfall was a clear demonstration of the impossibility it encountered of maintaining a political structure on an economic base which was no longer able to support the load.

That economic base of the State, as of society, was from this time on the landed proprietor. Just as the Carolingian Empire was an inland State without foreign markets, so also was it an essentially agricultural State. The traces of commerce which were still to be found there were negligible. There was no other property than landed property, and no other work than rural work. As has already been stated above, this predominance of agriculture was no new fact. It existed in a very distinct form in the Roman era and it continued with increasing strength in the Merovingian era. As early as the close of antiquity, all the west of Europe was covered with great demesnes belonging to an aristocracy the members of which bore the title of senators. More and more, property was disappearing in a transformation into hereditary tenures, while the old free farmers were themselves undergoing a transformation into "coloni," bound to the soil, from father to son. The Germanic invasions did not noticeably alter this state of things. We have definitely given up the idea of picturing the Germanic tribes in the light of a democracy of peasants, all on an equal footing. Social distinctions were very great among them even when they first invaded the Empire. They comprised a minority of the wealthy and a majority of the poor. The number of slaves and half-free was considerable.

The arrival of the invaders in the Roman provinces brought with it, then, no overthrow of the existing order. The newcomers preserved, in adapting themselves thereto, the status quo. Many of the invaders received from the king or acquired by force or by marriage, or otherwise, great demesnes which made them the equals of the "senators." The landed aristocracy, far from disappearing, was on the contrary invigorated by new elements.

The disappearance of the small free proprietors continued. It seems, in fact, that as early as the start of the Carolingian period only a very small number of them still existed in Gaul. Charlemagne in vain took measures to safeguard those who were left. The need of protection inevitably made them turn to the more powerful individuals to whose patronage they subordinated their persons and their possessions.

Large estates, then, kept on being more and more generally in evidence after the period of the invasions. The favor which the kings showed the Church was an additional factor in this development, and the religious fervor of the aristocracy had the same effect. Monasteries, whose number multiplied with such remarkable rapidity after the seventh century, were receiving bountiful gifts of land. Everywhere ecclesiastical demesnes and lay demesnes were mixed up together, uniting not only cultivated ground, but woods, heaths and wastelands.

The organization of these demesnes remained in conformity, in Frankish Gaul, with what it had been in Roman Gaul. It is clear that this could not have been otherwise. The Germanic tribes had no motive for, and were, furthermore, incapable of, substituting a different organization. It consisted, in its essentials, of classifying all the land in two groups, subject to two distinct forms of government. The first, the less extensive, was directly exploited by the proprietor; the second was divided, as tenurial holdings, among the peasants. Each of the *villae* of which a demesne was composed comprised both seignorial land and censal land, divided in units of cultivation held by hereditary right by manants or villeins in return for the prestation of rents, in money or in kind, and statute-labor.

As long as urban life and commerce flourished, the great demesnes had a market for the disposal of their produce. There is no room for doubt that during all the Merovingian era it was through them that the city groups were provisioned and that the merchants were supplied. But it could not help be otherwise when trade disappeared and therewith the merchant class and the municipal population. The great estates suffered the same fate as the Frankish Empire. Like it, they lost their markets. The possibility of selling abroad existed no longer because of the lack of buyers, and it became useless to continue to produce more than the indispensable minimum for the subsistence of the men, proprietors or tenants, living on the estate.

For an economy of exchange was substituted an economy of

consumption. Each demesne, in place of continuing to deal with the outside, constituted from this time on a little world of its own. It lived by itself and for itself, in the traditional immobility of a patriarchal form of government. The ninth century is the golden age of what we have called the closed domestic economy and which we might call, with more exactitude, the economy of no markets.

This economy, in which production had no other aim than the sustenance of the demesnial group and which in consequence was absolutely foreign to the idea of profit, can not be considered as a natural and spontaneous phenomenon. It was, on the contrary, merely the result of an evolution which forced it to take this characteristic form. The great proprietors did not give up selling the products of their lands of their own free will; they stopped because they could not do otherwise. Certainly if commerce had continued to supply them regularly with the means of disposing of these products abroad, they would not have neglected to profit thereby. They did not sell because they could not sell, and they could not sell because markets were wanting. The closed demesnial organization, which made its appearance at the beginning of the ninth century, was a phenomenon due to compulsion. That is merely to say that it was an abnormal phenomenon.

This can be most effectively shown by comparing the picture, which Carolingian Europe presents, with that of Southern Russia at the same era.

We know that bands of sea-faring Norsemen, that is to say of Scandinavians originally from Sweden, established their domination over the Slavs of the watershed of the Dnieper during the course of the ninth century. These conquerors, whom the conquered designated by the name of Russians, naturally had to congregate in groups in order to insure their safety in the midst of the populations they had subjected.

For this purpose they built fortified enclosures, called *gorods* in the Slavic tongue, where they settled with their princes and the images of their gods. The most ancient Russian cities owe their origin to these entrenched camps. There were such camps at Smolensk, Suzdal and Novgorod; the most important and the most civilized was at Kiev, the prince of which ranked above all the other princes. The subsistence of the invaders was assured by tributes levied on the native population.

It was therefore possible for the Russians to live off the land, without seeking abroad to supplement the resources which the country gave them in abundance. They would have done so, without doubt, and been content to use the prestations of their subjects if they had found it impossible, like their contemporaries in Western Europe, to communicate with the exterior. But the position which they occupied must have early led them to practice an economy of exchange.

Southern Russia was placed, as a matter of fact, between two regions of superior civilization. To the east, beyond the Caspian Sea, extended the Caliphate of Bagdad; to the south, the Black Sea bathed the coasts of the Byzantine Empire and pointed the way towards Constantinople. The barbarians felt at once the effect of these two strong centers of attraction. To be sure, they were in the highest degree energetic, enterprising and adventurous, but their native qualities only served to turn circumstances to the best account. Arab, Jewish and Byzantine merchants were already frequenting the Slavic regions when they took possession, and showed them the route to follow. They themselves did not hesitate to plunge along it under the spur of the love of gain, quite as natural to primitive man as to civilized.

The country they occupied placed at their disposal products particularly well suited for trade with rich empires accustomed to the refinements of life. Its immense forests furnished them with a quantity of honey, precious in those days when sugar was still unknown, and furs, sumptuousness in which was a requisite, even in southern climes, of luxurious dress and equipment.

Slaves were easier still to procure and, thanks to the Moslem harems and the great houses or Byzantine workshops, had a sale as sure as it was remunerative. Thus as early as the ninth century, while the Empire of Charlemagne was kept in isolation after the closing of the Mediterranean, Southern Russia on the contrary was induced to sell her products in the two great markets which exercised their attraction on her. The paganism of the Scandinavians of the Dnieper left them free of the religious scruples which prevented the Christians of the West from having dealings with the Moslems. Belonging neither to the faith of Christ nor to that of Mahomet, they only asked to get rich, in dealing impartially with the followers of either.

The importance of the trade which they kept up as much with the Moslem Empire as with the Greek, is made clear by the extraordinary number of Arab and Byzantine coins discovered in Russia and which mark, like a golden compass needle, the direction of the commercial routes.

From the region of Kiev they followed to the south the course of the Dnieper, to the east the Volga, and to the north the direction marked by the Western Dvina or the lakes which abut the Gulf of Bothnia. Information from Jewish or Arab travelers and from Byzantine writers fortunately supplements the data from archaeological records. It will suffice here to give a brief résumé of what Constantine Porphyrogenetus[2] reports in the tenth century. He shows the Russians assembling their boats at Kiev each year after the ice melts. Their flotilla slowly descends the Dnieper, whose numerous cataracts present obstacles that have to be avoided by dragging the barks along the banks. The sea once reached, they sail before the wind along the coasts towards Constantinople, the supreme goal of their long and perilous voyage. There the Russian merchants had a special quarter and made commercial treaties, the oldest of which dates back to the ninth century, regulating their relations with the population. Many of them, seduced by its attractions, settled down there and took service in the Imperial Guard, as had done, before that time, the Germans in the legions of Rome.

The City of the Emperors (*Czarograd*) had for the Russians a fascination the influence of which lasted across the centuries. It was from her that they received Christianity (957–1015); it was from her that they borrowed their art, their writing, the use of money and a good part of their administrative organization. Nothing more is needed to demonstrate the role played by Byzantine commerce in their social life. It occupied so essential a place therein that without it their civilization would remain inexplicable. To be sure, the forms in which it is found are very primitive, but the important thing is not the forms of this traffic; it is the effect it had.

Among the Russians of the late Middle Ages it actually determined the constitution of society. By striking contrast with what has been shown to be the case with their contemporaries of Carolingian Europe, not only the importance but the very idea of real estate was unknown to them. Their notion of wealth comprised only personal property, of which slaves were the most valuable. They were not interested in land except insofar as, by their control of it, they were able to appropriate its products. And if this conception was that of a

---

[2] Byzantine Emperor (912–959) and scholar who wrote or inspired several works which provide much of our knowledge of his time.—Ed.

class of warrior-conquerors, there is but little doubt that it was held for so long because these warriors were, at the same time, merchants. We might, incidentally, add that the concentration of the Russians in the *gorods,* motivated in the beginning by military necessity, is itself found to fit in admirably with commercial needs. An organization created by barbarians for the purpose of keeping conquered populations under the yoke was well adapted to the sort of life which theirs became after they gave heed to the economic attraction of Byzantium and Bagdad. Their example shows that a society does not necessarily have to pass through an agrarian stage before giving itself over to commerce. Here commerce appears as an original phenomenon. And if this is so, it is because the Russians instead of finding themselves isolated from the outside world like Western Europe were on the contrary pushed or, to use a better word, *drawn* into contact with it from the beginning. Out of this derive the violent contrasts which are disclosed in comparing their social state with that of the Carolingian Empire: in place of a demesnial aristocracy, a commercial aristocracy; in place of serfs bound to the soil, slaves considered as instruments of work; in place of a population living in the country, a population gathered together in towns; in place, finally, of a simple economy of consumption, an economy of exchange and a regular and permanent commercial activity.

That these outstanding contrasts were the result of circumstances which gave Russia markets while depriving the Carolingian Empire of them, history clearly demonstrates. The activity of Russian trade was maintained, indeed, only as long as the routes to Constantinople and Bagdad remained open before it. It was not fated to withstand the crisis which the Petchenegs brought about in the eleventh century. The invasion of these barbarians along the shores of the Caspian and the Black Seas brought in their train consequences identical to those which the invasion of Islam in the Mediterranean had had for Western Europe in the eighth century.

Just as the latter cut the communications between Gaul and the East, the former cut the communications between Russia and her foreign markets. And in both quarters, the results of this interruption coincide with a singular exactitude. In Russia as in Gaul, when means of communication disappeared and towns were depopulated and the populace forced to find near at hand the means of their subsistence, a period of agricultural economy was substituted for a period of commercial economy. Despite the differences in details, it was the same picture in both cases. The regions of the south, ruined and troubled by the barbarians, gave way in importance to the regions of the north. Kiev fell into a decline as Marseilles had fallen, and the center of the Russian State was removed to Moscow just as the center of the Frankish State, with the Carolingian dynasty, had been removed to the watershed of the Rhine. And to end by making the parallel still more conclusive, there arose, in Russia as in Gaul, a landed aristocracy, and a demesnial system was organized in which the impossibility of exporting or of selling forced production to be limited to the needs of the proprietor and his peasants.

So, in both cases, the same causes produced the same effects. But they did not produce them at the same date. Russia was living by trade at an era when the Carolingian Empire knew only the demesnial regime, and she in turn inaugurated this form of government at the very moment when Western Europe, having found new markets, broke away from it. We shall examine further how this break was accomplished. It will suffice for the moment to have proved, by the example of Russia, the theory that the economy of the Carolingian era was not the result of an internal evolution but must be attributed to the closing of the Mediterranean by Islam.

Henri Pirenne

MOHAMMED AND CHARLEMAGNE

WESTERN EUROPE BEFORE ISLAM

From whatever standpoint we regard it, then, the period inaugurated by the establishment of the Barbarians within the Empire introduced no absolute historical innovation.[1] What the Germans destroyed was not the Empire, but the Imperial government *in partibus occidentis.* They themselves acknowledged as much by installing themselves as *foederati.* Far from seeking to replace the Empire by anything new, they established themselves within it, and although their settlement was accompanied by a process of serious degradation, it did not introduce a new scheme of government; the ancient *palazzo,* so to speak, was divided up into apartments, but it still survived as a building. In short, the essential character of "Romania" still remained Mediterranean. The frontier territories, which remained Germanic, and England, played no part in it as yet; it is a mistake to regard them at this period as a point of departure. Considering matters as they actually were, we see that the great novelty of the epoch was a political fact; in the Occident a plurality of States was replacing the unity of the Roman State. And this, of course, was a considerable novelty. The aspect of Europe was changing, but the fundamental character of its life remained the same. These States, which have been described as national States, were not really national at all, but were merely fragments of the great unity which they had replaced. There was no profound transformation except in Britain.

There the Emperor and the civilization of the Empire had disappeared. Nothing remained of the old tradition. A new world had made its appearance. The old law and language and institutions were replaced by those of the Germans. A civilization of a new type appeared, which we may call the Nordic or Germanic civilization. It was

From Henri Pirenne, *Mohammed and Charlemagne* (London, 1939), pp. 140–44, 147–50, 265–85. Translated from the French by George Miall. By permission of George Allen & Unwin Ltd. Some changes have been made in the Miall translation with the assistance of Professor Paul Archambault. Documentation is, for the most part, omitted.

[1] These things were retained: the language, the currency, writing (papyrus), weights and measures, the kinds of foodstuffs in common use, the social classes, the religion—the role of Arianism has been exaggerated—art, the law, the administration, the taxes, the economic organization.

opposed to the Mediterranean civilization syncretized in the Late Empire, that last form of antiquity. Here was no trace of the Roman State with its legislative ideal, its civil population, and its Christian religion, but a society which had preserved the blood tie between its members; the family community, with all the consequences which it entailed in law and morality and economy; a paganism like that of the heroic poems; such were the things that constituted the original- ity of these Barbarians, who had thrust back the ancient world in order to take its place. In Britain a new age was beginning, which did not gravitate towards the South. The man of the North had con- quered and taken for his own this extreme corner of that "Romania" of which he had no memories, whose majesty he repudiated, and to which he owed nothing. In every sense of the word he replaced it, and in replacing it he destroyed it.

The Anglo-Saxon invaders came into the Empire fresh from their Germanic environment, and had never been subjected to the in- fluence of Rome. Further, the province of Britain, in which they had established themselves, was the least Romanized of all the provinces. In Britain, therefore, they remained themselves: the Germanic, Nor- dic, Barbarian soul of peoples whose culture might almost be called Homeric has been the essential factor in the history of this country.

But the spectacle presented by this Anglo-Saxon Britain was unique. We should seek in vain for anything like it on the Continent. There "Romania" still existed, except on the frontier, or along the Rhine, in the decumate lands, and along the Danube—that is to say, in the provinces of Germania, Raetia, Noricum and Pannonia, all close to that Germania whose inhabitants had overflowed into the Empire and driven it before them. But these border regions played no part of their own, since they were attached to States which had been established, like that of the Franks or the Ostrogoths, in the heart of "Romania." And there it is plain that the old state of affairs still existed. The invaders, too few in number, and also too long in contact with the Empire were inevitably absorbed, and they asked nothing better. What may well surprise us is that there was so little Germanism in the new States, all of which were ruled by Germanic dynasties. Language, religion, institutions and art were entirely, or almost entirely, devoid of Germanism. We find some Germanic in- fluences in the law of those countries situated to the north of the Seine and the Alps, but until the Lombards arrived in Italy these did not amount to very much. If some have held a contrary belief, it is because they have followed the Germanic school and have wrongly applied to Gaul, Italy, and Spain what they find in the *Leges Barbarorum* of the Salians, the Ripuarians and the Bavarians. They have also extended to the period which preceded the Carolingians what is true only of the latter. Moreover, they have exaggerated the role of Merovingian Gaul by allowing themselves to be governed by the thought of what it later became, but as yet was not.

What was Clovis as compared with Theodoric? And let it be noted that after Clovis the Frankish kings, despite all their efforts, could neither establish themselves in Italy, nor even recapture the Narbonnaise from the Visigoths. It is evident that they were tending towards the Mediterranean. The object of their conquest beyond the Rhine was to defend their kingdom against the Barbarians, and was far from having the effect of Germanizing it. But to admit that under the conditions of their establishment in the Empire, and with the small forces which they brought with them, the Visigoths, Burgundi, Ostrogoths, Vandals and Franks could have intended to Germanize the Empire is simply to admit the impossible.

Moreover, we must not forget the part played by the Church, within which Rome had taken refuge, and which, in imposing itself upon the Barbarians, was at the same time imposing Rome upon them. In the Occident, in the Roman world which had become so disordered as a State, the Germanic kings were, so to speak, points of political crystallization. But the old, or shall we say, the classic social equilibrium still existed in the world about them, though it had suffered inevitable losses.

In other words, the Mediterranean unity which was the essential feature of this ancient world was maintained in all its various manifestations. The increasing Hellenization of the Orient did not prevent it from continuing to influence the Occident by its commerce, its art, and the vicissitudes of its religious life. To a certain extent, as we have seen, the Occident was becoming Byzantinized.

This explains Justinian's impulse of reconquest, which almost restored the Mediterranean to the status of a Roman lake. And regarding it from our point of view, it is, of course, plainly apparent that this Empire could not last. But this was not the view of its contemporaries. The Lombard invasion was certainly less important than has been supposed. The striking thing about it is its tardiness.

Justinian's Mediterranean policy—and it really was a Mediterranean policy, since he sacrificed to this policy his conflicts with the Persians and the Slavs—was in tune with the Mediterranean spirit of European civilization as a whole from the fifth to the seventh century. It is on the shores of this *mare nostrum* that we find all the specific manifestations of the life of the epoch. Commerce gravitated toward the sea, as under the Empire; there the last representatives of ancient literature—Boëtius, Cassiodorus—wrote their works; there, with Caesarius of Arles, and Gregory the Great, the new literature of the Church was born and began to develop; there writers like Isidore of Seville made the inventory of civilization from which the Middle Ages obtained their knowledge of antiquity; there, at Lérins, or at Monte Cassino, monasticism, coming from the Orient, was acclimatized to its Occidental environment; from the shores of the Mediterranean came the missionaries who converted England, and it was there that arose the characteristic monuments of that Hellenistico-Oriental art which seemed destined to become the art of the Occident, as it had remained that of the Orient.

There was as yet nothing, in the seventh century, that seemed to announce the end of the community of civilization established by the Roman Empire from the Pillars of Hercules to the Aegean Sea and from the shores of Egypt and Africa to those of Italy, Gaul, and Spain. The new world had not lost the Mediterranean character of the ancient world. All its activities were concentrated and nourished on the shores of the Mediterranean.

There was nothing to indicate that the millenary evolution of society was to be suddenly interrupted. No one was anticipating a catastrophe. Although the immediate successors of Justinian were unable to continue his work, they did not repudiate it. They refused to make any concession to the Lombards; they feverishly fortified Africa; they established their themes there as in Italy; their policies took account of the Franks and the Visigoths alike; their fleet controlled the sea; and the Pope of Rome regarded them as his Sovereigns.

The greatest intellect of the Occident, Gregory the Great, Pope from 590 to 604, saluted the Emperor Phocas, in 603, as reigning solely over free men, while the kings of the Occident reigned only over slaves. . . .

THE EXPANSION OF ISLAM IN THE
MEDITERRANEAN BASIN

The Islamic Invasion

Nothing could be more suggestive, to enable us to understand the expansion of Islam in the seventh century, than to compare its effect upon the Roman Empire with that of the Germanic invasions. These latter invasions were the climax of a situation which was as old as the Empire, and indeed even older, and which had weighed upon it more or less heavily throughout its history. When the Empire, its frontiers penetrated, abandoned the struggle, the invaders promptly allowed themselves to become absorbed in it, and as far as possible they maintained its civilization, and entered into the community upon which this civilization was based.

On the other hand, before the time of Mohammed the Empire had had practically no dealings with the Arabian peninsula. It contented itself with building a wall to protect Syria against the nomadic bands of the desert, much as it had built a wall in the north of Britain in order to check the invasions of the Picts; but this Syrian *limes,* some remains of which may still be seen on crossing the desert, was in no way comparable to that of the Rhine or the Danube.

The Empire had never regarded this as one of its vulnerable points, nor had it ever massed there any large proportion of its military forces. It was a frontier of inspection, which was crossed by the caravans that brought perfumes and spices. The Persian Empire, another of Arabia's neighbors, had taken the same precaution. In short, there was nothing to fear from the nomadic Bedouins of the Peninsula, whose civilization was still in the tribal stage, whose religious beliefs were hardly better than fetishism, and who spent their time in making war upon one another, or pillaging the caravans that traveled from south to north, from Yemen to Palestine, Syria and the Peninsula of Sinai, passing through Mecca and Yathreb (the future Medina).

Preoccupied by their century-old conflict, neither the Roman nor the Persian Empire seems to have anticipated the propaganda by which Mohammed, amidst the confused conflicts of the tribes, was to give his own people a religion which he would presently cast upon the world, while imposing his own dominion. The Empire was already in deadly danger when John of Damascus was still regarding Islam as a sort of schism, of much the same character as previous heresies.

When Mohammed died, in 632, there was as yet no sign of the peril which was to manifest itself in so overwhelming a fashion a couple of years later. No measures had been taken to defend the frontier. It is evident that whereas the Germanic menace had always attracted the attention of the Emperors, the Arab onslaught took them by surprise. In a certain sense, the expansion of Islam was due to chance, if we can give this name to the unpredictable consequence of a combination of causes. The success of the attack is explained by the exhaustion of the two Empires adjacent to Arabia, the Roman and the Persian, at the end of the long struggle between them, which had at last culminated in the victory of Heraclius over Chosröes (d. 627).

Byzantium had just regained its prestige, and its future seemed assured by the fall of the age-old enemy and the restoration to the Empire of Syria, Palestine and Egypt. The Holy Cross, which had long ago been carried off, was now triumphantly restored to Constantinople by the conqueror. The sovereign of India sent his felicitations to Heraclius, and the king of the Franks, Dagobert, concluded a perpetual peace with him. After this it was natural to expect that Heraclius would continue the Occidental policy of Justinian. It was true that the Lombards had occupied a portion of Italy, and the Visigoths, in 624, had recaptured from Byzantium its last outposts in Spain; but what was that compared with the tremendous recovery which had just been accomplished in the Orient?

However, the effort, which was doubtless excessive, had exhausted the Empire. The provinces which Persia had just surrendered were suddenly wrested from the Empire by Islam. Heraclius (610–641) was doomed to be a helpless spectator of the first onslaught of this new force which was about to disconcert and bewilder the Western world.

The Arab conquest, which brought confusion upon both Europe and Asia, was without precedent. The swiftness of its success is comparable only with that by which the Mongol Empires of Attila, Jenghiz Khan and Tamerlane were established. But these Empires were as ephemeral as the conquest of Islam was lasting. This religion still has its faithful today in almost every country where it was imposed by the first Caliphs. The lighting-like rapidity of its diffusion was a veritable miracle as compared with the slow progress of Christianity.

Compared to this irruption, what were the conquests, so long delayed, of the Germans, who, after centuries of effort, had succeeded only in nibbling at the edge of "Romania"? The Arabs, on the other hand, took possession of whole sections of the crumbling Empire. In 634 they seized the Byzantine fortress of Bothra (Bosra) in Transjordania; in 635 Damascus fell before them; in 636 the battle of Yarmok gave them the whole of Syria; in 637 or 638 Jerusalem opened its gates to them, while at the same time their Asiatic conquests included Mesopotamia and Persia. Then it was the turn of Egypt to be attacked; and shortly after the death of Heraclius (641) Alexandria was taken, and before long the whole country was occupied. Next the invasion, still continuing, submerged the Byzantine possessions in North Africa.

All this may doubtless be explained by the fact that the invasion was unexpected, by the disorder of the Byzantine armies, disorganized and surprised by a new method of fighting, by the religious and national discontent of the Monophysites and Nestorians of Syria, to whom the Empire had refused to make any concessions, and of the Coptic Church of Egypt, and by the weakness of the Persians. But all these reasons are insufficient to explain so complete a triumph. The magnitude of the results was out of all proportion to the numerical strength of the conquerors. . . .[2]

MEROVINGIANS AND CAROLINGIANS

Political Organization

Many historians regard what they call the Frankish epoch as constituting an unbroken whole, so that they describe the Carolingian period as the continuation and development of the Merovingian. But in this they are obviously mistaken, and for several reasons.

1. The Merovingian period belongs to a *milieu* entirely different from that of the Carolingian period. In the sixth and seventh centuries there was still a Mediterranean with which the Merovingians

---

[2] For further analysis of the Arab conquest the student is referred to the selections from *Medieval Cities*, which summarize the more comprehensive treatment in *Mohammed and Charlemagne.*—Ed.

were constantly in touch, and the Imperial tradition still survived in many domains of life.

2. The Germanic influence, confined to the vicinity of the Northern frontier, was very feeble, and made itself felt only in certain branches of the law and of legal procedure.

3. Between the glorious Merovingian period, which lasted until nearly the middle of the seventh century, and the Carolingian period, there was a full century of turbid decadence, in the course of which many of the features of the ancient civilizations disappeared, while others instead developed; and it was here that the Carolingian period had its origin. The ancestors of the Carolingians were not the Merovingian kings, but the mayors of the palace. Charlemagne was not in any sense the successor of Dagobert,[3] but of Charles Martel and Pippin.

4. We must not be misled by the identity of the name *regnum Francorum*. The new kingdom stretched as far as the Elbe and included part of Italy. It contained almost as many Germanic as Romanic populations.

5. Lastly, its relations with the Church were completely modified. The Merovingian State, like the Roman Empire, was secular. The Merovingian king was *rex Francorum*. The Carolingian king was *Dei gratia rex Francorum*,[4] and this little addition indicates a profound transformation. So great was this transformation that later generations did not realize the significance of the Merovingian usage. Later copyists and forgers embellished what seemed to them the inadmissible title of the Merovingian kings with a *Dei gratia*.

Thus, the two monarchies—the second of which, as I have endeavored to show in these pages, was due in some sort to the submersion of the European world by Islam—far from being continuous, were mutually opposed.

In the great crisis which led to the collapse of the State founded by Clovis, the Roman foundations crumbled away to nothing.

The first to go was the very conception of royal power. This, of course, in the form which it assumed under the Merovingians, was not a mere transposition of Imperial absolutism. I am quite willing to

---

[3] Dagobert, Frankish king, ca. 629–639, was the last of the Merovingians to rule as well as reign.—Ed.

[4] This had not yet become the regulation formula under Pippin, but it was always employed from the beginning of Charlemagne's reign. Giry, *Manuel de Diplomatique*, p. 318.

admit that the royal power was, to a great extent, merely a *de facto* despotism. Nevertheless, for the king, as for his subjects, the whole power of the State was concentrated in the monarch.

All that belonged to him was sacred; he could put himself above the law, and no one could gainsay him; he could gouge out the eyes of his enemies and confiscate their estates under the pretext that they were guilty of *lèse-majesté*. There was nothing, there was no one that he need spare. The power most resembling his own was that of the Byzantine Emperor, if we take into account the enormous differences due to the unequal levels of the two civilizations.

Every Merovingian administration preserved, for good or ill, the bureaucratic character of the Roman administration. The Merovingian chancellery, with its lay referendaries, was modeled upon that of Rome; the king picked his agents where he chose, even from among his slaves; his bodyguard of *antrustions* was reminiscent of the Pretorian guard. And in fact, the populations over whom he reigned had no conception of any other form of government. It was the government of all the kings of the period, Ostrogothic, Visigothic, Vandal. It should be noted that even when the kings assassinated one another the people did not revolt. Ambitious men committed murder, but there were no popular risings.

The cause of the Merovingian decadence was the increasing weakness of the royal power. And this weakness, by which the Carolingians profited, was due to the disorder of the financial administration, and this again was completely Roman. For, as we have seen, the king's treasury was nourished mainly by the impost. And with the disappearance of the gold currency, during the great crisis of the eighth century, this impost also disappeared. The very notion of the public impost was forgotten when the *curiales* of the cities disappeared.

The *monetarii* who forwarded this impost to the treasury in the form of gold *solidi* no longer existed. The last, I believe, is mentioned during the reign of Pippin. Thus the mayors of the palace no longer received the impost. The monarchy which they established by their *coup d'état* was a monarchy in which the Roman conception of the public impost was abolished.

The kings of the new dynasty, like the kings of the Middle Ages long after them, had no regular resources apart from the revenues of their domains. There were still prestations, of course, which dated from the Roman epoch, and in particular the *tonlieu*. But all these were diminishing. The *droit de gîte* was exercised by the functionaries rather than by the king.[5] As for the *tonlieu,* which brought in less and less as the circulation of goods diminished, the kings made donations of it to the abbeys and the *grandi.*

Some writers have attempted to prove the existence of an impost under the Carolingians. As a matter of fact, there was a custom of annual "gifts" in the Germanic portion of the Empire. And, further, the kings decreed collections and levies of silver at the time of the Norman invasions. But these were expedients which were not continued. In reality, it must be repeated, the basis of the king's financial power was his domain, his fisc, if you will. To this, at least, in the case of Charlemagne, we must add the booty taken in time of war. The ordinary financial basis of the royal power was purely rural. This was why the mayors of the palace confiscated so many ecclesiastical estates. The king was, and had to remain, if he was to maintain his power, the greatest landowner in the kingdom. No more surveys of lands, no more registers of taxes, no more financial functionaries; hence no more archives, no more offices, no more accounts. The kings, therefore, no longer had any finances; this, it will be realized, was something new. The Merovingian king bought or paid men with gold; the Carolingian king had to give them fragments of his domain. This was a serious cause of weakness, which was offset by booty as long as the country was at war under Charlemagne, but soon after his reign the consequences made themselves felt. And here, let it be repeated, there was a definite break with the financial tradition of the Romans.

To this first essential difference between the Merovingians and the Carolingians another must be added. The new king, as we have seen, was king by the grace of God. The rite of consecration, introduced under Pippin, made him in some sort a sacerdotal personage. The Merovingian was in every sense a secular king. The Carolingian was crowned only by the intervention of the Church, and the king, by virtue of his consecration, entered into the Church. He had now a religious ideal, and there were limits to his power—the limits imposed by Christian morality. We see that the kings no longer indulged in the arbitrary assassinations and the excesses of personal power which were everyday things in the Merovingian epoch. For proof we have only to read the *De rectoribus Christianis* of Sedulius

---

[5] The *tonlieu* was a market toll; the *droit de gîte* was the feudal right of lodging.—Ed.

of Liège, or the *De via regia* of Smaragdus, written, according to Ebert, between 806 and 813.

Through the rite of consecration the Church obtained a hold over the king. Henceforth the secular character of the State disappeared. Here two texts of Hincmar[6] may be cited. "It is to the unction, an episcopal and a spiritual act," he wrote to Charles the Bald in 868; "it is to this benediction, far more than to your earthly power, that you owe the royal dignity." We read further, in the Acts of the Council of Sainte-Macre: "The dignity of the pontiffs is above that of the kings: for the kings are consecrated by the pontiffs, while the pontiffs cannot be consecrated by the kings." Consecration imposed on the king certain duties to the Church. According to Smaragdus, he had to endeavor with all his might to remedy any defects that had crept into it. But he had also to protect it and to see that the tithe was paid to it.

It will be understood that under these conditions the monarchy acted in association with the Church. We have only to read the Capitularies to realize that these were as much concerned with ecclesiastical discipline and morality as with secular administration.

In the eyes of the Carolingian kings to administer their subjects meant to imbue them with ecclesiastical morality. We have already seen that their economic conceptions were dominated by the Church. The bishops were their councilors and officials. The kings entrusted them with the functions of *missi* and filled their chancellery with clerics. Here is a striking contrast with the Merovingians, who rewarded their lay referendaries by making them bishops. From the time of Hitherius, the first ecclesiastic to enter the chancellery under Charlemagne, no more laymen were employed there for centuries. Bresslau is mistaken in his belief that the invasion of the palace offices by the Church is explained by the fact that the first Carolingians wished to replace the Roman personnel of the Merovingians by an Austrasian personnel, and that they had to engage Austrasian clerics as being the only Austrasians who could read and write. No: they wanted to make sure of the collaboration of the Church.

Moreover, they could find educated men only among the clerics. During the crisis the education of laymen was discontinued. The mayors themselves were unable to write. The platonic efforts of Charlemagne to spread education among the people came to nothing,

---

[6] Hincmar was a celebrated Archbishop of Rheims, 845–882; Charles the Bald was the West Frankish King, 840–877.—Ed.

and the palace academy had only a few pupils. A period was commencing in which "cleric" and "literate man" were synonymous; hence the importance of the Church, which, in a kingdom where hardly anyone had retained any knowledge of Latin, was able for centuries to impose its language on the administration. We have to make an effort to understand the true significance of this fact; it was tremendous. Here we perceive the appearance of a new medieval characteristic: here was a religious caste which imposed its influence upon the State.

And in addition to this religious caste, the king had to reckon with the military class, which comprised the whole of the lay aristocracy, and all such freemen as had remained independent. Of course, we have glimpses of the rise of this military class under the Merovingian kings. But the aristocracy of the Merovingian epoch was strangely unlike that of the Carolingian era. The great Roman landowners, the *senatores,* whether they resided in the cities or in the country, do not give one the impression that they were primarily soldiers. They were educated. Above all things, they sought employment in the palace or the Church. It is probable that the king recruited his army leaders and the soldiers of his bodyguard more particularly among his Germanic *antrustions.* It is certain that the landowning aristocracy lost no time in attempting to dominate him. But it never succeeded in doing so.

We do not find that the king governed by means of this aristocracy, nor that he allowed it any share in the government as long as he remained powerful. And even though he conferred immunity upon it, he did not surrender either to the aristocracy or to the churches any of the rights of the crown. As a matter of fact, he had at his disposal two terrible weapons against it: prosecution for *lèse-majesté* and confiscation.

But in order to hold his own against this aristocracy it is obvious that the king had to remain extremely powerful: in other words, extremely wealthy. For the aristocracy—like the Church, for that matter—was constantly increasing its authority over the people. This social development, which began in the days of the late Empire, was continuing. Powerful individuals had their private soldiers, numerous *vassi* who had recommended themselves to them (had applied to them for protection), and who constituted a formidable following.

In the Merovingian period the seignorial authority of the landowners was manifested only within the limits of their private rights. But in the period of anarchy and decadence, when war broke out between the mayors of the palace, who were backed by factions of aristocrats, the institution of vassalage underwent a transformation. It assumed an increasing importance, and its military character became plainly apparent when the Carolingian triumphed over his rivals. From the time of Charles Martel the power exercised by the king was essentially based on his military vassals in the North.

He gave them benefices—that is to say, estates—in exchange for military service, and these estates he confiscated from the churches. "Now," says Guilhiermoz,[7] "owing to their importance, these concessions to vassals were henceforth found to tempt, not only persons of mean or moderate condition, but the *great*."

And this was entirely in the interest of the grantor, who henceforth gave large benefices "on the condition that the grantee served him, not only with his own person, but with a number of vassals in proportion to the importance of the benefice conceded." It was undoubtedly by such means that Charles Martel was able to recruit the powerful Austrasian following with which he went to war. And the system was continued after his time.

In the ninth century the kings exacted an oath of vassalage from all the magnates of the kingdom, and even from the bishops. It became increasingly apparent that only those were truly submissive to the king who had paid homage to him. Thus the subject was disappearing behind the vassal, and Hincmar went so far as to warn Charles the Bald of the consequent danger to the royal authority. The necessity in which the first mayors of the palace found themselves, of providing themselves with a loyal following, consisting of sworn beneficiaries, led to a profound transformation of the State. For henceforth the king would be compelled to reckon with his vassals, who constituted the military strength of the State. The organization of the countries fell into disorder, since the vassals were not amenable to the jurisdiction of the count. In the field they commanded their own vassals themselves; the count led only the freemen to battle. It is possible that their domains were exempt from taxation. They were known as *optimates regis*.

The chronicle of Moissac, in 813, called them *senatus* or *majores natu Francorum,* and together with the high ecclesiastics and the counts they did indeed form the king's council. The king, therefore,

---

[7] Guilhiermoz, *Essai sur les origines de la noblesse,* p. 125.

allowed them to partake of his political power. The State was becoming dependent on the contractual bonds established between the king and his vassals.

This was the beginning of the feudal period.

All might still have been well if the king could have retained his vassals. But at the close of the ninth century, apart from those of his own domain, they had become subject to the suzerainty of the counts. For as the royal power declined, from the time of the civil wars which marked the end of the reign of Louis the Pious, the counts became more and more independent. The only relation which existed between them and the king was that of the vassal to his suzerain. They collected the *regalia* for the king; and sometimes they combined several counties into one.[8] The monarchy lost its administrative character, becoming transformed into a *bloc* of independent principalities, attached to the king by a bond of vassalage which he could no longer force his vassals to respect. The kings allowed the royal power to slip through their fingers.

And it was inevitable that it should be so. We must not be misled by the prestige of Charlemagne. He was still able to rule the State by virtue of his military power, his wealth, which was derived from booty, and his *de facto* preeminence in the Church. These things enabled him to reign without systematic finances, and to exact obedience from functionaries who, being one and all great landowners, could very well have existed independently. But what is the value of an administration which is no longer salaried? How can it be prevented from administering the country, if it chooses, for its own benefit, and not for the king's? Of what real use were such inspectors as the *missi?* Charles undoubtedly intended to administer the kingdom, but was unable to do so. When we read the capitularies, we are struck by the difference between what they decreed and what was actually done. Charles decreed that everyone should send his sons to school; that there should be only one mint; that usurious prices should be abolished in time of famine. He established maximum prices. But it was impossible to achieve all these things, because to do so would have presupposed the obedience— which could not be assured—of the *grandi,* who were conscious of their independence, or of the bishops, who, when Charlemagne was

[8] In this connection the history of the formation of the county of Flanders is highly characteristic.

dead, proclaimed the superiority of the spiritual over the temporal power.

The economic basis of the State did not correspond with the administrative character which Charlemagne had endeavored to preserve. The economy of the State was based upon the great domain without commercial outlets.

The landowners had no need of security, since they did not engage in commerce. Such a form of property is perfectly consistent with anarchy. Those who owned the soil had no need of the king.

Was this why Charles had endeavored to preserve the class of humble freemen? He made the attempt, but he was unsuccessful. The great domain continued to expand, and liberty to disappear.

When the Normans began to invade the country, the State was already powerless. It was incapable of taking systematic measures of defense, and of assembling armies which could have held their own against the invaders. Everyone was going his own way. . . .

What was left of the king's *regalia* he misused. He relinquished the *tonlieu,* and the right of the mint. Of its own accord the monarchy divested itself of its remaining inheritance, which was little enough. In the end, royalty became no more than a form. Its evolution was completed when in France, with Hugh Capet, it became elective.

Intellectual Civilization

As we have seen, the Germanic invasions had not the effect of abolishing Latin as the language of "Romania," except in those territories where Salic and Ripuarian Franks, Alamans, and Bavarians had established themselves *en masse.* Elsewhere the German immigrants became Romanized with surprising rapidity.

The conquerors, dispersed about the country, and married to native wives who continued to speak their own language, all learned the Latin tongue. They did not modify it in any way, apart from introducing a good many terms relating to law, the chase, war, and agriculture, which made their way southwards from the Belgian regions, where the Germans were numerous.

Even more rapid was the Romanization of the Burgundi, Visigoths, Ostrogoths, Vandals and Lombards. According to Gamillscheg, nothing was left of the Gothic language when the Moors conquered Spain except the names of persons and places.

On the other hand, the confusion into which the Mediterranean world was thrown by the invasion of Islam resulted in a profound transformation where language was concerned. In Africa Latin was replaced by Arabic. In Spain, on the other hand, it survived, but was deprived of its foundations: there were no more schools or monasteries, and there was no longer an educated clergy. The conquered people made use of a Roman patois which was not a written language. Latin, which had survived so successfully in the Peninsula until the eve of the conquest, disappeared; people were beginning to speak Spanish.

In Italy, on the other hand, it resisted more successfully, and a few isolated schools survived in Rome and Milan.

But it is in Gaul that we can best observe the extent of the confusion, and its causes.

The Latin of the Merovingian epoch was, of course, barbarously incorrect; but it was still a living Latin. It seems that it was even taught in the schools where a practical education was given, while here and there the bishops and senators still read and sometimes even tried to write classical Latin.

Merovingian Latin was by no means a vulgar language. It showed few signs of Germanic influence. Those who spoke it could make themselves understood, and understand others, in any part of "Romania." It was perhaps more incorrect in the North of France than elsewhere, but nevertheless, it was a spoken and written language. The Church did not hesitate to employ it for the purposes of propaganda, administration, and justice.

This language was taught in the schools. Laymen learned and wrote it. Its relation to the Latin of the Empire was like that of the cursive in which it was written to the writing of the Roman epoch. And since it was still written and extensively employed for the purposes of administration and commerce, it became stabilized.

But it was destined to disappear in the course of the great disorders of the eighth century. The political anarchy, the reorganization of the Church, the disappearance of the cities, of commerce and of administration, especially the financial administration, and of the secular schools, made its survival, with its Latin soul, impossible. It became debased, and was transformed, according to the region, into various Romanic dialects. The details of the process are lost, but it is certain that Latin ceased to be spoken about the year 800, except by the clergy.

Now, it was precisely at this moment, when Latin ceased to be a living language, and was replaced by the rustic idioms from which the national languages are derived, that it became what it was to remain through the centuries: a learned language: a novel medieval feature which dates from the Carolingian epoch.

It is curious to note that the origin of this phenomenon must be sought in the only Romanic country in which the Germanic invasion had completely extirpated Romanism: in Britain, among the Anglo-Saxons.

The conversion of this country was organized, as we have seen, on the shores of the Mediterranean, and not in the neighboring country of Gaul. It was the monks of Augustine, dispatched by Gregory the Great in 596, who promoted the movement already commenced by the Celtic monks of Ireland.

In the seventh century Saint Theodore of Tarsus and his companion Adrian enriched the religion which they brought with them with the Graeco-Roman traditions. A new culture immediately began to evolve in the island, a fact which Dawson rightly considers "the most important event which occurred between the epoch of Justinian and that of Charlemagne." Among these purely Germanic Anglo-Saxons the Latin culture was introduced suddenly, together with the Latin religion, and it profited by the enthusiasm felt for the latter. No sooner were they converted, under the influence and guidance of Rome, than the Anglo-Saxons turned their gaze toward the Sacred City. They visited it continually, bringing back relics and manuscripts. They submitted themselves to its suggestive influence, and learned its language, which for them was no vulgar tongue, but a sacred language, invested with an incomparable prestige. As early as the seventh century there were men among the Anglo-Saxons, like the Venerable Bede and the poet Aldhelm, whose learning was truly astonishing as measured by the standards of Western Europe.

The intellectual reawakening which took place under Charlemagne must be attributed to the Anglo-Saxon missionaries. Before them, of course, there were the Irish monks, including the greatest of all, Saint Columban, the founder of Luxeuil and Bobbio, who landed in Gaul about 590. They had preached asceticism in a time of religious decadence, but we do not find that they exercised the slightest literary influence.

It was quite otherwise with the Anglo-Saxons; their purpose was to propagate Christianity in Germania, for which the Merovingian

Church had done little or nothing. And this purpose coincided with the policy of the Carolingians; hence the enormous influence of Boniface, the organizer of the Germanic Church, and, by virtue of this fact, the intermediary between the Pope and Pippin the Short.

Charlemagne devoted himself to the task of literary revival simultaneously with that of the restoration of the Church. The principal representative of Anglo-Saxon culture, Alcuin, the head of the school of York, entered Charlemagne's service in 782, as director of the palace school, and henceforth exercised a decisive influence over the literary movement of the time.

Thus, by the most curious reversal of affairs, which affords the most striking proof of the rupture effected by Islam, the North in Europe replaced the South both as a literary and as a political center.

It was the North that now proceeded to diffuse the culture which it had received from the Mediterranean. Latin, which had been a living language on the continental side of the Channel, was for the Anglo-Saxons, from the beginning, merely the language of the Church. The Latin which was taught to the Anglo-Saxons was not the incorrect business and administrative language, adapted to the needs of secular life, but the language which was still spoken in the Mediterranean schools. Theodore came from Tarsus in Cilicia, and had studied at Athens before coming to Rome. Adrian, an African by birth, was the abbot of a monastery near Naples, and was equally learned in Greek and in Latin.

It was the classic tradition that they propagated among their neophytes, and a correct Latin, which had no need, as on the Continent, to make concessions to common usage in order to be understood, since the people did not speak Latin, but Anglo-Saxon. Thus, the English monasteries received the heritage of ancient culture without intermediary. It was the same in the fifteenth century, when the Byzantine scholars brought to Italy, not the vulgar Greek, the living language of the street, but the classical Greek of the schools.

In this way the Anglo-Saxons became simultaneously the reformers of the language and also the reformers of the Church. The barbarism into which the Church had lapsed was manifested at once by its bad morals, its bad Latin, its bad singing, and its bad writing. To reform it at all meant to reform all these things. Hence questions of grammar and of writing immediately assumed all the significance of an apostolate. Purity of dogma and purity of language went together. Like the Anglo-Saxons, who had immediately adopted it, the

Roman rite made its way into all parts of the Empire, together with the Latin culture. This latter was the instrument *par excellence* of what is known as the Carolingian Renaissance, although this had other agents in such men as Paulus Diaconus, Peter of Pisa, and Theodulf.[9] But it is important to note that this Renaissance was purely clerical. It did not affect the people, who had no understanding of it. It was at once a revival of the ancient tradition and a break with the Roman tradition, which was interrupted by the seizure of the Mediterranean regions by Islam. The lay society of the period, being purely agricultural and military, no longer made use of Latin. This was now merely the language of the priestly caste, which monopolized all learning, and which was constantly becoming more divorced from the people whose divinely appointed guide it considered itself. For centuries there will be no learning save in the Church. The consequence was that learning and intellectual culture, while they became more assertive, were also becoming more exceptional. The Carolingian Renaissance coincided with the general illiteracy of the laity. Under the Merovingians laymen were still able to read and write; but not so under the Carolingians. The sovereign who instigated and supported this movement, Charlemagne, could not write; nor could his father, Pippin the Short. We must not attach any real importance to his ineffectual attempts to bestow this culture upon his court and his family. To please him, a few courtiers learned Latin. Men like Eginhard, Nithard and Angilbert[10] were passing luminaries. Generally speaking, the immense majority of the lay aristocracy were unaffected by a movement which interested only those of its members who wished to make a career in the Church.

During the Merovingian epoch the royal administration called for a certain culture on the part of those laymen who wished to enter it. But now, insofar as it still required literate recruits—as it did, for example, for the chancellery—it obtained them from the Church. For the rest, since it no longer had a bureaucracy, it had no further need

---

[9] Paulus Diaconus (Paul the Deacon) wrote the very important *History of the Lombards;* Peter of Pisa was a grammarian first at Pavia and then at the Palace School at Aachen; Theodulf was a Spanish Goth who became Bishop of Orléans and is recognized as the best poet of the "Carolingian Renaissance." All were contemporaries of Charlemagne.—Ed.

[10] Angilbert, d. 814, was a poet and probably one of the authors of the "Royal Annals" of Charlemagne's period, drawn up in the monastery at Lorsch. Nithard was a son of Angilbert and a grandson of Charlemagne, who wrote several histories of the first half of the ninth century; these contain the famous Oath of Strasbourg (842) in both French and German.—Ed.

of men of education. The immense majority of the counts were no doubt illiterate. The type of the Merovingian senator had disappeared. The aristocracy no longer spoke Latin, and apart from a very few exceptions, which prove the rule, it could neither read nor write. . . .

Thus we observe the same phenomenon in every domain of life. The culture which had hitherto flourished in the Mediterranean countries had migrated to the North. It was in the North that the civilization of the Middle Ages was elaborated. And it is a striking fact that the majority of the writers of this period were of Irish, Anglo-Saxon or Frankish origin: that is, they came from regions which lay to the north of the Seine. . . .

Thus we see that Germany, being converted, immediately began to play an essential part in the civilization to which she had hitherto been a stranger. The culture which had been entirely Roman was now becoming Romano-Germanic, but in point of fact it was localized in the bosom of the Church.

Nevertheless, it is evident that a new orientation was unconsciously effected in Europe, and that in this development Germanism collaborated. Charlemagne's court, and Charlemagne himself, were certainly much less Latinized than were the Merovingians. Under the new dispensation many functionaries were recruited from Germany, and Austrasian vassals were settled in the South. Charlemagne's wives were all German women. Certain judicial reforms, such as that of the *échevins,* had their origin in the regions which gave birth to the dynasty. Under Pippin the clergy became Germanized and under Charlemagne there were many German bishops in Romanic regions. Angelelmus and Heribald, at Auxerre, were both Bavarians; Bernold, at Strasbourg, was a Saxon; at Le Mans there were three Westphalians in succession; Hilduin, at Verdun, was a German; Herulfus and Ariolfus, at Langres, came from Augsburg; Wulferius, at Vienne, and Leidrad, at Lyons, were Bavarians. And I do not think there is any evidence of a contrary migration. To appreciate the difference we have only to compare Chilperic,[11] a Latin poet, with Charlemagne, at whose instance a collection was made of the ancient Germanic songs!

All this was bound to result in a break with the Roman and Mediterranean traditions. And while it made the West more and more

[11] Chilperic was King of the Franks, 561–584.—Ed.

self-sufficing, it produced an aristocracy of mixed descent and inheritance. Was it not then that many terms found their way into the vocabulary to which an origin too early has often been attributed? There were no longer any Barbarians. There was one great Christian community, coterminous with the *ecclesia*. This *ecclesia*, of course, looked toward Rome, but Rome had broken away from Byzantium and was forced to look toward the North. The Occident was now living its own life. It was preparing to unfold its possibilities, its virtualities, taking no orders from the outer world, except in the matter of religion.

There was now a community of civilization, of which the Carolingian Empire was the symbol and the instrument. For while the Germanic element collaborated in this civilization, it was a Germanic element which had been Romanized by the Church. There were, of course, differences within this community. The Empire would be dismembered, but each of its portions would survive, since the feudality would respect the monarchy. In short, the culture which was to be that of the period extending from the early Middle Ages to the Renaissance of the twelfth century—and this was a true renaissance—bore, and would continue to bear, the Carolingian imprint. There was an end of political unity, but an international unity of culture survived. Just as the States founded in the West in the fifth century by the Barbarian kings retained the Roman imprint, so France, Germany, and Italy retained the Carolingian imprint.

GENERAL CONCLUSION

From the foregoing data, it seems, we may draw two essential conclusions:

1. The Germanic invasions destroyed neither the Mediterranean unity of the ancient world, nor what may be regarded as the truly essential features of the Roman culture as it still existed in the fifth century, at a time when there was no longer an Emperor in the West.

Despite the resulting turmoil and destruction, no new principles made their appearance; either in the economic or social order, or in the linguistic situation, or in the existing institutions. Whatever civilization survived was Mediterranean. It was in the regions by the seacoast that culture was preserved, and it was from them that the innovations of the age proceeded: monasticism, the conversion of the Anglo-Saxons, the *ars Barbarica*, etc.

The Orient was the fertilizing factor: Constantinople, the center of the world. In 600 the physiognomy of the world was not different in quality from that which it had revealed in 400.

2. The cause of the break with the tradition of antiquity was the rapid and unexpected advance of Islam. The result of this advance was the final separation of East from West, and the end of Mediterranean unity. Countries like Africa and Spain, which had always been parts of the Western community, gravitated henceforth in the orbit of Bagdad. In these countries another religion made its appearance, and an entirely different culture. The Western Mediterranean, having become a Moslem lake, was no longer the thoroughfare of commerce and of thought which it had always been.

The West was blockaded and forced to live on in isolation. For the first time in history the axis of history was shifted northwards from the Mediterranean. The decadence into which the Merovingian monarchy lapsed as a result of this change gave birth to a new dynasty, the Carolingian, whose original home was in the Germanic North.

With this new dynasty the Pope allied himself, breaking with the Emperor, who, engrossed in his struggle against the Musulmans, could no longer protect him. And so the Church allied itself with the new order of things. In Rome, and in the Empire which it founded, it had no rival. And its power was all the greater inasmuch as the State, being incapable of maintaining its administration, allowed itself to be absorbed by the feudality, the inevitable sequel of the economic regression. All the consequences of this change became glaringly apparent after Charlemagne. Europe, dominated by the Church and the feudality, assumed a new physiognomy, differing slightly in different regions. The Middle Ages—to retain the traditional term—were beginning. The transitional phase was protracted. One may say that it lasted a whole century—from 650 to 750. It was during this period of anarchy that the tradition of antiquity disappeared, while the new elements took control.

This development was completed in 800 by the constitution of the new Empire, which consecrated the break between the West and the East, inasmuch as it gave to the West a new Roman Empire—the manifest proof that it had broken with the old Empire, which continued to exist in Constantinople.

Norman H. Baynes

M. PIRENNE AND THE UNITY OF THE MEDITERRANEAN WORLD

Norman H. Baynes (1877–1961), in his day dean of Byzantine scholars in Britain, came to the field of history as he was approaching middle age. A barrister-at-law, during World War I he was confronted with a choice of continuing in the teaching and practice of law, or turning to the teaching and writing of history. For English historical scholarship his decision was a happy one; for close to thirty years he was a member of the teaching staff of University College, London, where he was held in great affection and high esteem. His scholarly work, extensive and arresting, which brought him many honors, including honorary degrees from Oxford and Cambridge, was largely devoted to Byzantine studies, or, as he preferred to call it, East Roman History. The selection which follows is from a book review, published in 1929, of the French edition of Pirenne's Medieval Cities.

For M. Pirenne the unity of the Mediterranean world was maintained unbroken into the eighth century of our era: that unity was only shattered as a result of the Arab conquest of Africa. Upon the Continent that theory has been vigorously canvassed and directly challenged; it gave rise, I understand, to the debate which most successfully enlivened the proceedings of the International Congress of Historical Studies at Oslo. To it British scholarship has paid little attention—a disquieting sign of that general lack of interest in the early European Middle Age which is now prevalent in this country. Yet the problem raised by M. Pirenne is of the greatest significance alike for the history of the later Roman Empire and for the understanding of the whole period of transition which separates the reign of Theodosius the Great from the age of Charlemagne. The central issue at stake is the position of Merovingian Gaul, and in particular the question of the part played by the Syrian merchants of the West in the economic life of the Merovingian kingdom. Here Gregory of Tours[1] is, of course, our principal authority. The *History of the Franks*

From "M. Pirenne and the Unity of the Mediterranean World," in Norman H. Baynes, *Byzantine Studies and Other Essays* (University of London, The Athlone Press, London, 1955), pp. 310–16. Reprinted from *Journal of Roman Studies,* 19 (1929), by permission of the Society for the Promotion of Roman Studies.

[1] Gregory of Tours, 539–594. His *History of the Franks* is regarded as one of the most important historical works of the early Middle Ages.—Ed.

is an extensive work and it will probably be admitted that it has its *longueurs:* the most blood-thirsty reader can become sated by the story of incessant assassinations. Thus it may be suspected that the *History* is more often consulted than it is read through from beginning to end. Yet it is only by such a reading that one can gain an impression of the range of Gregory's interests and contacts. After such a reading I should like to take this opportunity to record my own personal impressions. M. Pirenne writes "La Mediterranée ne perd pas son importance après la période des invasions. Elle reste pour les Germains ce qu'elle était avant leur arrivée: le centre même de l'Europe, le *mare nostrum.*" ["The Mediterranean did not lose its importance after the period of the invasions. It remained for the Germans what it had been before their arrival: the very center of Europe, the *mare nostrum.*"] In what sense and to what extent is this true? How far can we prove direct contact between, let us say, Antioch or Alexandria and the ports of Merovingian Gaul?

In the first place two remarks must be made: (1) Students of economics have been tempted to give to terms used in our medieval sources a modern significance which is foreign to their context. If a "merchant" is mentioned, they tend to presume that he is engaged in far-reaching, even transmarine, transactions. . . . [But] the merchant may be solely concerned with local trade. (2) From the mention of "Syrians" in the Western sources during the early Middle Ages there is not infrequently drawn the inference that these eastern immigrants remained in close commercial relations with their country of origin, or that the population of these colonies was being constantly reinforced by new arrivals from the East . . . this presupposition underlies all M. Bréhier's work upon the subject.[2] That there was such commercial intercourse under the early Empire cannot be doubted: this it was which brought the Orientals to Western Europe. . . . Such intercourse continued through the fourth and into the early fifth century, but its persistence into the Middle Age of Merovingian Gaul cannot simply be assumed; the prior question must be asked: is there any justification for such an assumption?

Perhaps the best method of approach is to study Gregory's knowledge of foreign countries:[3] what is the range of his information? Of affairs in Visigothic Spain he was fully informed: embassies were

[2] Louis Bréhier is a French authority on Byzantine history. His best known work is *Le Monde Byzantin,* 3 vols. (Paris, 1947–1950).—Ed.
[3] The references to *The History of the Franks,* supplied by Baynes, are omitted.—Ed.

frequent, and he himself questioned Chilperic's envoys to Leuvigild on the condition of the Spanish Catholics. Agilan, Leuvigild's envoy, passed through Tours and disputed with Gregory, and the bishop was present at the banquet given by Oppila. Of N. Italy Gregory naturally knew something owing to the Frankish invasions of the country, but of S. Italy he seems to have known little: he can make the remarkable statement that Buccelin[4] captured Sicily and exacted tribute from it. Of Rome and of the Popes of the time we hear nothing, save of the appeal to John III in the case of the bishops Salonius and Sagittarius. [In the next book] however, we are given a long account of affairs in Rome, showing Gregory's readiness to be interested in the subject when information could be obtained. The reason for this sudden extension of the range of Gregory's vision lies in the fact that a deacon of Tours, who had been sent on a mission to Rome to acquire relics of the saints, had just returned from Italy. If the reader will consider the character of the information there recorded, and Gregory's general silence on Roman matters he will, I think, infer that Gaul was at this time not in regular contact with Italy. I myself cannot believe that ships and traders were customarily passing between Italy and Merovingian Gaul.[5]

If we pass to the history of the Roman Empire in the Eastern Mediterranean the result is curiously similar. Of Justinian we hear nothing save the appointment of Narses in place of Belisarius in Italy and the campaign in Spain. But of Justin's reign we learn more: of his character, of the capture by the Persians of Syrian Antioch—Antioch is placed in Egypt!—of the Persian War and of the association by Justin of Tiberius as colleague. This sudden expansion of the narrative is due to the fact that envoys of Sigebert returned at this time to Gaul from an embassy to the imperial court at Constantinople. From the reign of Tiberius we are given legends of the emperor's liberality, an account of the plot to dethrone him in favor of Justinian, Justin's nephew, and of his Persian War; but of the stubborn defense of Sirmium against the Avars Gregory knows noth-

---

[4] Buccelin was a German chieftain; he and his men were crushed by Narses (one of Justinian's generals), near Capua in 554.—Ed.

[5] Individuals mentioned in this and subsequent paragraphs: Leuvigild was king of the Visigoths, 568–586. Chilperic and Sigebert were sons of the Merovingian king of the Franks, Chlotar I; they and their two brothers waged civil war over the division of the kingdom following their father's death in 561. Tiberius II (578–582) and Maurice (582–602) were Eastern Roman Emperors. Childebert II, son of Sigebert and of the famous Brunhild (Visigoth princess) was king of the Franks, 575–596. Gundovald, illegitimate son of Chlotar I, revolted against Childebert II and was crushed by Brunhild.—Ed.

ing. The source of his information and the reason for his silence may be conjectured from the fact that Chilperic's embassy to Tiberius returned to Gaul, it would appear, in the year 580. The operations against the Avars belong to the years 580–582. We take up the eastern story once more with the death of Tiberius and the accession of Maurice. Here again the information doubtless came through the imperial envoys who brought a subsidy of 50,000 pieces of gold to induce Childebert to attack the Lombards in Italy. Gregory's interest in the affairs of the East when he could obtain first-hand knowledge of happenings there is shown from his account of the capture of Antioch by the Persians derived from the refugee bishop Simon, the Armenian. The conclusion which would seem to result from this analysis is that Gregory had no regular source of information for eastern affairs such as would have been furnished by traders had they been in continued relation with the ports of the eastern empire. . . .

Nowhere, so far as I can see, in the work of Gregory of Tours is there any suggestion of a *direct* contact of Merovingian Gaul with the eastern Mediterranean. If Justinian was constrained to resort to measures of fiscal oppression to compel shipowners to trade with the new imperial conquests in Italy and Africa, it is hardly likely that East Roman merchants would readily sail to the port of Gaul. That products from the East reached Merovingian Gaul is clear, but the problem is whence did they come *directly?* Was it from imperial territory in Spain or from Carthage?

My own belief is that the unity of the Mediterranean world was broken by the pirate fleet of Vandal Carthage and that the shattered unity was never restored. A Merovingian might have pepper to his meat, the wine of Gaza might be a bait to lure a man to his assassination but Gaul of the Merovingians, so far as vital contacts with the empire were concerned, was from the first marooned. Gregory with all his advantages only gained occasional fragments of information upon the doings of Romania. . . .

If, then, the view which I have endeavored to set forth has any foundation, it is misleading to state that for the Franks of the sixth century the Mediterranean still remained *"mare nostrum"*; we can only accept with qualifications the statement that "the great Mediterranean commerce which flourished in Gaul during the Late Empire subsisted into the sixth and even into the seventh century"; it is only true at a remove that "of Byzantium, of Asia Minor and of Egypt

Jewish merchants, but more especially Syrian merchants continued
to supply it (Gaul) with luxury goods, with precious fabrics, with fine
wines."[6]

[6] The quotations are from F. Vercauteren (another Belgian historian) and from Pirenne.
Baynes quotes them in French.—Ed.

H. St. L. B. Moss

ECONOMIC CONSEQUENCES OF THE BARBARIAN INVASIONS

*Henry St. Lawrence Beaufort Moss was long associated in historical writing
with Professor Norman H. Baynes. In Britain they opened up the study of
Byzantine history. The selection which follows reprints in large part an
article by Mr. Moss in a series on "Revisions in Economic History," in the
British journal,* The Economic History Review. *Mr. Moss wrote this article in
1937 as a summary of historical investigation at that time. For his extensive
documentation the student is referred to the original article.*

During the past generation a substantial literature has accumulated
around one of the central problems of European history—the transition from the ancient world to medieval civilization. By the end of the
nineteenth century what may be called the "catastrophic" view had
been definitely abandoned. Since then the complexity of the change
has become steadily more apparent. How distant any general agreement still is, even on its main features, was shown by the debates of
the Historical Congress at Oslo in 1928; and detailed reexamination
of its many aspects proceeds unceasingly in a score of periodicals
and a steady flow of monographs. A cursory and superficial survey of
some of the principal points of controversy is all that will be attempted in the following pages.

  The economic approach to history is a comparatively recent development. Ancient and medieval writers were seldom directly con-

From H. St. L. B. Moss, "The Economic Consequences of the Barbarian Invasions," *The
Economic History Review* 7 (May 1937): 209–16. Published for The Economic History
Society by A. & C. Black Ltd., London. Reprinted by permission of the Economic
History Society and Mr. Moss.

cerned with the subject, and not until the last century did it emerge as a definite subdivision of historiography. A revaluation of many historical judgments followed, based on a fresh sifting of the sources. But an important obstacle to the new studies, so far as the "dark ages" are concerned, soon made its appearance. Deficient in general as the sources for these centuries are, nowhere is their poverty more threadbare than in the economic data which they provide. Scanty references, often of purely local application, in the writings of annalists, orators, monkish chroniclers or theologians must be collected, interpreted, and assessed in the light of a background which is often only too obscure, before any general picture can be formed. Population statistics, estimates of money-values, even, in many cases, identification of place-names—these, and much else, are highly problematical. Epigraphic and archaeological evidence is notably insufficient, as compared with that of the preceding centuries. It is no disservice to the results achieved by recent scholarship to point out that the material at its disposal is lamentably small in proportion to the difficulty and extent of the problem. This being so, it is arguable that comprehensive theories should be regarded at present rather as working hypotheses to be tested and possibly modified by gradually accumulating data, than as definite solutions to which all such data must necessarily conform.

"Barbarian Invasions" is a wide term, covering more than a millennium. For our present purpose we may define it as the Germanic settlements which, during the fifth and sixth centuries A.D., led to the breakdown of Roman government in the western provinces. This will exclude such later developments as the Slavs, the Northmen, the Magyars, and (except incidentally) the Arabs. The eastern Mediterranean, where Roman administration continued to operate, is also excluded, though it was undoubtedly, during the whole of this period, the commercial focus of Europe. Spain and Africa, owing to the Islamic conquests, stand apart; and evidence concerning them is in any case insufficient for any brief generalizations. Britain is also, at this time, removed from the main course of Western European history, and its special problems will not be entered upon here.

The economic significance of the invasions has been presented in a fresh light by the results of recent investigation, which has led to a general softening down of climaxes and contrasts. *Kulturcäsur,* an abrupt break of cultural continuity, is no longer in question: for Rostovtzeff "what happened was a slow and gradual change, a shifting of values in the consciousness of men," though he admits the virtual disappearance of the Graeco-Roman city organization, and a reduction of ancient civilization to some essential elements. Chronologically, he adds, this "coincides with the political disintegration of the Roman Empire, and with a great change in its social and economic life." This simplification of the complex structure of the ancient world can be traced from the unsettled conditions which succeeded the Antonine Age, at the close of the second century; it is from this period, in F. Lot's view,[1] that the Middle Ages should properly be dated. The pace of regression was therefore slow; and the continued contact and gradual fusion of the Roman and Germanic worlds, which was made possible by the survival, until the opening of the fifth century, of the Roman Empire in the West— thanks largely to the measures of Diocletian and Constantine— enabled many Roman institutions to pass into the structure of the barbarian kingdoms.

The details of this fusion have received much attention. Early German settlements within the frontiers have been noticed; the careers of Germans in Roman service have been traced. Economic and cultural relations between the Empire and the barbarians have been studied. . . . The agrarian systems of the later Roman Empire and of the Teutonic peoples have given rise to much controversial literature. The contrast formerly drawn between the free association of the "Mark" of primitive German agriculture and the despotic control of the great Roman estates had been abandoned, or seriously modified, by the end of last century, and emphasis is now laid by certain writers on the inequalities of German social classes and the essential continuity in landholding arrangements, from the ancient to the medieval worlds. Thus H. Sée, developing the teaching of Fustel de Coulanges, claims that in France "le personnel des propriétaires pourra changer au cours des temps, mais la villa et le manse subsisteront pendant des siècles, souvent avec leur dimensions primitives."[2] Italian authorities have similarly dwelt on the Roman survivals in their country, not only in the organization of the great estates, but

---

[1] This view was developed by Ferdinand Lot in his *The End of the Ancient World and the Beginnings of the Middle Ages* (London, 1931).—Ed.

[2] "the personnel of the owners will change in time, but the villa and the 'manse' will persist for centuries, often with their original boundaries." Henri Sée (1864–1930) was a leading French economic historian. Fustel de Coulanges (1830–1889) developed a theory of Roman origins of feudalism, which though not generally accepted had a significant influence on historical interpretations in his day.—Ed.

in the city-centered life of the Lombards, and, as has been suggested, in the continued existence, even so late as the tenth century, of "artisan corporations" akin to those which characterized the industrial system of the later Roman state.

Examination of the conditions prevailing in the Romano-German kingdoms has shown a compromise rather than a conquest, varying in the degree with the different peoples, but—such is the trend of much recent theory—with a considerably larger admixture of Roman elements than was formerly believed. Legal codes, marriage customs and social divisions exhibit many examples of interaction and even, perhaps, convergence of similar institutions, while the role played by the Church in the preservation of Roman legal and juridical methods has lately been brought into full prominence. Nor has the view of an unbroken economic regression, a steady drift towards "natural economy" from the third century onwards, been left unchallenged. It had already been noticed that the currency reforms of Constantine I were followed by a return to the monetary conditions of the earlier Empire, and G. Mickwitz has shown that these continued to exist throughout the fourth century; even the State itself, in whose interests it was to maintain the payments in kind stabilized by Diocletian, had finally to capitulate before the demands of the army and civil service. The Ostrogothic kingdom in Italy, as Hartmann[3] had proved, was still organized on a money basis, the details of which have recently been elucidated by H. Geiss, and Italian writers have even maintained that no real breach is observable between the financial arrangements of the later Roman Empire and those of the Lombard government. Stress, in fact, is in general laid on the prevalence of a "money economy" throughout these centuries, and the denial of any decisive economic change caused by the barbarians has involved the theory that commerce and finance suffered no serious setback.

Two celebrated theories must be mentioned in this connection, those of H. Pirenne and A. Dopsch, though space forbids more than a brief description. . . .[4]

To summarize briefly the work of Dopsch is an even more hazardous task in view of the wide range of his theories and the considerable development which they have undergone. Covering the whole

---

[3] Ludo M. Hartmann (1865–1924), a German historian who applied the evolutionary approach to the problem of the transition from Rome to Europe. Other historians mentioned in this paragraph are more recent writers.—Ed.
[4] The remainder of this paragraph is a summary of Pirenne's views with quotations from his writings.—Ed.

field of economic life from Caesar to Charlemagne, Dopsch has surveyed in detail the evidence for the relations between the German and Roman worlds, the importance of which had been first brought into full prominence in O. Seeck's brilliant work.[5] Emphasis is laid on the recent findings of archaeology, especially in the districts of the Rhine and upper Danube, as showing continuity on the occupied sites, and on the smallness of the difference in cultural level which, it is claimed, separated the German from the Roman population at the time of the invasions. It is no longer possible to regard the German as a mere peasant, or a follower of nomad raiding chiefs; he was also a settled farmer, a seafarer, a skilled merchant, even a city-dweller. The general conclusion, which resembles that of Seeck, is reached that the German peoples pervaded the Roman Empire from within, by a kind of peaceful penetration; with the coming of the German kingdoms, the old-established firm, as it were, changed its name to that of the long predominant partner. The continuity is worked out in great detail; land-holding, social classes, political organization are traced in the various kingdoms up to the time of the Carolingian ascendancy in Western Europe. Industry and commerce are likewise held to show no hiatus, save for the temporary disturbances caused by the invasions. Trade still circulated along the Roman roads, carrying not only the luxuries, but the necessities of life. The nobility may have retreated to their country estates, but they remained in contact with the towns (which continued for the most part to exist) and produced for the local market. The whole theory of a regression to "natural economy" and the doctrine of a "closed domestic economy" must therefore be abandoned. The Germans had for centuries been accustomed to the handling of money, and even in the invasion period had carried on extensive trading activities. The Germanic kingdoms were therefore conducted on a currency basis, and financial policy formed part of their political programs. The Carolingian period, far from showing a decline, as in Pirenne's view, witnessed a considerable extension of trade and industry, and even the dissolution of Charlemagne's Empire was not followed by any regression to autarchic conditions. "The Carolingian development is a link in the unbroken chain of living continuity which leads, without any cultural break, from the late antiquity to the German Middle Ages."

What, it may be asked, has become of "the great change in social

---

[5] Otto Seeck (1850–1921) wrote an important six-volume work on the period from Diocletian to 476.—Ed.

and economic life" to which Rostovtzeff refers? From the studies which we have been analyzing, it would seem that nothing of the sort took place, and that the early Middle Ages preserved intact the fabric of later Roman economic organization. Some reservations may be suggested as regards the theories outlined above. In the first place, none of the attempts to provide a general economic "pattern" for these centuries has succeeded in establishing itself beyond the reach of controversy. M. Weber and others had pointed to the recession to conditions of "natural economy" which took place in the third century A.D., and to the settlement of nobles on country estates which supplied all their own needs. . . . Trade was only thinly spread, and the requirements of the State were not met, on the whole by monetary means. K. Bücher, building on this position, then formed his theory of stages, in which three main phases of development were traced in the economic history of Europe. The first, most primitive, stage, that of a "closed house-economy," covered the whole ancient world, and persisted until the tenth century A.D. His view was based, as regards ancient history, on an incomplete analysis, which examined principally the early Greek and late Roman periods. Subsequent work by Beloch and Eduard Meyer, among others, invalidated his conclusions. It was shown that the economic life of the ancient world, especially in the Hellenistic and Roman periods, attained a complexity of organization which was not reached again until many centuries had passed. These views have been reinforced by epigraphic and archaeological research, and especially by the papyrus evidence from Egypt. Thus the theory of Bücher, as regards the Graeco-Roman world, has long ceased to find any general acceptance. Dopsch, however, complains that its influence continues to dominate the outlook of historical students upon the period under discussion.[6]

Yet the character of the later Roman organization precludes any unhesitating acceptance in their entirety of Dopsch's views. Perhaps the greatest administrative change in European history was the replacement of the *polis* system by the Roman world-empire. The organism of the self-governing city-state gave way to the new bureaucracy, supporting and supported by the central Imperial power, whose

---

[6] Historians mentioned in this paragraph: Max Weber (1864–1920) ranks as one of the most profound of German historians of his day; today we would call him a social scientist. Karl Bücher was a German economic historian. Beloch (1854–1929) and E. Meyer (1855–1930) were German authorities on the ancient world.—Ed.

origin lay not in the old *polis* world, but rather in the great "private economies" of the Hellenistic rulers. In the final stage, the constitution of Diocletian and Constantine, the bureaucracy became the executive of the absolutist central government in all breaches of administration. Society adapted itself to the new conditions, and the great landowners gained a large measure of control over their dependents. Trade and industry, as Rostovtzeff has shown, were progressively subordinated to the public services. . . . But whereas in the East the centralizing bureaucracy prevailed, in the West, through the weakness, and final breakdown, of the imperial government, it was the decentralizing landowners who gained the upper hand. Indeed, in western Europe the decline may have set in long before; but the immense contrast, which recent studies have not weakened, between the east Roman world—with its highly developed administration and civil service, its complex, and largely State-controlled, organization of trade and commerce—and the chaotic conditions, localized governments and decline of cultural standards in western Europe indicates more surely than anything else the changes wrought by the barbarian invasions.

The onus of proof, therefore, lies on those who would seek to show that industry and trade suffered no vital and permanent setback when the fall of the Empire in the West had removed the unified framework of civil and military defense, and left in its place a number of different, and often antagonistic, governmental units. Such proof, if it is to cover the economic life of western Europe, must be not only extensive, but representative, and typical of whole countries. The provinces of the later Roman Empire already exhibited marked variations, and the circumstances of the barbarian settlements greatly increased them. In Italy, the contrasting conditions of the Byzantine exarchate and the Lombard districts are well known, and for the latter the unsatisfactory nature of the sources has often been emphasized. . . . In France, regional differences are equally remarkable, and the unequal—and scanty—nature of the evidence forms an inadequate basis for the far-reaching conclusions of Pirenne's theory. The Germanic districts, for example, of the Merovingian realm rarely find mention in the sources, and the survival of Rhineland trade in the fifth and sixth centuries is incapable of proof. A principal part in that theory is played by the statements of Gregory of Tours, but the striking criticism of N. H. Baynes has gone far to invalidate the interpretation placed upon them, and his suggestion that the unity of the Mediterranean world was broken, not by the advance of Islam, but by the pirate fleet of Vandal Carthage, seems more in accordance with probability. Moreover, in face of the general picture of the barbarous conditions in France delineated by Gregory of Tours, stronger proofs than Pirenne has been able to adduce are required before we can be confident of the survival of a highly developed machinery of trade. It is not sufficient to point to examples of exotic imports as evidence of this. Easily portable luxuries—amber, jewels, beads—were carried enormous distances in prehistoric times, but such commerce belongs rather to the romance than to the everyday realities of economic life. Finally, the evidence for the continuance of the Roman educational system under the Merovings, to which Pirenne has devoted several studies, is not, in the opinion of the present writer, convincing.

Dopsch's theory has developed from his criticism of opposing views, and it may be suggested that this circumstance has led to a somewhat one-sided presentation of the facts, and not infrequently to overstatement. The quality of his voluminous evidence varies considerably, and much of it has already been called in question. In drawing attention to the immense variety of conditions which prevailed in western Europe during these centuries, and in modifying the generalizations which have been put forward concerning its social and economic life, Dopsch has performed an invaluable service. Whether these modifications are sufficiently far-reaching to establish a new and authoritative "pattern" of economic development is a more doubtful matter.

Robert S. Lopez

MOHAMMED AND CHARLEMAGNE:
A REVISION

*Robert S. Lopez, born and educated in Italy, came to the United States
shortly before World War II; during that conflict he served with the Italian
section of the Office of War Information. In the intervening years he has
taught at Brooklyn College and at Columbia University and is now Sterling
Professor of History at Yale. His well-known* The Birth of Europe *(New York,
1967), a translation of his* Naissance de l'Europe *(Paris, 1962), ranges over
the period 400 to 1400, and his more recent* The Commercial Revolution of
the Middle Ages: 950–1350 *(Englewood Cliffs, N.J., 1971) also reflects his
interest in both the Middle Ages and the Renaissance. Research in medieval
trade in the Mediterranean brought him early into the Pirenne controversy.
This article, here reproduced in its entirety, is particularly valuable in illus-
trating the character of the controversy in its early stages. If some of his
views have been questioned, this comes in part from further research by
Professor Lopez himself.*

It is not my purpose to challenge the core of Pirenne's conclusions. Mahomet et Charlemagne, and Dopsch's Grundlagen—however
much one may disagree on point of details and on range of implications—have helped historians to realize that their traditional division of ages was wrong: Germanic invasions did not mark the
beginning of a new era; Arab invasions did.

This is undoubtedly true insofar as history of culture is concerned.
The great push of the Germans had been preceded by long in-
terpenetration, and was followed by thorough fusion of the newcomers into the mass of the conquered people. The followers of Alaric,
Theodoric and Clovis neither wanted to nor could break the moral
unity of the Western Empire, and its connections with the East. They
only gave a political expression to those particularisms which were
already cracking the surface of the old Roman edifice without breaking its deep foundations. The Latin language and Latin literature,
however much their already advanced barbarization may have been
precipitated by the impact of rude invaders, remained as the common
background of European culture. The greatest achievements of the

From Robert S. Lopez, "Mohammed and Charlemagne: A Revision," *Speculum* 18
(January 1943): 14–38. By permission of the Medieval Academy of America, Cambridge,
Mass.

medieval "Germanized" world, the Church and the Empire, were either a heritage or an imitation of Roman institutions. As soon as Europe was again able to produce something great and original, Roman peoples again took the lead. *Niebelungennot* and the wooden buildings of the Germans were forgotten for Romanesque and French ("Gothic") architecture, and for the Italian *Divina Commedia.*

On the other hand, wherever the Arabs stepped on Romanic soil (except in Spain and in Sicily, outposts which they held for too short a time), they eradicated the classic roots forever. A slow but sweeping revolution won over the masses in Syria, Egypt, and North Africa to a new civilization, whose language and religion (these typical expressions of a people's soul) were the language and the religion of the conquerors. There was no Arab Romanesque architecture, and no Arab Imperium. Even where there was imitation, an original blend was formed out of three cultures—Graeco-Roman, Persian, and Semitic.

However, neither Pirenne nor Dopsch lays as much stress on cultural relations as they do on economic and social conditions. I shall not discuss here the views of Dopsch. Let us remark only that, while his thesis cannot be slighted as an element in the understanding of the early Middle Ages, his documentation has been recognized as too scanty and questionable for the wide inferences which many followers of Dopsch have drawn. Are the foundations of Pirenne's economic theory more solid? At first, one cannot but be struck by the four "disappearances" which he pointed out as the symptoms of a disruption of the economic unity of the Mediterranean countries after the Arabic invasions. Papyrus, Oriental luxury cloths, spices, and gold currency shrank gradually to the Eastern part of the Mediterranean; under the Carolingians, Europe had almost entirely abandoned their use. Pirenne's documentation is striking.

And yet, on a close examination, it appears that the four "disappearances" were not contemporary either with the Arab advance or with each other; indeed, it is not exact to speak of disappearances. Papyrus was manufactured exclusively in Egypt and this province was conquered by the Arabs between 639 and 641. But it was only in 692 that the Merovingian chancery ceased to use papyrus for its official documents. Other powers of the Christian world (as we shall see better later) continued to use papyrus for several centuries afterwards. Gold money ceased to be struck in France, apparently, only in the second half of the eighth century; in Italy, it came to an abrupt end in or about 800—a date of no importance for the Caliphate, but a great date for Europe. Furthermore, there was a brilliant resumption of gold currency under Louis the Pious; and gold kept an important place among the means of exchange, at least in Italy and in England, under the form of foreign and imitated coins, metallic dust, and ingots. A Belgian scholar, Sabbe, has recently proved that there was still a current of importation of Oriental cloth during the ninth and tenth centuries. Although his essay does not cover specifically the trade in spices, occasional references to it lead us to draw a similar conclusion.

In the presence of these circumstances, it seems difficult to maintain a "catastrophic" thesis, and to envisage Arab conquests as the cause of a sudden collapse in international trade—which, in turn, would have produced sweeping social and economic internal revolutions. In other words, there were no sudden changes as an immediate and direct repercussion of the Arab conquests. International trade was not swept away at one stroke, and "closed economy" did not spring up at once in the regions outside the gleam of the Moslem Crescent. However, new trends slowly asserted themselves in the economy of the Western world. These trends should be related to conditions existing in the Arab or Byzantine world, for any disturbance in the European supply of Oriental wares is likely to originate in events occurring somewhere in the East.

We shall have a first clue if we take into account a circumstance which Pirenne and his followers seem to have overlooked: Three of the "disappearing" goods—gold currency, luxury fabrics, and papyrus—were state monopolies, and their sale had been subjected to special restrictions ever since the Roman Empire. A short survey of these restrictions will be necessary to understand the whole problem.

Currency has been, and still is, a public monopoly in almost all civilized states. This depends chiefly on two causes. On the one hand, it is felt that issuing the most tangible and popular symbol of wealth should be a prerogative of the sovereign power. On the other hand, it is deemed that state control is the best means to give to the paramount instrument of exchanges universal credit, a stable standard, and a surety against counterfeiting. Thus currency is at the same time a sovereign function—what the Middle Ages called a "regale"—and a device of public interest.

Besides, money can become a source of public income (in other words, a fiscal monopoly) if the state can make the people accept coins at a higher price than the actual content of their bullion plus cost of coinage. But this development of currency, no matter how often a state can resort to it, is a pathologic phenomenon which sooner or later defeats the very aims of currency, and makes it unfit as a means of exchange. In the Roman Republic and Empire, money had always been both a symbol of sovereign power and a device for public interest. Debasements had taken place repeatedly, but the notion that coinage might be a mere source of income for the state, variable at the will of the rulers, was never accepted.

However, there was a distinction and a hierarchy of metals, the origins of which can be traced back to similar regulations of the Persian and Seleucid monarchies. The state mints for copper and silver were sometimes leased out, at least until a law (393 A.D.) prohibited such a practice and revoked all the earlier grants; but gold mints were never leased out. Silver and copper money, with both standard and types different from those of the state currency, were allowed to some autonomous municipalities for local use; but gold was never struck in local mints. The Senate of the Republic struck every sort of money; but after the rise of Augustus, it was left with the right to strike copper only. Gold and silver state coinage became a monopoly of the Emperor, who also had coppers struck occasionally in the provinces.

When the "Principate" was transformed into a "Dominate," both Senate coppers and autonomous municipal coinage of silver and copper were driven out in a few years by the extraordinary emissions of debased coins in the imperial mints. No definite order of dissolution seems to have been enacted; but the mint of the Senate was never reopened (except under the Ostrogoths), and local coinage had only sporadic and short-lived reappearances, as long as the Roman and the Byzantine Empires lasted. This extension of imperial monopoly to every kind of money and every metal must be connected with the progress of absolutism. Forging coins, striking them in private work-shops, refusing old and worn imperial money was regarded as a "sacrilegium," or an act of "laesa maiestas," because it implied an outrage to the effigy of the sovereign impressed on the coins. But motives of public interest were almost as influential as this new stress on the sacred character of money-regale, for in the fourth, fifth, and sixth centuries there was such an increase in forgeries, that the only remedy seemed to be a thorough and undiscriminating state monopolization.

The rise of barbaric autonomous states formally subjected to imperial suzerainty again raised the problem of local currency. Once more, the view of the Emperors (as stated by Procopius and confirmed by the extant coins) was that barbarian kings should be entitled to strike both copper and silver with their own effigies and names; but gold could be lawfully struck only with the portrait and name of the *Roman* Emperor. Along with this pretension went the Byzantine claim that no foreign prince could call himself Emperor (Basileus) on equal terms with the autocrat of Constantinople.

Altogether, these pretensions suffered no serious challenge for a long time. The Vandals and the Ostrogoths never struck gold coins with the effigies of their sovereigns. The Visigoths and the Lombards began to issue gold with their king's portrait only very late, when they had no longer anything to fear from the Emperor's wrath. Theodebert I, the Merovingian, while at war against Justinian the Great, struck some personal gold coins which roused the indignation of Procopius; it is true that Justinian, on his side, hurt the feelings of the Frankish ruler by assuming the title of "Francicus"; which amounted to a claim to a triumph over him. After Theodebert, no Merovingian king struck gold with his own portrait for some years. When this "usurpation" was committed again, the Emperor needed Frankish alliance against the Lombards, too badly to raise complaints. A similar calculation must have led the Basileis not only to overlook the gold coinage of the Ethiopian kings of Aksum, but to bestow on them the title of Basileis in the official correspondence. The common rival of Byzantium and Aksum, the Sasanian "Shahan Sha" (King of the Kings), was also called Basileus and regarded as an equal by the Basileus of Constantinople. But he eventually abandoned gold currency, to the great satisfaction of the Byzantine court. His pride could find a compensation in the yearly tribute that the Empire had to pay to him.

The success of Constantinople in matters of money-regale was not entirely due to the prestige and the power of the Emperors. In Western Europe not only gold, but even the less valuable metals continued to be struck in large amounts with the portrait of the Emperor, because the populace, accustomed to the traditional types, was reluctant to accept coins of an unusual appearance. In Persia and in some of the barbaric states, gold was of little use anyway, because the exchanges were generally of a modest amount, and silver was more suitable for the common needs. Finally, the title of "rex" had an equivalent in all the Indo-European languages, while that of "imperator" was proper to Latin only.

Nonetheless, it is an undoubted fact that the early Germanic rulers recognized some moral hierarchic superiority of the Emperors in several other respects. As for gold currency, we cannot say that German kings did not care about it because they had no "regalian" notion. On the contrary, the barbaric states of Western Europe as a rule maintained a state monopoly of money. Even more, both Visigoths and Lombards apparently followed closely the developments of eastern Roman law on that matter. As soon as the Byzantine Empire changed the penalty to be enforced on money-counterfeiters, the same modification was introduced by Receswinth in Spain and by Rothari in Italy.[1] Besides, Rothari seems to have reorganized the Lombard mints according to an administrative reform of emperor Heraclius. Only the Merovingian state followed an opposite course: the very notion of state monopoly was slowly forgotten, and private moneyers began to strike on private order coins bearing no other marks than the moneyer's signature, the customer's name, and the place of emission. This was because the Merovingian monarchies during the seventh century underwent a steady decline of internal cohesion and international relations.

The inclusion of some kinds of cloths and jewelry in the "regalian" monopolies will not seem surprising, if we remember that in the late Roman and Byzantine Empires the sovereign impersonated the state, and made himself a superhuman being to the eyes of the populace, even by his exterior appearance. Thus imperial garments and jewelry were symbols of the nation, almost like our flag. An offense against them was really a threat to the stability of the regime, and the protection extended to them could be regarded as a matter of public interest. This notion had already appeared in the Oriental monarchies, where the worship of the sovereign was taken as a matter of course. But the Romans were proud of their personal freedom and dignity. As long as they were allowed, they spoke of "our plebeian purple" (as opposed to the other peoples' "royal pur-

[1] Receswinth (d. 672) was king of the Visigoths; Rothari (d. 652) was king of the Lombards, particularly important for his codification of Lombard customary law.—Ed.

ple") with a satisfaction similar to our pride in free speech and popular government.

Only the Late Empire introduced the worship of the living autocrat, and destroyed even the exterior forms of liberty. Purple-dyed and gold-embroidered cloths, and jewelry of several categories were brought under "regalian" restrictions. A hierarchy of materials, parallel to the hierarchy of offices, was established in this monopoly, as it had been established in currency. A certain kind of purple and some special jewels were allowed only to God, to the saints, and to the sovereigns. Other ceremonial garments were reserved to high officers; by that means, they shared in the veneration owed to the Emperor. Other cloths—even some dyed with purple or embroidered with gold and silk—continued to be permitted to the commoners. This arrangement was subject to fluctuations, for, in the fifth century, there were innumerable crimes of "majesty"—that is, private use of imperial garments and jewels. The only remedy appeared to be to extend the state monopoly to a much larger field than the strictly "tabooed" objects. Little by little, as the citizens made up their minds to reserve some ornaments to the sacred person of the sovereign and to his dignitaries, unnecessary restrictions were lifted.

When the Western Empire was dismembered, the Byzantine Emperors were able to defend their monopoly of ceremonial garments better than that of gold currency. As a matter of fact, some of the raw materials (silk, several qualities of purple-dyes, pearls and other precious stones) could not be found in Western Europe. Furthermore, the goldsmiths and clothiers of the Barbarians were often very skilled in their own way, but they could not reproduce the patterns of Roman aulic art. Thus the Empire had practically a monopoly of production and supply. Control of exportation was sufficient to prevent Barbarian leaders from robing themselves in garments which they were not supposed to wear. Not only "regalian" considerations, but a "premercantilistic" outlook led the Emperors to enforce on exporters even more drastic restrictions than those enforced at home. It was not convenient to allow gold, precious stones, and secrets of textile industries to be taken out of the state.

On the other hand, the Emperors themselves used to buy off Barbarian rulers by gifts of ceremonial garments and jewels. Such gifts were cautiously dealt out, lest their value depreciated. Besides, no imperial mantles and crowns were given, but only ornaments allowed to Byzantine high officers. Thus the donors could feel that they were enlisting Barbarians in the army of Byzantine officers and vassals, while the grantees usually felt pleased and exalted with the gifts. Likewise, the gift of regalian ornaments to churches and clergy in the West was one of the weapons of the Byzantine ecclesiastic diplomacy. But the amount of objects obtained by that means, captured as war prizes, or smuggled into Western Europe with the help of bribed imperial manufacturers and customs-officers, could never be very large. Furthermore, some of the Barbaric peoples (although *not* all of them) cared little for the shining, but somewhat effeminate apparel of the Basileis. They took more pride in their national fur garments, spurned by the Romans, and in Germanic parade armors.

The situation was different in Persia and in Ethiopia, where both raw materials and finished objects could be secured without Byzantine intermediaries. In these countries, the local ceremonial costumes were similar to those of the Eastern Empire; indeed, the latter repeatedly borrowed Persian aulic fashions. Apparently the Basileis were wise enough not to put forward any monopolistic claims as regards Ethiopia and Persia. At any rate, it was less wounding to see the sovereigns of those very ancient states dressed in purple than the unpedigreed rulers of provinces recently belonging to the Romans.

Papyrus had also been subject to restrictions under the Ptolemies, but on a different ground. In Hellenistic Egypt nearly all the wares of some value were under fiscal monopoly, no matter whether the stability of the regime or the public welfare required it or not. While some of these goods were directly produced and sold by state agents, more often private entrepreneurs leased out portions of the monopolistic rights in one or more provinces. There was no absolute monopoly on papyrus production, although many fields were directly cultivated and exploited by the crown. But the private producers, apparently, could sell only to the king the best qualities of papyrus ("basilikē chartē," royal papyrus). Moreover, public notaries were expected to write their instruments on this kind of papyrus, and to pay a tax on every deed.

It seems that these provisions did not aim at protecting against forgeries of documents; they were only one of the numberless restrictions by which the Ptolemies fleeced their flock. This is why the Romans, systematically opposed to fiscal monopolies, seem to have removed the obstacles against free commerce. But they maintained the duty on notarial instruments as a sort of certification fee.

This tax, however, contained the germ of the elements for the later growth of a state monopoly with a purpose of public interest. As a matter of fact, during the fifth and sixth centuries the increasing forgeries of documents led the Emperors to issue a set of provisions which revived and completed the ancient restrictions. Notaries public were obliged again to use only "basilikē chartē" for their deeds. This time, the restrictions did not aim primarily at securing an outlet for the state production of papyrus, but rather at bringing under state control the drawing of legal documents. The right of selling state papyrus apparently had been leased out to private citizens in the provinces; now such leases were revoked. Justinian ordered that no notarial instrument drawn in Constantinople should be recognized as authentic, unless each roll of papyrus had an untouched first sheet, which contained the subscription of the state officers attached to papyrus administration. Another guarantee of authenticity was the heading, to be compiled according to a definite formula, with the names of both the ruling sovereign and the consuls. Particular cautions were adopted for state documents: Purple ink must be used for the signature of the Emperor; golden seals, with an effigy of the sovereign like that on golden coins, were also attached to the most important imperial documents. Again, for state documents issued by members of the imperial family or by subordinate officers a special, but inferior set of precautions was adopted. Silver ink, silver, leaden or clay seals, and other exterior features pointed out the importance of the various writs, in proportion to the authority of the writer.

By that way a new field of monopolies was opened. Obviously their aim could be qualified as one of public interest. The fact that the Emperor, and his officers, lent in different ways the prestige of their names and portraits, caused restrictions and cautions concerning state and notarial instruments to take on the character of regales. Forging imperial documents signed with purple ink, or even using such an ink for private writing, was regarded as a crime of majesty, committed "tyrannico spiritu," and liable to capital penalty. Forgeries of less solemn charters were punished by maiming of a hand.

These laws apparently were taken over, in a simplified form, both by the Visigoths and the Lombards, at the same time as Heraclius's legislation on currency. The Pope and the bishops, who followed Roman law, seem to have uniformed their correspondence to the rules set in Constantinople. Since the production of papyrus was strictly localized in the Byzantine province of Egypt, whoever used papyrus (even outside the borders of the Empire) had to bow to the imperial monopoly. On the other hand, as the monopoly was one of production, and not of use like the clothing monopoly, the supply of lawful writing material to the Western chanceries and notaries went on unhampered.

The appearance of the Arabs among the great powers of the Mediterranean did not, at first, bring about such a revolution in the system of regalian monopolies as it could have. To be sure, the conquerors could seize in Egypt and in Syria two Byzantine state mints, a number of dye-houses for ceremonial garments, and the whole output of papyrus. But work was carried on almost as usual, with unchanged staff and unaltered standard of production. The Arabs, as a rule, conserved the existing state of things wherever they had no definite reasons to change it. They were slow in setting up regalian monopolies, for they had none at home. When they did, however, they were not awkward and half-hearted imitators, like the Germans. On the contrary, the Arabs built a solid state organization out of an original blend of Byzantine, Persian and national institutions.

According to an early tradition, the Prophet praised himself for having "left to Mesopotamia its dirhem and its hafīz, to Syria its mudd and its dīnār, to Egypt its ardeb and its dīnār." As a matter of fact, the bulk of circulation in the early Arab Caliphate was formed by pre-Arabic Sasanian, Byzantine and a few Himyarite (South-Arabic) coins, plus new money of the Empire which was currently imported by merchants. This currency of foreign origin was soon augmented with domestic imitations, privately struck, of Persian and Byzantine coins.

We have already remarked that the same phenomenon occurred with the Germans. But in the Arab Empire, where civilization was older and money exchanges were larger, the period before autonomous currency would not have lasted so long, but for peculiar delaying reasons. All the moneys in use at the time of the Arab conquest bore some representations of living objects, and such figures were unwelcome (although not altogether prohibited) because of the Islamic religious principles. On the other hand, it would have been almost impossible to get the subject peoples to accept suddenly money with simple inscriptions. 'Ali,[2] the champion of the old in-

---

[2] 'Ali was a son-in-law of Mohammed and was caliph, 655–661.—Ed.

digenous orthodoxy, tried to put out some nonfigured coins but his attempt died with him.

The simplest solution by far was tolerating the maintenance of the traditional, unofficial currency. Thus the blame for the figures could fall upon the foreign rulers and the unauthorized private moneyers who had struck the coins. At the most, some emblems of the Gentile religion were completed (or replaced after erasure) with legends praising Allah and Mohammed. Moreover, even this practice was not altogether immune from the censure of the most rigid lawyers, because such coins with their sacred formula were exposed to falling into the hands of men legally impure. At last, under Caliph Mu'āwiyah,[3] a few coppers were issued on which the portrait of the Basileus holding a cross was replaced by that of the Caliph brandishing a sword. But gold currency, the pride of the Empire, was not affected; and Mu'āwiyah gave a greater satisfaction to the Emperor, by binding himself to the payment of a yearly tribute.

While the currency, destined mainly to be handled by the Gentile subjects, was not modified for a long time, the Arabs soon conformed the drawing of their own state documents to the precepts of Islam. Seals had been largely used, even for private correspondence, before Mohammed; therefore we may cast some doubt on a tradition, according to which the Prophet had a seal engraved only when he was told that the Emperor would not read his letters if unsealed. At any rate, we have full evidence that the seal of the Caliphate was protected by a special "regalian" notion, as early as the time of 'Umar I,[4] the conqueror of Syria and Egypt. A little later, Mu'āwiyah organized an Office of the State Seal, on the model of a similar Sasanian institution. The Byzantine papyrus manufacturers in Egypt were maintained under state control, although it is not clear whether or not the imperial regulation for monopoly of the best qualities of papyrus was enforced by the Arabs without modifications.

For internal use the Arabs adapted the preparation of chancery materials and records to the needs of their own state and religious organization. It is true that some figures of animals (and, occasionally, even of men), as well as the cross, were left on the seals and the protocols, as merely decorative adornments. But the name of the

[3] Mu'āwiyah was the first Omayyad caliph (661–680) and one of the great Moslem statesmen. He developed a centralized autocratic administration, with headquarters at Damascus, which unified the Moslem world.—Ed.
[4] 'Umar I was the caliph (634–644) under whom Islam expanded religiously and politically over Syria, Egypt, and Persia.—Ed.

Basileus and the Christian formulae were soon replaced by the name of the Caliph and Islamic sentences. However, on the papyri which were exported to the Empire the Christian workers of the papyrus factories replaced the name of the Basileus, which obviously could not be written on the protocol (in Arabic "tirāz"), by an invocation to the Trinity. This arrangement, worked out or tolerated by the Islamic officers, was advantageous for both the Empire and the Caliphate. The former secured the usual supply of a material necessary to the chancery and the notaries—for Justinian's laws, which ordered the use of papyrus with untouched protocols, were still in force. The Arabs, on their side, drew large profits from this exportation, and, in that way, secured a continuous inflow of that Byzantine gold which formed the bulk of their currency.

An arrangement of the same kind was worked out for embroidered ceremonial cloths. It was an Arabic use—modeled, apparently, on a Persian custom, for no evidence of a similar practice can be found on Byzantine cloths before the so-called Byzantine Middle Ages—that a "tirāz" with the name of the Caliph and religious sentences should be embroidered on all ceremonial cloths. But on the tissues which were exported into Christian countries only an invocation to the Trinity was applied.

This unwritten compromise was broken by the real founder of the Arab administrative machinery, 'Abd al-Malik.[5] He could not think of reforms in the first years of his reign, for he was engaged in an all-out civil war against 'Abdallāh ibn-az-Zubair; indeed, for the sake of peace he had even to increase the yearly tribute to the Emperor (686 or 687 A.D.). But, as soon as the danger was overcome, the Caliph resolutely inaugurated a new policy, with the double aim of consolidating the central power, and of offering some satisfaction to the orthodox Arab element, from which came the main support of the enemies of his dynasty. The brother of ibn-az-Zubair had coined a number of small silver dirhems; 'Abd al-Malik ordered them to be broken up, thus showing a decidedly "regalian" viewpoint. Then he ordered the invocation to the Trinity and the cross on the "tirāz" of the papyri and cloths destined for export replaced by Moslem formulae. Emperor Justinian II, who evidently did not want to break the advantageous treaty of 686–687, tried repeatedly to obtain the withdrawal of those provisions by large gifts; he always met with a refusal. Finally his rash and violent character prevailed over diplomatic tact. He threatened the Caliph with putting an outrageous inscription against the Prophet on his gold coins, which (as he thought) the Arabs could not help using.

But the Caliph was now the stronger. As a reprisal, he entirely prohibited the exportation of papyrus, and inaugurated a national gold and silver currency, of the same type as the figured coppers of Mu'āwiyah. He thought of making the new coins acceptable to the Byzantine pride (or was it a refinement of jest?) by sending the first specimen of this new money as a part of the yearly tribute; besides, he promised to keep accepting the Byzantine gold currency in his own states. But when Justinian saw his own humiliation brought home to him, under the form of the coins bearing the name and the portrait of 'Abd al-Malik, he decided that the only issue left was war. Unfortunately, he was abandoned on the battlefield by the contingent of Slavs, on whom he relied. The Arabs, who had hoisted on their lances the broken treaty, gained a complete victory.

Nevertheless, the pretensions of the Byzantine rulers were satisfied in a way. The portrait of a Caliph on coins hurt the feelings of the orthodox "fukaha" as much as those of the Basileus, although the reasons for complaint were different. 'Abd al-Malik had succeeded in introducing into circulation a national type of coin; he soon took a further step, and had money coined like that of 'Ali, without any figure or personal symbol. After a short period of transition, when both figured and nonfigured coins circulated together, the new type, bearing only pious inscriptions, affirmed itself. Ever since, the currency of Moslem dynasties has been without figures, with only a few exceptions. Even the recollection that there had been Islamic figured coins was eventually lost.

It would be incautious to dismiss the whole history of this "regalian" war by ascribing it to the "foolishness" of Justinian and to the "diabolic shrewdness" of 'Abd al-Malik, as do some later Byzantine chroniclers, bitterly adverse to the Emperor. To be sure, Justinian II was one of the worst men who ever sat on the Byzantine throne. But the war was more tha a collision between a hot and cool head. It was a challenge between an old civilization, proud of its religious tradition and world power, and a new state, which had to make room for the set-up of its own sacred formulae and sovereign prerogatives. A few years later, when the successor of Justinian, Philippicus, inaugurated a religious policy sharply hostile to the Pope, the Romans

showed their solidarity with the latter by rejecting all the documents
and the coins bearing the seal or the portrait of the impious Basileus.
This proves that now the respect for the regalian character of
moneys was not merely an artificial imposition of the rulers, but—let
us repeat it—a popular feeling comparable with our reverence for the
national flag.

The regalian notion of currency and of "tirāz" (both on ceremonial
cloths and on public documents) almost at once took deep roots in
the Caliphate, and in the various Moslem states which sprang up on
its farthest provinces. Monopolistic state factories were established
everywhere, with the same functions as those of the Byzantine Empire. The sovereign, and some members of his family or of his court
appointed by him, reserved to themselves the right to put their names
on the inscriptions of regalian objects. A hierarchy of materials in
each kind of monopolies, corresponding to the hierarchy of officers,
was established by custom if not, perhaps, by law: Gold—silver—
copper for coins; different qualities of garments; probably, also different kinds of charters. To be sure, restrictions were never as extended as in the Empire. To give only some instances, mints were
often leased out; in Egypt, state textile manufactures were set up
only to give the finishing touch to cloths prepared in private work-
shops; the maiming penalty for infringers of regalian monopolies was
suggested and enforced on several occasions, but it could never
prevail against the stubborn hostility of nationalistic lawyers. But,
altogether, the new regalian policy of Moslem rulers after 'Abd al-
Malik stressed the same points which so far had been maintained by
the Greeks.

As regards papyrus, the Arabs were in the same position as the
Byzantine Empire before the loss of Egypt. They had the monopoly of
production; if the other countries wanted any papyrus at all, they had
to accept it as it was produced by the Moslem factories. Rather than
waive the old laws on chancery and notarial instruments, the Basileis
seem to have adapted themselves to the new situation. They continued to use papyrus, as is demonstrated by the earliest letter of a
Byzantine Emperor of which an original fragment has come down to
us (beginning of the ninth century). But, since the manufacturers no
longer inscribed on the protocols the invocation to the Trinity, the
Emperors transferred this invocation to the heading of the documents. Only in the tenth century, when Egypt itself ceased to man-

ufacture papyrus because paper had replaced it all over the Arab states, was it necessary for the Greek chancery to adopt parchment.

The Roman regulation for the drawing of authentic documents was generally observed by the Popes, the Church, and the Byzantine territories of Italy. For instance, the consular date is found on most of the Papal documents, and on many private sources of the Roman region, until the first years of the tenth century. Papyrus was the only material used for formal Papal charters until the end of that century—with only one exception—and did not disappear entirely until 1057. A bull of John VII (year 876), which has been preserved with parts of the original protocol, bears on it the invocation to Allah, according to the regulation of 'Abd al-Malik. Papyrus was also widely used by bishops until the late eighth century; indeed, we know at least one episcopal letter written on that material as late as 977. We know many Roman private documents on papyrus of the same period; the last one is of 998. Urban documents of Ravenna, a Byzantine city until 751, and, later a center of studies in Roman Law, are on papyrus until the middle of the tenth century. Those are the instances which we can ascertain; on the other hand, the very largest part of papyri from Western Europe has certainly not come down to us, because this writing material, unlike parchment, is extremely perishable except in a dry climate. In conclusion, we can well say that *wherever the Roman regulation was observed, the disappearance of papyrus was not caused by the Arab conquests, but by the victory of paper three centuries later.*

In the barbaric states, however, Roman law was melting away. No consular dates are found in the secular documents of Lombard, Italy, France, and Germany. In a few private charters the words "sub die consule," without any indication of the consul's name, are the only relics of a forgotten formula, added by sheer force of habit. Force of habit led the Merovingian royal chancery to use imported papyrus *until 692*, although parchment, which could be easily produced at home, began occasionally to be used from 670 on. But *in 692* the embargo enforced by 'Abd al-Malik cut the supply entirely for some time. When this embargo was lifted, the Merovingian chancery did not go back to a costly material which had been purchased only out of respect to a vanishing tradition.

Unfortunately, no original documents of the Lombard chancery have come down to us. But all our knowledge of them, although indirect, leads us to think that not only the royal charters, but even those of the dukes were written on papyrus. This may explain why they all have perished. On the other hand, the earliest Italian private document on parchment which has come down to us, a notarial deed from Piacenza, dates from 716—that is, twenty-eight years later than the Arab embargo. We may infer that the tradition of Roman law was still the stronger in Italy, insofar as state and church documents were concerned. But the reform of 'Abd al-Malik probably affected private instruments in Italy in the same way as it affected royal charters in France. In Germany, too, the earliest documents on parchment which have been preserved are of the second quarter of the eighth century. Thus it would seem that *where Roman legal traditions declined, the introduction of parchment for royal or notarial documents was not brought about directly by the Arab conquest of Egypt, but by the organization of Arab state monopolies, fifty years later.*

When we compare Merovingian and Carolingian currency, we are naturally led to regard those two periods as separated by a sharp contrast. First we have mainly golden coins with a portrait; then we find chiefly silver coins with an inscription. However, the transition took place over a long time. The output of silver coins became abundant in France as early as the last years of the sixth century—long before Mohammed and the decline of the Merovingians. On the other hand, it is true that the proportion of gold in circulation decreased steadily under the late Merovingians, and that no gold at all seems to have been struck by Pepin the Short (though we cannot exclude that some such coin may be eventually yielded by a new find); but gold money was struck under Charlemagne and, even more, under Louis the Pious. Likewise, the shift from figured to nonfigured money was gradual and progressive during the sixth and seventh centuries. We have no figured coins of Pepin, but we have many of Charlemagne and Louis the Pious.

A connection of this gradual, though interrupted decrease of gold coins with a steady decrease in the volume of exchanges cannot be doubted. On the other hand, the decline of portraiture on coins must be connected with both the general decline of art, and the decadence of the sovereign power. Silver is more convenient than gold for small exchanges; unskilled moneyers will prefer easy epigraphic types, unless a sovereign insists on advertising his own portrait on coins. These trends, let us repeat it, appeared earlier than the Arab invasions, and therefore cannot have been caused directly and exclusively by them. Pepin the Short was the first who tried to bring back some uniformity in currency, and to restore partially the regalian monopoly, which the "rois fainéants" had allowed to melt away. The easiest path towards uniformity obviously was to stress the existing trends, and to suppress altogether the figured golden coins, relics of a dying past. The political, artistic and economic renaissance under Charlemagne and Louis I was incomplete and ephemeral; so was the revival of figured and golden currency during their reigns.

These observations take into no account the possible influence of Arab invasions, but do not exclude that there may have been such an influence. However, we must remark again a circumstance that Pirenne and his followers seem to have overlooked: the period of Arab conquest in the East and even in Spain, is not one of sudden changes in the Merovingian currency. Comparatively sweeping changes occurred only when an autonomous dynasty took power over Spain. This region had gold currency under both the Visigoths and the officers of the central Caliphate. But the first independent Cordovan ruler, 'Abd al-Rahmān I—*a contemporary of Pepin the Short*—seems to have refrained both from striking gold and from assuming the title of Caliph, because another man ruled as Caliph (although unlawfully) over the Holy Cities of the Moslems. Only in the tenth century, after the Eastern Caliphate was practically dominated by the Turkish guard, did 'Abd al-Rahmān III assume the title of Caliph at Cordova. At the same time, he began regularly to strike gold. It is quite possible that the influence of the silver standard in a neighbor state led Pepin to carry out the complete abandonment of the gold standard in his own kingdom.

Likewise, the example of the epigraphic currency of the Arabs very likely encouraged Frankish moneyers to abandon entirely the striking of figured coins, inasmuch as these coins were struck mainly in Provence, at the doorstep of Spain. This influence could not be felt before the second quarter of the eighth century, for in Spain the Arabs did not suppress at once the figured coins. To sum up, we may assume that *the new trends in Frankish currency, begun before the Arab conquests, were not influenced by the trade disruption that these conquests may have caused, but by parallel trends of Arab currency in Spain.*

Islamic epigraphic currency not only influenced silver and copper coinage in the barbaric states of Western Europe, but even those gold coins, which had been regarded as the paramount show-place for the royal effigy. The only coins of this metal that Charlemagne struck in France (at Uzès, not far from the Arab border) are epigraphic. His contemporary, Offa, the Mercian king, struck gold with his name in Latin letters and a legend in Arabic, copied from an Abasside dīnār; even the date was that of the Hegira, 157 (774 A.D.). Imitations of this kind grew more and more abundant until the thirteenth century. Thus the Arab dīnār partly replaced the Byzantine nomisma as a model for the currency of Western Europe. Now this phenomenon is certainly not the symptom of a crisis in trade brought about by the Arabs; on the contrary, it shows that the Arab merchants for some time surpassed the Greeks.

Once more, the Lombard kingdom presented a different picture. While the Arabic states had no common borders with it, the Byzantine Empire enveloped it from almost every side, and even wedged into its central part. There was a continuous exchange of influences between the barbaric and the Byzantine mints of Italy; the mint of Ravenna passed from the Greeks to the Lombards a few months before Pepin began his work of restoration of state control on money in France. State control was never waived in the Lombard kingdom, and coinage remained faithful to the figured type, although, here too, artistic decadence caused legends to cover a larger and larger part of the coins. Furthermore, the predominance of the gold standard was never challenged; indeed, the quantity of silver in circulation seems to have been very scanty, as it was in the Empire. On the other hand, figured coins and the gold standard had remained paramount also in the Visigothic kingdom until it was conquered by the Arabs. Gold emissions took place more than once in England from the time of Offa to that of Edward the Confessor. Thus we may conclude that *the new trends in Merovingian and early Carolingian currency were only local phenomena.*

It must be pointed out that Lombard gold coinage after Rothari did not bear the portrait of the Byzantine Emperor (except for the local currency of the dukes of Benevento), but that of the national king. Therefore, it constituted a challenge to the imperial regalian pretensions—the only challenge still existing since the Arabs and the Franks had adopted epigraphic types, and the Visigothic kingdom had been overrun. This challenge was not removed by Charlemagne when he conquered Italy. Lombard mints merely replaced on golden coins the portrait and the name of the national king with those of the new ruler. Meanwhile, in France, only epigraphic coinage was carried on as before. But there was a sudden change after Charlemagne was crowned emperor. Gold currency was discontinued all over his states, except for the epigraphic coins of Uzès, which were still in circulation in 813, despite some complaints of a council. The epigraphic currency of silver and copper was withdrawn, and replaced everywhere by coins of classic inspiration, bearing the portrait of the Emperor crowned with laurels, his name, and the imperial title.

There can be doubt that the establishment of uniform standards for the whole empire was a step towards centralization. But it remains to be explained why the Byzantine figured type was chosen for silver and copper, and why such little gold as was still in circulation kept the epigraphic type. We are more likely to find a clue in Charlemagne's relations with the Byzantine Empire, than in the consequences of Arab invasions which occurred one century earlier or more! In fact, Charlemagne's assumption of the imperial title was certainly a hard blow to the Byzantine pretensions. Since the disappearance of the Sasanian and Aksumite monarchies, no foreign ruler had yet dared to style himself an Emperor. All the contemporary sources agree in pointing out that Charlemagne realized the gravity of his act. He made every possible effort to appease the Byzantine pride, and to secure some recognition of his title from the legitimate emperor of Constantinople. On the other hand, it has been remarked that he did not call himself "Romanorum imperator," like the Basileus, but "Imperator . . . Romananorum gubernans imperium."[6] This title, being a little more modest than the other one, could possibly sound more acceptable to Constantinople than a formula implying absolute parity.

It may be suggested that the abandonment of figured gold currency, which removed the last challenge to the Byzantine monopoly, was another good-will move, intended to pave the way for an understanding. A similar arrangement had been worked out between Byzantium and Persia, and its memory had not been forgotten. Thus, in Italy, gold coinage was abandoned altogether, for it would have been difficult to persuade Italians to accept unusual nonfigured coins. In France, epigraphic golden money was not a new thing; still, even there, it aroused complaints, apparently because it lent itself to forgery.

[6] "Roman Emperor," like the Basileus, but "Emperor . . . governing the empire of he Romans."—Ed.

If our interpretation may be accepted, we shall infer that *Char-lemagne's monetary reforms were not prompted by the progress of Arab invasions, but, primarily, by considerations of good-neighbor policy towards the Byzantine Empire.* Obviously this does not imply that the economic background had nothing to do with these reforms. Probably Charlemagne would not have sacrificed figured gold coinage to reconciliation with the Basileis unless the prestige and the economic usefulness of gold had already lost so much ground in France; to a large extent, his reforms were the completion of those of Pepin. But in Italy the economic situation did not justify the abandonment of gold. Since no new coins of this metal were produced at home after Charlemagne, foreign gold coins (Arabic and Byzantine) took the place of the old Lombard currency all over the peninsula.

In 806, when the relations with the Eastern Empire were at their worst, Charlemagne did not even mention the imperial dignity in his division of his states among his sons. But an understanding, implying the recognition of Charlemagne as "imperator et basileus" by the Byzantine ambassadors, was finally reached in 812 at Aix-la-Chapelle. In the same place (not in Rome!), one year later, the old emperor placed the crown on the head of Louis the Pious and ordered him to be called "imperator et Augustus." In 814 Louis succeeded to the throne; he maintained passably good diplomatic relations with the Emperors of the East. The Basileis were drawn to a friendly attitude by their hope of securing the help of the second Carolingian "emperor" against the Arabs and the Bulgarians; but this hope was not realized. Much worse (at least, worse to the eyes of the ceremonial-conscious Byzantine Emperors), Louis felt bold enough to strike gold coins with his own name and portrait, of the same type as Charlemagne's imperial silver and copper. The obverse of these coins bore a crown with the words "minus divinum," implying that Louis was emperor by the grace of God, and not a sort of a cadet of his Eastern brother. It is true that this affirmation of power was not made from an Italian mint, even though Italy would have been the most appropriate soil on which to start gold currency again. The gold coinage of Louis was struck in that part of his empire which was the farthest from the Byzantine border, and the nearest to those uncivilized Germanic tribes which were still likely to be dazzled by the prestige of figured gold money. But, on their side, the Basileis Michael and Theophilus called themselves, in a letter to Louis, "in ipso Deo imperatores Romanorum." They branded him as "regi Francorum et Langobardorum et *vocato eorum* Imperatori!"[7]

The ecclesiastic conflict for the parity of Constantinople with Rome, and for the Bulgarian church, gave the last blows to the crumbling compromise of Aix-la-Chapelle. When the balance of powers was definitely broken by the partition of the Western Empire, and by the accession of the energetic Macedonian dynasty in the East, Basil I formally withdrew the Byzantine recognition of the imperial rank of the Carolingian monarchs. Louis II could only send a diplomatic note, where he reminded Basil that, at any rate, the title of "basileus" had been granted in the past to many rulers—both heathen and Christians. But his protest remained unanswered. Under these circumstances, Louis II could well have retaliated by resuming gold currency. The princes of Benevento struck regularly gold money, and we know that for some years Louis II had silver struck in Benevento with his own name and imperial title. No golden coins of Louis have come down to us; but we cannot make much of a proof "ex silentio," since his power over Benevento lasted seven years only. Afterwards, Benevento recognized Byzantine overlordship; it is remarkable that no gold seems to have been struck there after this recognition.

At any rate, gold has always been essentially the instrument of international trade—as Marc Bloch has pointed out. For local trade silver was usually sufficient. Gold coins, if internationally accepted, were a vehicle of prestige for the ruler whose name and effigy they bore; but not every ruler's name could give international credit to golden coins. Already in the eighth century, the long intermission of gold coinage in France had caused Frankish money to disappear from those internationally accepted. Louis the Pious tried to go against the stream; but only the Frisians and the Saxons were impressed by his prestige enough to use widely his golden coins, and even to carry on for some time domestic imitations of them. But the powerless successors of Louis, who were even able to maintain the sovereign monopoly of currency, could have no hope of persuading international merchants to carry along Frankish gold instead of the famous Byzantine *nomismata* and Moslem *dīnār*. In conclusion, *the definitive abandonment of the gold standard after Louis the Pious*

---

[7] "By God himself, emperors of the Romans." They branded him as "king of the Franks and the Lombards and called their Emperor!"—Ed.

*was not directly connected with the Arab invasions, but depended on
the insufficient prestige of the Western monarchs.* Only when the
prestige of both the Greeks and Arabs declined, in the thirteenth
century, was it possible to resume the striking of gold in Western
Europe.

If neither the "disappearance" of papyrus nor that of gold currency is connected with a sudden regression in trade caused by the
Arab conquests, the thesis of Pirenne has little support left. As a
matter of fact, the evidence collected in the above-mentioned essay
of Sabbe is more than sufficient to prove that the trade of Oriental
purple-dyed and embroidered cloths was never interrupted in Western Europe. At the most, we can suppose that this trade suffered a
temporary depression—although there are no grounds for this sup-
position, and, at any rate, no comparative statistics can be drawn
when sources are casual, scant, and far between. Nevertheless, for
the sake of a further demonstration, we shall assume that there was a
depression. Must such a hypothetical trend be connected with a
general disruption of trade?

First of all, we should take into account the trends in matters of
etiquette and costumes. Let us repeat that the value of a symbol does
not reach farther than the convention on which the symbol is based.
A flag would have been a scrap of cloth in the Roman Republic. The
Huns and most of the early Germans did not care for imperial purple.
Now we may agree with Halphen in discounting as a sheer invention
the witty anecdote of the Monk of Saint Gall, where Charlemagne is
shown playing a cunning trick on his officers, who had preferred
refined Oriental garments to the simple national costumes. Still the
anecdote is doubtless evidence of a widespread attitude of the
Franks when the Monk was writing, in the second half of the ninth
century. Another source relates that Charles the Bald, after being
crowned by John III, wore a Byzantine ceremonial dress, and drew
upon himself the blame of his subjects for spurning "the tradition of
the Frankish kings for the Greek vanity." Again the source is unfair to
Charles—although the "Hellenism" ·of this sovereign, expecially in
regalian matters, is an undoubted fact. But the ground chosen to put
blame on Charles must express an actual sentiment.

In conclusion, *the diminished use of Oriental cloths among the
laymen* (if there was a diminution) *depended to a great extent on a
change in fashions. The Church did not change fashions,* and, in fact,

the largest part of the existing evidence of Oriental cloths in Western Europe relates to the Church.

On the other hand, we must remember that the regalian monopoly of cloths and jewelry—unlike the monopolies of currency and papyrus—did not cover only manufacturing and trade, but the use itself of many qualities of these objects. The expressions of the Byzantine "kommerkiarioi" (customs-officers), as related by Liudprand[8] in the tenth century, are significant. The Greeks maintained that the wearing of cloths dyed with special qualities of purple (including some which were not reserved to the emperor and to the high officers) should be allowed only to the Byzantine nation, "as we surpass all other nations in wealth and wisdom." Thus the monopoly of cloths, like that of gold currency, had ceased to be an arbitrary imposition of the government, and had taken roots in popular feelings.

A very meticulous and complex set of provisions (which we know in detail only for the tenth century, but based to a large extent on laws of the late Roman Empire) established various categories of cloths, according to qualities of dye and to size. Some categories could be exported without restrictions, some were vetoed to exporters, some could be purchased only in limited amounts. Subjects of the Empire (such as the Venetians and the citizens of some Southern Italian cities) and merchants of some allied countries (such as Bulgarians and Russians) enjoyed special facilities by treaty. But in no case was unlimited exportation granted. Even churches and monasteries, if located in foreign countries, could not get Byzantine ceremonial objects for their shrines without special permission by the Basileus. Foreign ambassadors had to submit their luggage to the visit of the "kommerkiarioi," whose final inspection completed the usual, permanent contol of the cloth market and of the jewelry-shops entrusted to special city officers.

Under these circumstances, the largest source of supply for Western Europe probably was the already mentioned custom of the Emperors of sending ceremonial objects as diplomatic gifts. Some Emperors dispensed such gifts lavishly both to foreign princes and to churches. But those monarchs who felt little necessity to win over allies or to conciliate the Western Church—for instance, the great

---

[8] Liudprand (ca. 922–972), Bishop of Cremona and an important historian. The work here cited is an account of his mission (for Otto I) to Constantinople in 968.—Ed.

Iconoclasts, contemporary of Charles Martel and Pepin the Short—
were much stricter. As late as the tenth century, Constantinus Porphyrogenitus warned his son against complying with the requests for
imperial crowns, stoles and cloths, which were so frequently advanced by the Mongolic and Slavonic neighbors of the Empire. These
stoles and crowns, he said (and he almost believed it) were not made
by human hands, but sent from Heaven by the Angels themselves.

To be sure, there was another source of supply: smuggling. Vigi-
lant and numerous as they were, the controllers could not see everything; and they were only too often bribable at will. If we should
believe the unfair account of Liudprand, at the time of Constantine
Porphyrogenitus even the prostitutes in Italy could bestow on themselves the very ornaments which the Angels had intended for the
august Basileus only. But Liudprand grossly exaggerates. The price
itself of Oriental cloths, the cost of transportation, and the bribe for
the complaisant officers must have reserved to very few Westerners
the pleasure of bootlegged goods, even under as weak an emperor
as Constantine VII. When the power was in the hands of a man
"tachucheir," with a long reach (such as Nicephorus Phocas),
smuggling must have been practically impossible.

However, Oriental cloths could be purchased in Arabic-ruled countries, too. It is true that since 'Abd al-Malik a monopoly had been
established, and that Moslem rulers, in general, were more sparing
than the Basileis in their diplomatic gifts of cloths. But, as a rule, the
restrictions enforced by Islamic princes were not as tight as those
of the Eastern Empire. This explains why many great personages
of Western Europe—including clergymen and crusaders—displayed
on many occasions glowing ceremonial garments, where the praise
of Allah was embroidered in the "tirāz," in words luckily unintelligi-
ble to most of the bearers of such a cloth!

To sum up, *any fluctuation which may be noticed in the supply of
Oriental cloths is likely to stem from a fluctuation in the efficiency of
state control or in the system of alliances of the Byzantine and Arab
governments. The rise of the Arab Empire, far from curtailing supply,
made it a little less difficult to obtain cloth, because of the Arabs'
looser notion of regalian monopoly.*

Of fluctuations in the trade of spices we know but little. Some of
the documents quoted by Sabbe show that spices too were occasionally imported into Western Europe, right at the time when Pirenne speaks of disappearance. But, unfortunately, we have no

specific essay on that question. I shall give only a few general re-marks, which are a suggestion of fields for investigation, rather than matter-of-fact statements.

Once more, the evolution of taste should be taken into account. Were the tough noblemen and the rough ecclesiastic grandees of early medieval Western Europe as fond of spiced food as the Romans and the men of the Renaissance? We know that the latter were persons of a nice palate. The gastronomic history of the early Middle Ages has not been expounded as yet in detail, but the hypothesis of a coarser taste may be not altogether unlikely.

On the other hand, the spices arrived from countries so different and far apart, that it is not enough to connect the fluctuations in supply with the general relations between the Arab world and West-ern Europe. Revolutions which occurred in the Asiatic Far East, or in Dark Africa, may have affected the spice trade very deeply. In 1343, according to an Italian chronicler, a war between the Golden Horde and the Genoese colonies in Crimea caused spices to rise from 50 to 100 percent in price. It should be expected that crises of the same kind were caused by Asiatic wars of the early Middle Ages. Now the eighth century, which saw the rise of the Carolingians in Western Europe, was an epoch of troubles for Eastern Asia. India was going through the crisis which followed the defeat of Buddhism and the triumph of Rajput "feudalism." While the Arabs invaded the Sindh in 712, Hindustan was being split into a great number of petty states. The Chinese T'ang dynasty, after reaching the peak of its power in the seventh century, suffered severe blows. In 751 the Arabs stopped the Chinese expansion in Central Asia (battle of Talas). Between 755 and 763 the emperors, driven out of their capital by a revolution, asked the help of the Uighurs to retake the city—a remedy worse than the sore. In 758, the Moslems sacked and burned Canton. These do not seem very favorable circumstances for the continuity of trade relations. But the situation gradually improved in the ninth century, and, in fact, evidence of spices in Western Europe grows less scant in that century.

Daniel C. Dennett, Jr.

PIRENNE AND MUHAMMAD

Editorial note attached to the article in Speculum: *"The author of this article was killed when the plane in which he was traveling on government service crashed over Ethiopia on March 22, 1947. An able scholar, expert in the languages and history of the Near East, Dr. Dennett had served as instructor in history at Harvard previous to his appointment in 1942 as Cultural Relations Attaché at the American Legation in Beirut, a post he held until his untimely death at the age of thirty-seven."*

A critic of Pirenne's theses must begin by asking the following six questions:

1. Was it the policy and the practice of the Arabs to prohibit commerce either at its source or on the normal trade routes of the Mediterranean? Can we indicate an approximate date, accurate within twenty-five years, for the ending of commerce between the Christian Occident and the Orient?
2. Is it possible to find another explanation for the disappearance of the wines of Gaza, the papyrus of Egypt, and the spices of the Orient?
3. Is it true that Gaul had no appreciable foreign commerce after the beginning of the Carolingian period?
4. Is it true that the civilization of Merovingian Gaul, considered in its broadest social and political aspects, was determined by trade? Is it possible that internal factors conversely may have been of importance in determining the prosperity of industry and trade? How extensive was Mediterranean commerce before 650?
5. Was "Romania" in fact a true cultural unity of ideas, law, language, foreign policy, common interest?
6. What is the real significance and true cause of the transition from a gold to a silver coinage?

I

We must affirm that neither in the Koran, nor in the sayings of the Prophet, nor in the acts of the first caliphs, nor in the opinions of

From Daniel C. Dennett, Jr., "Pirenne and Muhammad," *Speculum* 23 (April 1948): 167–90. By permission of The Mediaeval Academy of America, Cambridge, Mass. Dr. Dennett's extensive documentation, save for a few references for quotations, has been omitted.

Muslim jurists is there any prohibition against trading with the Christians or unbelievers. Before Muhammad, the Arabs of the desert lived by their flocks and those of the town by their commerce. To these two sources of livelihood the conquest added the income of empire and the yield of agriculture, but the mercantile career remained the goal of many, as the caravan still crossed the desert and the trading vessel skirted the coastline of the Red Sea, the Persian Gulf, and the Indian Ocean. Pirenne had asserted that "it is a proven fact that the Musulman traders did not install themselves beyond the frontiers of Islam. If they did trade, they did so among themselves." This statement is a serious misrepresentation of fact. Arab merchants had established trading colonies which were centers not only for the exchange of goods but the propagation of the faith in India, Ceylon, the East Indies, and even China, by the close of the eighth century, and if one wishes to know why they did not establish similar centers in Gaul, let him ask the question—would Charlemagne have permitted a mosque in Marseilles?

In this respect the Muslims themselves were more tolerant and placed few obstacles in the path of Christian traders who came to their territory. Within the lands that had formerly submitted to the Emperor, the Christians were now subjects of the Muslim state, yet they were protected by law, and in return for the payment of their taxes and the discharge of obligations stipulated in the original terms of capitulation, they were specifically and formally guaranteed the freedom of Christian worship, the jurisdiction of Christian bishops in cases not involving Muslims, and the pursuit of trades and professions. The civil service and the language of administration remained Greek, and Arabic did not universally displace Greek in the government bureaus until the end of the first century following the conquest. In Egypt, at least, the change of rule brought an improvement in the social and economic life of the population, and the church of Alexandria enjoyed a liberty of faith which it had hitherto not experienced.

In consideration of the fact that it has formerly been believed that internal causes produced a decline of industry and trade in Gaul, the burden of proof in Pirenne's thesis must show that the Arab raids were of a frequency and intensity *in themselves* to destroy the commerce of the western Mediterranean. It is not a just argument merely to assert that these raids were disastrous because commerce in Gaul declined. We have already noticed that in order to connect the decline of the Merovingian monarchy with the activity of the Arabs, Pirenne has been obliged to assign the date 650 as that point when Arab naval activity became formidable. What are the facts?

There may have been a raid on Sicily in 652. We are told that it was led by Muawia ibn Hudaij and resulted in taking much booty from unfortified places, but was called off when plague threatened the invaders. As Amari shows, there is a great deal of confusion among the Muslim authorities both as to the date (for an alternative, 664 A.D. is given), as to the leader (since it is highly probable that not Muawia but his lieutenant Abdallah ibn Qais commanded the actual expedition), and as to the port of embarkation (either Tripoli in Syria or Barka in North Africa). Becker does not accept the date 652 and argues that the first raid took place only in 664, but it is possible that there were two different expeditions, one in 652, the second in 664.[1]

Three years after the presumed earliest assault on Sicily, the Emperor Constans II, in 655, received a serious blow to his prestige when the Byzantine fleet was beaten in the Aegean by the new Muslim navy in the first real test of sea power. The Arabs did not follow up their victory, but its consequence demonstrated to the Emperor the need for a vigorous naval policy, for, although Constantinople and the straits might be held against siege, the strategically vulnerable point of the Empire was not in the Aegean, but in the West, since (as events were to show two centuries later) once the enemy had a base in Sicily, South Italy would then be within easy grasp, and if South Italy were securely held, only immense naval exertions could protect Greece proper, and if Greece fell under Muslim control, a combined blockade by land and sea of the imperial city would be possible. Bury[2] holds that this consideration, the guarding of the rear against attack from the West, was a strong motive in inducing Constans to concentrate naval power in the West and to go himself to Sicily in 662, where he reigned for six years until his assassination in 668.

The Arabs took advantage of the chaos following the assassination to raid the coasts of Sicily the next year, but when order was reestablished Sicily remained at peace again for thirty-five years.

Meanwhile the Greek fleet itself was far from inactive, raiding

---

[1] Amari is an Italian historian and C. H. Becker was Professor of Oriental History in the Colonial Institute of Hamburg. Dennett's references to their writings have been omitted.—Ed.

[2] J. B. Bury (d. 1927) was a distinguished British historian, an authority on the later Roman Empire and the Byzantine era.—Ed.

Egypt in 673 and, in a successful attack on Barka in 689, putting the Arabs to rout in which the governor of North Africa, Zuheir ibn Qais, perished. Early attempts to take Carthage were frustrated because the Greeks had control of the seas, and the city fell in 698 only because the Arabs had constructed a fleet for the purpose and the Greek naval force was in the Aegean. Following Bury's argument, if the Emperor had established a permanent naval base at Carthage, the city would never have been taken.

Therefore, in view of the facts that the Arabs made only two (possibly three) raids on Sicily before 700, that these raids resulted in a vigorous naval policy of the Greeks in the West, that it was not until 698 that the Arabs had a fleet strong enough to operate at Carthage, and that they had not yet seized the straits of Gibraltar or occupied Spain, we are bound to acknowledge the absence of any evidence to indicate the closing of the Mediterranean thereby weakening the basis of royal power in Gaul before 700. Pirenne himself acknowledges this fact by admitting that spices and papyrus could be procured by the monks of Corbie in 716. Indeed, anyone who reads Pirenne closely will notice that he is careless with chronology and mentions results which were produced by the Arab conquest as beginning at various points within a period of 150 years.

What progress was made in the eighth century? In 700 the Arabs took Pantellaria and constructed a naval base in Tunis with the intention of undertaking the conquest of Sicily, but after some preliminary raids in 703–705, for the purpose of reconnoitering, the new governor, Musa ibn Nusair, turned westwards and launched a campaign which was to culminate in the Spanish conquest, begun in 711.

Papyri dated 710 to 718 give us considerable information about shipbuilding in the Nile delta, where vessels were constructed for service not only in Egypt but in the West and in Syria as well, and mention raids of which, unfortunately, we know neither the destination nor the results. We do not know of any raids against Sicily until 720. Thereafter there were attacks in 727, 728, 730, 732, and 734. It must be emphasized that these were not attempts at conquest nor were they successful against fortified ports. A raid in 740 was recalled when civil war, due to tribal and religious factions, broke out throughout the entire territory under Muslim sway, a war which ended all hopes of an Arab offensive and resulted in the destruction of the Umayyad Caliphate at Damascus. In the meantime the Greek fleet led attacks on Egypt in 720 and 739, won a naval victory in 736, and annihilated the principal Arab force off Cyprus in 747. Only three Arab ships escaped this disaster.

After 751 the new Arab capital was 700 miles from the sea, and the Abbasids neglected the navy. Spain became independent under a rival Umayyad, and the political control of North Africa weakened sensibly. Henceforth naval operations could be undertaken only by virtually independent governors who lacked the organization and collective resources of the Caliphate. A last abortive assault on Sicily in 752–753 was frustrated by the Greek fleet. A fifty-years peace followed, perpetuated in 805 in a treaty signed by Ibrahim ibn Aghlab for a term of ten years and renewed by his son for a similar period in 813. The Arab conquest of Sicily did not commence until 827 and then only on invitation of a rebel Greek who had assassinated the governor.

Sardinia was first raided in 710 and Corsica in 713. The Arab control of the latter ended with its reconquest by Charlemagne in 774, and the Arab occupation of Sardinia was never complete. We have no evidence that these islands were used as bases for raids on commerce.

Pirenne grants that after 717 there was no question of Arab superiority in the Aegean but argues that before that time Arab naval activity had serious consequences. We have already noted that during the seventh century the Greeks for much of the time were sure enough of their Aegean position to conduct raids against Egypt and North Africa and to operate in the West. Let us review briefly the situation.

In 655, an Arab fleet routed the Greeks led by Constans II. This was the first and only *important* naval defeat. The following year the caliph Uthman was murdered, and in the ensuing struggle for power between Ali and Muawia, the latter, to secure his rear and the Syrian coasts against a Greek assault, entered into an arrangement in 659 with the Emperor by which he agreed to pay tribute. In 666, according to Theophanes,[3] the Mardaites, an unconquered people inhabiting the Amanus mountains in Northwest Syria, broke out in a series of attacks which secured for them all the strategic points from northern Syria to Palestine. It is presumed that Muawia, after being recognized as caliph, had ceased to pay tribute, but this new situation made it impossible to defend the Syrian ports should the Greek

---

[3] Theophanes, 758–817, a Byzantine chronicler.—Ed.

fleet determine to attack, and again the caliph, to secure his position, resumed the payment of tribute.

During the years 674–680 men witnessed the first "siege" of Constantinople. The Arab fleet established a winter base at Cyzicus in the Propontis and raided the Aegean in the summer. We have no evidence that their operations severed communications between Constantinople and the West, which could be maintained by land anyway, and trade with the East was still possible via the Black Sea port of Trebizond.

Armenia during the Sassanid rule of Persia was obligatory neutral territory for the exchange of goods between East and West, inasmuch as a national of the one country was prohibited from setting foot on the territory of the other. Trebizond on the Black Sea was the port of entry, and Dwin, among other towns, was a principal mart of the interior. After the Muslim conquest, Armenia, the friend of the Greeks and the vassal of the Arabs, continued to remain a center for the exchange of goods.

In 685, Abdul Malik, faced with a civil war in Iraq, resumed payment of the tribute of Muawia to protect his western flank, and the agreement was renewed for a five-year period in 688 with the condition, among others, that the tribute from the island of Cyprus, which had been recovered by the Greeks, should be equally divided between the Greeks and the Arabs. The truce was violated in 691–692 by the Emperor when he declined to accept the new Arab coinage and violated the Cyprus convention. The last great assault on Constantinople was the siege of 716–718. Greek fire terrified the enemy, and the failure of the Arab fleet to provision the besiegers resulted in catastrophe. Only five Muslim vessels escaped destruction and but a remnant of the army reached Syria.

When we consider that the three attempts on Constantinople all failed, that only during the years 774–780 did a Muslim fleet dominate the Aegean, that the Greeks had recovered Cyprus, and that for long periods the two most powerful caliphs, Muawia and Abdul Malik, paid tribute to the Greeks to preserve the Syrian ports from attack, we are not justified in saying that Arab naval supremacy broke up the Greek lines of communication in the Aegean during the seventh century.

Finally, let us consider the possibility that Gaul was cut off from the East by military occupation.

The Arabs crossed the Pyrenees in 720, occupied Narbonne, and controlled the extreme southern part of the country bordering on the Mediterranean—Septimania. In 726 they occupied Carcassonne. The next great advance, coming in 732, was turned back by Charles Martel in the celebrated battle of Tours. In 736 they reached the Rhone for the *first* time at Arles and Avignon but were hurled back the next year by Charles. We have already mentioned the period of chaos after 740 which shelved all plans of aggression; when domestic order was restored, a new power existed in Gaul; Pippin recaptured Narbonne in 759. Pirenne himself says, "This victory marks, if not the end of the expeditions against Provence, at least the end of the Musulman expansion in the West of Europe." Charlemagne, as is well known, carried the war with indifferent success across the Pyrenees, but the Arabs did not again renew their assaults until after his death. In 848 they raided Marseilles for the first time, and later, spreading out from the base at Fraxinetum, pushed into Switzerland, where in 950 they held Grenoble and the St. Bernard Pass. The consequences of this activity, however, fall long after the period under discussion and need not be considered here.

To summarize: It is not correct to assume, as Pirenne does, that a policy of economic blockade played as principal a role in the warfare of antiquity and the Middle Ages as it does today, unless there is a positive testimony to that effect, as for example, the instance when the Persians cut the Greeks off from the supply of Eastern silk. With the exception of two brief intervals, the Byzantine fleet was master of the Aegean and the eastern Mediterranean not only in the seventh century but in the following centuries. This same fleet defended the West so well that only two raids are known to have been attempted against Sicily before 700. After the conquest of Spain had been accomplished, the Arabs embarked in 720 on an ambitious policy which took them for one brief year to the Rhone, and exactly coinciding in time with these military attacks came a series of raids on Sicily; but by 740 dismal failure was the reward everywhere, and throughout the last fifty years of the century the Arabs were either at peace or on the defensive.

We cannot admit that this evidence permits one to say, "Thus, it may be asserted that navigation with the Orient ceased about 650 as regards the regions situated eastward of Sicily, while in the second half of the seventh century it came to an end in the whole of the Western Mediterranean. By the beginning of the eighth century it had completely disappeared." . . .

II

Did the Arab conquest of Egypt in 640–642 end the exportation of papyrus? The evidence is to the contrary. It was not until 677 that the royal chancery of Gaul adopted parchment and it would be difficult to imagine that the Frankish government had a supply on hand to last for thirty-seven years. Actually, papyrus was employed in Gaul until a much later epoch, since the monks of Corbie obtained fifty rolls in 716, but the last specimen, dated 787, discovered in the country, had been written in Italy. Papyrus was traditionally employed by the papacy. Still preserved on papyrus are numerous papal documents, together with a letter of Constantin V to Pippin and a breviary of Archbishop Peter VI (927–971) describing the possessions of the Church of Ravenna. That papyrus was the customary material used by the popes seems to be indicated by numerous references, e.g., the glossator of the panegyrist of Berengar comments on the word papyrus "secundum Romanum morem dicit, qui in papiro scribere solent."[4]

In light of the evidence, there can be no other conclusion than that "the conquest of Egypt by the Arabs brought no immediate change. The manufacturing of papyrus continued." Relying on a statement of Ibn Haukal who referred to the cultivation of papyrus in Sicily in 977, some have held that in the tenth and eleventh centuries, the papal chancery obtained its supplies in Sicily and not in Egypt. In this connection it is worth noting that the process of making rag paper was introduced from China into the Eastern Caliphate shortly after 750, and we hear of a paper factory in Bagdad in 794. About this time there was a decline in Egyptian production of papyrus, and political disturbances in the country so interfered with a supply which paper had not yet made dispensable, that the caliph was forced to establish his own papyrus factory at Samarra in 836. T. W. Allen suggests that inasmuch as the earliest known Greek minuscule occurs in the Uspensky Gospels of 835, one may accept as a hypothesis that a known temporary shortage of papyrus may have induced the world of the Isaurian monarchy to give up the use of papyrus, to write on vellum only, in book form, on both sides, in a small hand permitting the most to be made of the space. Papyrus continued to be produced until the competition of paper finally de-

---

[4] "He is talking according to the fashion of the Romans who are accustomed to writing on papyrus."—Ed.

stroyed the industry in the middle of the eleventh century, and the fact that the last Western document to employ it, a bull of Victor II, is dated 1057 and coincides with the end of production in Egypt, leads us to believe that it was on Egypt, and not on Sicily, that the papacy depended.

Parchment, of course, was not unknown in Merovingian Gaul. Gregory of Tours mentions it, as Pirenne points out. It was regularly employed in preference to papyrus in Germany from the earliest times.

Since the Arab conquest of Egypt did not cut off the supply of papyrus at its source, because this material was still found in Gaul a century later and was regularly employed by the papacy until the eleventh century, it is difficult to say that its disappearance in Gaul is a conclusive proof that the Arabs had cut the trade routes. In the absence of all direct evidence one way or another, it would appear that as a possible hypothesis one might conclude that because parchment could be locally produced, because it was preferable as a writing material, and because, owing to a depreciated coinage, it *may* not have been more expensive than papyrus, the people of Gaul preferred to employ it.

The wines of Gaza undoubtedly were no longer exported, or even produced on a large scale, since it is a not unreasonable assumption that the Arabs, following the well-known Koranic injunction against wine, discouraged its manufacture. Some vineyards certainly remained, for the Christian churches of Palestine and Syria still used wine in celebrating the mass, and certain of the later Umayyad Caliphs were notorious drunkards. But inasmuch as papyrus and (as we shall presently show) spices were still exported, the *argumentum ad vinum* cannot be seriously advanced.

III

Is it true that with the Carolingians the former commerce of Gaul came to an end and the importation of Eastern luxuries ceased?

Everyone agrees—even Pirenne—that Gaul was surrounded by countries actively engaged in commerce. In Italy, for example, Venetian traders were selling velvet, silk, and Tyrian purple in Pavia by 780. Early in the ninth century they had trading connections with Alexandria, since the Doge issued an edict in conjunction with Leo V (813–820) forbidding this trade—an edict which had little effect in view of the fact that Venetian merchants translated the body of St. Mark in 827. Venice exported armor, timber for shipbuilding, and slaves—the latter despite the interdicts of Charlemagne and Popes Zacharias and Adrian I and imported all the usual Eastern products: spices, papyrus, and silks, large quantities of which were purchased by the Papacy.

Confronted with the alternative of defending Christendom or cooperating with the Saracens in return for trading rights, Naples, Amalfi, Salerno, and Gaeta chose the latter course.

North of Gaul, the Scandinavian countries and the region about the Baltic maintained an active intercourse with Persia via the water routes of Russia. The Arabs purchased furs (sable, ermine, martin, fox, and beaver), honey, wax, birch bark (for medicinal purposes), hazel nuts, fish glue, leather, amber, slaves, cattle, Norwegian falcons, and isinglas (made from sturgeons' bladders), and they sold jewelry, felt, metal mirrors, luxury goods, and even harpoons for the whale fisheries, besides exporting large quantities of silver coin to balance an unfavorable trade. The evidence for the really great prosperity of this commerce is to be found in the enormous coin hoards, the contents of tombs excavated in Scandinavia, the accounts of Arab geographers, and the incidental references in the writings and lives of men like Adam of Bremen and St. Ansgar.[5] Pirenne testifies to the importance of commerce in this period for the Netherlands.

We now come to the crucial point. If Gaul was surrounded by neighbors actively engaged in commerce, did not some of their activity embrace Gaul as well? Pirenne denies this and asserts that no mention of spices is to be found after 716 in Gaul and that no *negotiator* of the Merovingian type—a man who lent money at interest, was buried in a sarcophagus, and bequeathed property to the poor and the church—existed.

Now spices could be obtained at the time of Charlemagne, but at a high price, according to a statement of Alcuin, "Indica pigmentorum genera magno emenda pretio."[6] Augsburg, from the beginning of the tenth century, imported oriental products via Venice. In 908 we read of a gift of Tyrian purple by the bishop of Augsburg to the monastery of St Gall. . . .

---

[5] Adam of Bremen (eleventh century) wrote *The Deeds of the Bishops of Hamburg-Bremen,* a valuable source for North German history. St. Ansgar (ninth century) was the first Christian missionary to the Swedes; his life was written by Rimbert, a contemporary.—Ed.

[6] "Indian kinds of pigment bought only at a great price."—Ed.

Einhard, in his account of the translation of the blessed martyrs, Marcellinus and Peter, mentions that the holy relics on arrival were placed on *new* cushions of silk and that the shrine was draped with fine linen and silk. Abbo, in his epic of the siege of Paris by the Northmen in 885–886, scorned those whose manners were softened by Eastern luxuries, rich attire, Tyrian purple, gems, and Antioch leather. Similar references are to be found in the work of the celebrated monk of St. Gall.[7] Are we certain that this credulous retailer of myth completely falsified the local color as well? A far more interesting example is a long list of spices to be found appended to a manuscript of the statutes of Abbot Adalhard. These statutes are certainly dated in 822, but the manuscript is a copy of 986, so scholars have assumed the possibility that the list of spices may have been inserted at any period between 822 and 986. If this were true, Pirenne's case would certainly be shaken and he has not hesitated to deny the authenticity of the document, which he places in the Merovingian period. But he can produce not a single argument to support his view—except the usual one—the document could not date from 822 or after because the Arabs had cut the trade routes of the Mediterranean. Such a reason is inadmissible.

That Carolingian Gaul traded with her neighbors we may gather from a capitulation issued by Charlemagne in 805 regulating commerce with the East in which specific towns were named where merchants might go. Louis the Pious confirmed the bishop of Marseilles as collector of tariff at the port. An edict of Charles III in 887 mentions merchants at Passau on the Danube who were exempt from customs duties. A pact of Lothar in 840 regulated trade with Venice.

Charles the Bald in a charter of immunity given to St. Denis in 884 exempted from all exactions boats belonging to the monks engaged in trade or to their commercial agents. . . .

Sabbe has discovered an example of at least one *negotiator* who died in Bonn in 845 and disposed of a large estate—a man who certainly would seem to be included in Pirenne's definition of a Merovingian merchant. We have a continuous record of Mainz as a trading center from the ninth to the eleventh century: Einhard mentions grain merchants who were accustomed (*solebant*) to make purchases in Germany. The *Annales Fuldenses,* for the famine year of 850, mention the price of grain there. Frisian merchants founded a

[7] These were the *Annals of St. Gaul,* written in the famous monastery in Switzerland.— Ed.

colony in the city in 866. Otto I sent a wealthy merchant of Mainz as ambassador to Constantinople in 979. An Arab geographer of the next century describing the city says, "It is strange, too, that one finds there herbs which are produced only in the farthest Orient: pepper, ginger, cloves, etc." Sabbe has collected much evidence, from which he concludes that in the ninth and tenth centuries there were merchants, men of fortune, making long voyages, transporting cargoes in ships they owned personally and speculating on the rise of prices. . . .

Any notion that Gaul was separated from commercial contacts with the East in the ninth and tenth centuries can be contradicted by irrefutable evidence.

IV

Is it true that the culture and stability of Merovingian Gaul was largely determined by its commerce? The answer to this question is to be found in a brief survey of the economic history of the country. From the Roman conquest until the end of the second century of our era, Gaul enjoyed an immense prosperity based on natural products. Wheat and barley were produced in exportable quantities. Flax and wool were woven into textiles famous throughout the Mediterranean world. Cicero tells us (*De Republica*, III, 9, 16) that Rome, to safeguard Italian interests from competition, forbade the production of wine and olives, but the prohibition was ineffective as vineyards and olive orchards multiplied. The wine of Vienne was especially prized in Rome and in the middle of the second century Gaul exported both oil and olives. Forests yielded timber which was sawed into planking or exported to feed the fires of the baths of the imperial city. In Belgium horses were bred for the Roman cavalry. Ham, game birds, and the oysters of Medoc were prized by Roman gourmets.

Mines yielded copper, lead, and iron, and quarries in the Pyrenees, marble. Especially famous was Gallic pottery and glass, large quantities of which have been found at Pompeii and in Naples and Rome. The names of hundreds of free workers are known from autographs on sherds. The principal industries were textiles and ironware, for Gallic swords, armor, and metal utensils were highly valued. Leather and skin containers for oil were widely manufactured. One fact is of the *utmost* importance: the merchants and shipowners who carried this commerce were of Gallo-Roman birth. The merchants of Narbonne[8] had a *schola* at Ostia as did those of Arles. An inscription in Narbonne tells us that a native merchant of that city who traded in Sicily was an honorary magistrate of all the important Sicilian ports. Another inscription found in Beirut, dated 201, contains a letter of the prefect to representatives of the five corporations of *navicularii* of Arles. It should be especially noted that all the commodities mentioned above have one characteristic in common: they are either bulky or heavy objects of low intrinsic value which depend of necessity for profitable export on cheap transportation and relative freedom from onerous tariffs.

The accession of Commodus in 180 marks the beginning of serious civil disturbances in Gaul. Robber bands pillaged the country. After his assassination in 192, the struggle between Clodius and Septimus Severus was settled in the battle of Lyon, in the course of which the city was sacked and burned. Political disorder in this and ensuing periods was always an invitation for the barbarians to cross the frontier. They now came in bands, inflicting damage everywhere. Alexander Severus restored some semblance of order and initiated a policy of settling the new arrivals in military colonies on the frontier, but assassination stayed his hand and the infamous Maximin, who dominated the scene after 235, systematically confiscated all property within his grasp. He reduced the most illustrious families to poverty, seized the property of the different societies and charitable foundations, and stripped the temples of their valuables. A treasure hoard uncovered in 1909 in Cologne, of 100 gold aurei and 20,000 silver pieces, dating from Nero to 236, testifies to the unhappy fate of the owner, who preserved his goods but doubtless lost his life. Maximin shortly was slain, but civil war continued from 238 to 261, with new invasions of Franks and Alemans in 253–257. In 267 the German soldiery murdered the emperor, who had forbidden them the sacking of Mainz. When Aurelian died in 275 more barbarians entered Gaul, to be checked until Probus died in 282, when Alemans and Burgundians ravaged the country and pirates harried the coasts. At the same time the terrible Bagaudes, robber bands of peasants, wreaked havoc wherever they went. It is highly significant that in the debris scattered about Roman ruins in France today are to be found coins and scattered inscriptions dating about, but rarely after, the second half of the third century, thus fixing the date of the greatest damage. Adrian

---

[8] Narbonne, in southern France, in the Middle Ages had a port on the Mediterranean.—Ed.

Blanchet, in a study of 871 coin hoards uncovered in Gaul and northern Italy, by tabulating the results in chronological and geographical form has concluded that there is a remarkable correspondence between the places and periods of disorder and invasion, and the location, numbers, and size of the hoards.

When order was restored in the fourth century, the cities had been reduced to a size which could be easily fortified and defended, and they became important rather as military centers with a population of officials, soldiers, clerics, and a few merchants, than as the once thriving, proud, free cities of happier eras. An attempt was made at reconstruction, as in the case of Autun, ravaged in 269 and restored in the years after 296. Testifying to the lack of skilled labor was the importation of masons from Britain to assist in the rebuilding. Yet when Constantine visited Autun in 311 it was still poor and sparsely settled, while the citizens who survived complained of the crushing taxation.

Renewed civil war followed the death of Constantine in 337, culminating in the Frankish invasion of 355. Julian's campaigns brought peace and a revitalized life, but the year following his death, 363, the Alemans again invaded the country and in 368 sacked Mainz. After 395 Gaul was virtually abandoned by the Empire.

In addition to these civil disturbances, the depreciation of the Roman coinage in the third century was a powerful factor in leading to the institution of the colonnate and compulsory services of the fourth century with attendant hardships on the poor and middle classes. The severity of their circumstances urged them to seek relief through the relationship of the *precarium* and *patrocinium,* producing as the result the dominating class of the great landholders of the senatorial aristocracy and a general weakening of all imperial authority.

One would imagine that the final product of these disturbances and regulations would be the serious, if not catastrophic deterioration of the once flourishing economic activity of the country, and our information leads us to believe that such was the case. Some cloth was still made at Trèves, Metz, and Reims; but, if we except the beautiful jewelry of the Merovingian age, the glass industry alone may be said to have flourished, although the pieces that have survived are poor in quality and design and characterized by imperfect purification of the glass. Technical skill in masonry was limited, and the crudity of lettering on inscriptions bears witness to a decline of craftsmanship. During the earlier period of the empire, there were frequent references to Gallic sailors, as we have shown, but in the fourth century we hear only of African, Spanish, Syrian, and Egyptian sailors, and it is, of course, well known that Syrians and Orientals henceforth play an increasingly dominant role in trade and commerce. It would be a serious mistake to exaggerate this decline. Arles was still a busy port for the entrance of Eastern commodities, as an edict of Honorius of 418 testifies, and some possessors of large estates were extremely wealthy not only in land, but in large sums of gold; however, the accumulative testimony of writers, archaeology, and legislation indicates a far smaller scale of activity in industry and commerce then two centuries earlier.

Consequently, if after the Gothic invasions of North Italy, Southern Gaul, and Spain, and the Vandal conquest of North Africa and pirate raids in the western Mediterranean in the fifth century, we wish to speak of commerce as a determining factor in Merovingian Gaul, we would have to show that the reigns of Clovis and his successors produced a considerable economic revival, rather than that they maintained purely the status quo. This is, of course, one of the major parts of Pirenne's thesis: that there was an important identity in all the significant aspects of life, government, and culture between East and West, a true unity which effected a real survival—indeed revival—of prosperity until the Muslim conquest. Consequently, a comparison of West and East is necessary, and if possible an attempt should be made to show whether Merovingian government acted to encourage or discourage commerce.

V

The government of Merovingian Gaul was a monarchy, absolute in all respects, and if one may judge from the conduct of its rulers as revealed in the history of Gregory of Tours, the monarch had a very imperfect grasp of the "antique" notion of the state as an instrument designed to promote the common welfare. True, Clovis and his successors preserved many of the features of the Roman administrative system—particularly the method of deriving revenue, but there was certainly not the slightest reason for altering the machinery of an institution designed to raise the maximum of taxes when the principal aim of the ruler was to acquire as much wealth as possible. But even the operation of this part of the government became increasingly inefficient, particularly in the collection of the taxes on land, for the registers were in the greatest disorder and rarely revised, and the powerful did not pay at all. Thus, it came about that the easiest imposts to collect were the indirect tolls on commerce, for officers could be stationed on bridges, at crossroads, in the ports, and along the principal waterways to waylay all who passed. All the old levies of the later empire remained or were multiplied. . . . The internal free trade of a bygone era was a thing of the past, and it should be obvious that while such tariffs could be borne by goods of high intrinsic value and small bulk, or by goods going short distances, they would certainly put an intolerable burden on those products which once constituted the basis of Gaul's prosperity.

True, Latin was still the language of administration, but after the death of Justinian, Greek replaced Latin in the East.

Let us compare the position of King and Emperor. The sovereign of the East was the chief of a hierarchy of subordinate magistrates. He was not above the law, but held himself bound to conform to the accumulated tradition of Roman law and to his own edicts. As ruler, his main preoccupation was the preservation of his empire and its administrative machinery from attacks without and within the state, but he did not hesitate to introduce innovations when circumstances warranted a change. He maintained a standing army and fleet commanded by professional officers whose sworn duty it was to keep the empire secure from all threats. To accomplish all these ends the empire was organized into an administrative bureaucracy, carefully regulated, of extraordinary complexity and detail.

The King of Gaul, on the contrary, thought of himself rather less as a magistrate and rather more as a proprietor. The imperial office in the East was in theory elective, but the King in the West divided his kingdom after his death by rules of inheritance among his several sons without, as Lot has observed, any regard for geography, ethnography, or the desires of the people. Before 476 the unity of East and West, despite the presence of two emperors, was not only theory but fact, for both emperors issued laws under their joint names, and a general law promulgated by one emperor and transmitted to the other for publication was universally valid, but the division of Gaul among the King's sons shattered all legislative unity within the separate kingdoms, and such unity was restored only when and if a more powerful son succeeded in overwhelming and murdering his brothers. Furthermore, an edict issued in Constantinople was neither valid nor binding in Merovingian Gaul—indeed, was probably never heard of. In Gaul the army cost little or nothing, for it was neither professional nor standing, but was recruited by compulsion and without pay when the occasion or emergency warranted. Because a third of the proceeds of judgment went to the King, the courts were regarded more as a source of profit than as instruments of justice. In contrast to the complex bureaucracy of the East, in Gaul the King confided local administration to a few officials who combined executive, financial, and judicial functions in their one person, who commonly purchased their office, and who commonly exercised it to their own profit and the destruction and despair of the inhabitants submitted to their authority.

Pirenne is greatly impressed by the fact that the barbarian states had three features in common with the Empire: they were absolutist, they were secular, and the instruments of government were the fisc and the treasury. This seems to be a similarity without significance or value. Most states ruled by one man are absolutist, secular, and dependent on the treasury—yet that does not prove a derived and intentional identity with Byzantium. The personal role of Charles I before the summoning of the Long Parliament was absolutist; like the Byzantine Emperor, Charles was the head of the church, and his power was exclusively dependent on the treasury, but surely no one would dream of maintaining that there was a valid identity between Stuart England and the Eastern Roman Empire. What earthly reason would Clovis and his successors have had for setting up any other kind of state?

But, still more important, is this supposed identity, even if insignificant, really true? We have already indicated that the absolutism of the Emperor was different in some respects from that of the King. Were both governments *secular* in the same sense and spirit? Pirenne defines a secular government as one conducted without the aid or intervention of the church and its officials, and one in which the King was a pure layman whose power did not depend upon any religious ceremony, although the King might nominate bishops and other clergy and even summon synods.

It is, of course, true that the Byzantine Emperor was a layman in the sense that his power did not depend upon any religious ceremony. Ever since Leo I was crowned in 457 by the Patriarch, that ecclesiastic usually performed the act of coronation, yet, he did so as an important individual—not as a representative of the church—so that his presence was not legally indispensable.

The church, however, was most certainly subject to the state, in a manner utterly unlike that in Gaul, and the union of church and state which became always closer as time went on profoundly affected the character of both. It will be recalled that Constantine had established the principle that it was the emperor's duty and right to summon and preside over general councils of the church, and the later emperors considered themselves competent even to legislate in all religious questions. Justinian, who was a complete Erastian, did so. He issued edicts regulating the election of bishops, the ordination of priests, the appointment of abbots, and the management of church property, nor did he hesitate to pronounce and define his own views, on matters of faith. . . .

If the Emperor, then, played a major role in church affairs, it is also true that the bishops assumed an increasing importance in the civil administration of cities, and Justinian added to their civil functions. They had the right of acting as judges in civil suits when both parties agreed to submit to their arbitration, and judgment once given was not subject to appeal. In municipalities they had the duty of protecting the poor against the tyranny either of the agents of the Emperor or the nobles, and they could appeal directly over the heads of the administrative hierarchy to the Emperor himself. Throughout the territory of the exarchate of Ravenna, the bishops were general supervisors of the baths, granaries, aqueducts, and municipal finance. They protected the poor, prisoners, and slaves. They nominated to the Emperor the candidates for provincial magistracies and assisted at the installation of new governors. They examined for traces of illegality the acts of civil officials. They received notice before publication of all new laws. In short, they had the recognized power of continual intervention in all matters of secular policy.

Whereas the King of the Franks interfered in the appointment of church officers, he did not pretend to settle larger matters which were reserved for the authority of the Pope, and whereas the Pope's competence was acknowledged in the West, and his claim to be the chief of all bishops was admitted in the East, we have already seen that his authority was frequently challenged and defied by the Emperor, so that a closer examination reveals that far from the Pope and Emperor being mutually indispensable, as Pirenne asserts, the

Pope recognized the Emperor's intervention and definition of doctrine only when the temporal authority of the Exarchs was sufficient to compel obedience, or an alliance and cooperation with the Emperor were essential for an immediate papal aim, so that as a general thing it would be more correct to say that from the time of Gregory the Great, the Popes submitted when they must, but asserted their independence when they could. Thus, by Pirenne's own definition of *secular,* it will be seen that there was a very great difference between the state of the Franks and that of the Emperor.

No problem is more important than this: why did the Romans preserve the Empire in the East and lose it to the barbarians in the West? Various answers have been given: the impregnable situation of Constantinople and the more strongly fortified towns of the East, the more favorable geographical factors, the occupation of the throne by men of real ability in times of crisis, and the purely fortuitous turn of events at many times. Of the many factors one should not underestimate two: the character of the emperors and of the citizen population in the East. Both ruler and ruled composed a society which through the traditions of centuries had become accustomed to the idea of the State as an instrument for the very preservation and well-being of society, and to this concept of living under law administered by the officials of government both ruler and ruled paid homage and acknowledged the obligation. Thus there was a community of thought for self-preservation. Unfortunately in the West the same sentiments had not been a sufficient bulwark to keep out the invaders, and the newcomers to power, however much of the paraphernalia of the previous government they may have taken over, certainly failed to absorb, or absorbed but imperfectly, the old notions of the nature of the state and the value of its traditions. The principal fact of the Merovingian period was the decomposition of public power. The refinements of state-craft were an unappreciated art to the wielders of a purely personal power, and this blindness to realities led the kings to take those measures which resulted in the sapping of their own authority. The granting of immunities has long been recognized as a short-sighted act, productive of decay of royal absolutions. Inasmuch as we have already demonstrated that the Arabs did not cut off the trade routes at a time when the effects of their acts could have resulted in the granting of immunities due to weakening of power by the loss of revenue, Pirenne's interpretation of the proper sequence of cause and effect may be rejected. Indeed, we first learn of the granting of immunities in the sixth century, and after 623 the instances become increasingly numerous; the practice was well established long before anyone knew who Muhammad was, and Fustel de Coulanges has well remarked, "Immunity does not date from the decadence of the Merovingian; it is almost as ancient as the Frankish monarchy itself."[9]

In a wild and bloody period where one Merovingian fought another, the reckless expenditure of money, the destruction of property, the escape of the nobility from taxation, the conciliation of partisans by lavish gifts—these, and similar factors weakened the royal authority.

Pirenne asserts that "the foreign policy of the Empire embraced all peoples of Europe, and completely dominated the policy of the Germanic State." The fact that on certain occasions embassies were sent to Constantinople or that the Emperor at one time hired the Franks to attack the Lombards is the chief basis of this assertion. Clovis may have been honored by the title of "consul," but would anyone maintain that he considered himself answerable to the will of the Emperor? Insofar as for much of the time the conduct of the kings either in their domestic or foreign affairs can hardly be honored by the term "policy," it would be probably true to say that the Emperor was the *only* one to have a foreign policy.

Again, Pirenne makes a great point of the fact that the Merovingians for a long time employed the image of the Emperor on their coins. So did the Arabs, until Abdul Malik's reform, and for the same reason.

In fact, in matters of law, of policy domestic and foreign, of language, of culture, of statecraft and political vision, the kingdom of the Franks and the empire of the Greeks were as independent of one another as two different sovereign states can be, and if one is reduced to speaking of the mystical "unity of Romania" as a dominant historical fact, one has reduced history itself to mysticism.

Now to return again, after this digression, to the problem of commerce in Merovingian Gaul. It must be clear that there is nothing which one can indicate as calculated to improve the economic prosperity of the country. Furthermore, three characteristics dominate the picture:

9 Fustel de Coulanges, *Les Origines du Système Féodal* (Paris, 1907), p. 345.

1. People of Oriental origin appear to play the chief role in commerce.
2. These Syrians are dealing in luxury goods of eastern origin: spices, papyrus, wines.
3. We have practically no mention at all of exports from Gaul to the East.

Is there any connection between these three facts and the internal political and social condition of the country?

First: There is a physical factor in transportation too often ignored. Goods of high value and small compass may be transported long distances, in face of hardship and peril, and still be sold for a profit. This circumstance alone accounts for the survival and prosperity of the land route of five thousand miles across Central Asia, since tightly baled silk carried by camel and other pack animals was valuable enough to offset the cost of transportation. For the same reason, spices which had already passed through the hands of at least three or four middlemen before reaching a Mediterranean port could be taken to Gaul, either by sea or by land, and yield a satisfactory return to those who made the effort. What was true of spices was also true of papyrus and of silk from Byzantium. A merchant with capital enough to purchase a few hundred pounds of pepper, or of cinnamon, or of silk—even though he had to make wide detours, cover difficult terrain, take considerable risks, and pay innumerable tolls—might still expect to make a profit.

But we have already had occasion to point out that during the flourishing years of the late Republic and early Empire, the commercial prosperity of Gaul was founded principally upon the export of the natural products of the country: foodstuffs, cheaper textiles, timber, pottery, glass, skin bags, and so forth. These commodities could either be produced in the other parts of the empire, or could be dispensed with altogether. To compete favorably in the imperial marts their export depended on secure and relatively cheap transportation and the absence of oppressive tolls and restrictive legislation. Therefore, when we consider the destruction wrought by the barbarian invasions, the civil turmoil, the depreciation of the coinage, and the impoverishment of the empire in the third century, we should expect the foreign markets for Gallic products would be temporarily lost, and it would appear reasonable to conclude that the rigid economic and social legislation of the emperors after Diocletian's restoration, the collection of taxes in kind, the multiplication of indirect tolls and tariffs, compulsory services, the fiscal policy of the Frankish kings, and the absence of any policy to promote commerce and economic enterprise, would have made it virtually impossible, even if the desire had existed, to recover and reestablish lost or disorganized markets.

These assumptions have, in fact, commonly been held by most economic historians of the period, and no one has ever produced sufficient evidence seriously to threaten their validity. They are, of course, very inconvenient for Pirenne's thesis. He consequently challenges them, but unfortunately has been unable to find more than one direct piece of evidence: that Gregory the Great purchased some woollen cloth in Marseilles and had some timber sent to Alexandria. He also is "rather inclined" to believe that the Germanic invasions revived the prosperity of the slave trade.

VI

Since this evidence is scarcely convincing, and since it would be difficult to find more, Pirenne turns to the problem of money and says, "In any case, the abundant circulation of gold compels us to conclude that there was a very considerable export trade." Now, in the absence of any banking system for settling by the shipment of bullion an accumulated disparity between exports and imports, one would certainly be prepared to believe it quite possible that the export of some products would bring foreign gold into the country, although the total supply might be diminishing due to larger imports, and this was undoubtedly the case, but Pirenne goes much farther and makes it very plain that he believes the exports from Gaul in early Merovingian days exceeded in value, or at least equalled, the imports of eastern products, since "if it [gold] had been gradually drained away by foreign trade we should find that it diminished as time went on. But we do not find anything of the sort." He argues that when the Muslim conquest closed the trade routes, gold became a rarity and was abandoned for silver as a medium of exchange. The employment of silver was the real beginning of the Middle Ages and is a witness of a reversion to natural economy. When gold reappeared, the Middle Ages were over, and "Gold resumed its place in the monetary system only when spices resumed theirs in the normal diet."

A natural question arises. If gold remained the medium of currency, unimpaired in quantity due to a favorable export balance until the Arabs cut the trade routes, what happened to it then? It could not have flowed East after the catastrophe on the assumption that exports suffered before imports, because Pirenne is insistent, and all the evidence he has collected is designed to show that it was the import of Eastern products which first disappeared. If gold *could not* flow East, why did it not remain in Gaul as a medium of local exchange?

There are at least three factors in the problem.

1. From the earliest times small quantities of gold were found in the beds of certain streams flowing from the Pyrenees, and even in the sands of the Rhine, but the supply was so negligible that one may assert that the West produced no gold. On the other hand, there were substantial deposits of silver, and there were silver mines at Melle in Poitou and in the Harz mountains.

2. It should be unnecessary to point out that we have not the slightest idea of the total amount of gold in Gaul at any period. We occasionally hear of an amount confiscated by a king, of a loan given by a bishop, of a sum bequeathed the church by a landholder or merchant, of the size of booty or tribute, of a subsidy of 50,000 *solidi* sent by the Emperor, but that is all. In many cases, without doubt, a figure or instance is mentioned, not because it was usual, but because it was extraordinary. The number and importance of coin finds are not in any proportion to the probable facts and may not be relied on. Therefore when Pirenne speaks of "large" amounts of gold, he is merely guessing. Furthermore, as is well known, there was in general circulation a bronze and silver currency for use in smaller transactions.

3. Gregory the Great (590–604) testifies that Gallic gold coins were so bad that they did not circulate in Italy, and an examination of coins shows a progressive debasement before the Arab conquest. Since these coins did not come from the royal mint, but were struck by roving minters for people in more than a hundred known localities, one has evidence of the chaotic decentralization of the government and lack of interest in orderly financial administration, together with a possible indication of a growing scarcity of gold.

If gold disappeared in Gaul, this disappearance could be due to the following causes:

a. It might have been hoarded, buried, and lost.
b. It might have been exchanged or used for the purchase of silver.
c. It might have been drained off in purchase of commodities in a one-sided trade, or paid in tribute.
d. Through the operation of Gresham's law, foreign merchants might have hoarded and removed the good gold coinage, leaving a debased coinage in local circulation.

There is no evidence to support the first two hypotheses, and considerable evidence for the last two—both of which amount to this same fact: gold was drained out of the country. This hypothesis is strongly supported by the best known authority and Bloch gives good reasons for accepting it. Gold, of course, did not completely disappear in the West, as the manufacture of jewelry and occasional references show, and it would be interesting to possess the full facts about the gold coin counterfeiting the Arab dinar—the *mancus*. However, it is difficult to accept the thesis advanced by Dopsch that there was enough gold to constitute with silver a truly bimetallic currency. But it is even more difficult to accept the proposition of Pirenne that the change from gold to silver meant a change from money to natural economy. The numerous instances which prove conclusively that money continued as a medium of exchange have been diligently collected by Dopsch and need not be repeated. It is not clear why silver coinage should equal natural economy. China and Mexico use silver today, and the coins of Arab mintage found in the Baltic regions are also silver, yet no one would pretend that in these instances we are dealing with a system of natural economy. Had a system of natural economy prevailed we might have expected an absence of all kinds of money, and the fact that the Carolingians introduced a pure, standard, centrally minted silver coinage would seem logically to prove just the contrary of Pirenne's thesis. But Pirenne takes as a point the circumstance of the monasteries in those regions of Belgium where the soil will not support vineyards. "The fact that nearly all the monasteries in this region where the cultivation of the vine is impossible, made a point of obtaining estates in the vine-growing countries, either in the valleys of the Rhine and Moselle or in that of the Seine, as gifts from their benefactors, proves that they were unable to obtain wine by ordinary commercial means."[10] Pirenne has drawn his information from an article of Hans van Werveke.[11] The latter appears to have been a collaborator of Pirenne's and asserts, "The phenomenon which we signal is so general that we can say that it responds to an economic law." Now a superficial observer, intent on discovering for himself the likeliest place to observe the functioning of a system of natural self-sufficing economy, might very reasonably turn to a monastery as the logical place of all places, because of monastic rules themselves, to find such a system in operation. On the contrary, it is a well known fact that in the Middle Ages a good many monasteries were something more than self-sufficing and turned to advantage surplus commodities which they disposed of, or profited as toll collectors, if rivers, bridge, or roads were within their property. . . .

To conclude: There is no evidence to prove that the Arabs either desired to close, or actually did close the Mediterranean to the commerce of the West either in the seventh or eighth centuries. Islam was hostile to Christianity as a rival, not as a completely alien faith, and the Muslims were invariably more tolerant than the Christians, but Islam as a culture, as the common faith of those who submitted and who spoke Arabic, though not necessarily by any means of Arab blood, had far more in common with the Hellenized East and with Byzantium than did the Gaul of Pirenne's Romania. Much of what he says of Gaul was true of Islam. The Merovingians took over the administrative and particularly the taxation system of Rome intact. So did the Arabs. The Merovingians preserved Latin as the language of administration. The Arabs used Greek. Western art was influenced by Byzantine forms. So was Arab. But these are smaller matters. The crude Western barbarians were not able to develop—indeed, they were too ignorant to preserve the state and the culture they took by conquest, while the Arabs on the contrary not only preserved what they took but created from it a culture which the world had not known for centuries, and which was not to be equaled for centuries more. This culture was based on that of the Hellenized Eastern Mediterranean in one part and on that of Persia strongly permeated

[10] Pirenne, "The Place of the Netherlands in the Economic History of Medieval Europe," *Economic History Review*, II (1929), 23.
[11] Hans van Werveke, "Comment les établissements religieux belges se procuraient-ils du vin au haut moyen âge," *Revue Belge de Philologie et d'Histoire*, II (1923), 643–62.

with both Hellenic and Indian elements, on the other. Arab theology, Arab philosophy, Arab science, Arab art—none was in opposition to late antique culture, as Pirenne seems to imagine, but was a new, fertile, virile, and logical development of long established forms. The decadence of the West—the so-called Middle Ages—was due to a complexity of causes, mostly internal, and largely connected with social and political institutions. Rostovtzeff, writing of economic conditions of the later Roman Empire, frequently warns against mistaking an aspect for a cause, and most of the economic factors of the Middle Ages are aspects and not causes. Thus, the man—whether he be a Pirenne or a Dopsch—who attempts to understand and to interpret either the Merovingian or Carolingian period in terms *purely* of an economic interpretation of history will be certain to fail, for the simple reason that economic factors play a subsidiary role and present merely aspects in the great causative process.

Sture Bolin

MOHAMMED, CHARLEMAGNE AND RURIC

Professor Sture Bolin (1900–1963), a Swedish historian, tells us that "this study is based upon, and in part reproduces unchanged, the manuscript of a lecture which I delivered when I took up a chair of history at Lund University in February, 1939." In its original form it appeared in 1939 in Scandia *as "Muhammed, Karl den Store og Rurik." Professor Bolin's entire academic career, as undergraduate, graduate student (he received his Ph.D. in 1927), teacher, and scholar, was associated with the University of Lund. Professor Kristof Glamann of the University of Copenhagen remarks that Professor Bolin, "in a way was a local patriot with a far-ranging, however, rather abstract mind. His attitudes toward archeology and numismatics were those of the true historian. . . . His intention undoubtedly was to write a general history of currency down to about 1300, but only parts of it were ever published." His published writings include* Ledung och frälse *(1934), which concerns the debate about the structure of twelfth-century Scandinavian society, the chapter on Scandinavia in vol. I of the* Cambridge Economic History of Europe *(1942), and* State and Currency in the Roman Empire to 300 A.D., *vol. I (1958).*

The association of Charlemagne with Mohammed is familiar to all students of the Middle Ages. It has arisen particularly in the various attempts which have been made from about 1920 to assess the significance of the political and cultural changes which took place in the early Middle Ages and are ascribed to, or at least associated with, Mohammed and Charlemagne, and to estimate the connections between the events in the Arab and the Carolingian parts of the world. The two leading participants in the discussion are the Austrian Alfons Dopsch and the Belgian Henri Pirenne. Ruric, the Nordic viking chief in Russia, has, however, never been mentioned in the discussion.

There is no important difference between the interpretation of Dopsch and Pirenne of the transition from the ancient world to the Middle Ages. The collapse of the Roman Empire did not mean the end of an old world, nor did the Germanic migrations imply the birth of anything completely new. Neither the invasion of the Roman Em-

Excerpted from Sture Bolin, "Mohammed, Charlemagne and Ruric," *Scandinavian Economic History Review* 1 (1953): 5–12, 24–39. With permission of the Scandinavian Society for Economic and Social History and Historical Geography. Documentation is omitted.

pire by the Teutons, nor their assumption of political power led to any transformation of economic, social, political or cultural conditions. Changes had been continuously occurring in social, economic and intellectual life throughout the late Empire; these same processes continued during and after the barbarian invasions. Both Dopsch and Pirenne held that the similarities between the later Roman Empire and the Merovingian period were very significant while the differences were comparatively unimportant. Pirenne particularly stressed that the Mediterranean world remained a cultural and economic unit during the entire Merovingian period: the same religion and the same cultural influences still prevailed throughout; lively trading connections were still maintained across the Mediterranean between western Europe and the many coastal towns of the Near East.

But although Dopsch and Pirenne are in agreement on all essentials concerning the Merovingian period, their opinions are in sharp contrast when they turn to the Carolingian period.

Dopsch maintains that social and economic life in the Carolingian period rested on the same foundations as Merovingian society. No gulf separated the two epochs; there were no essential differences in character between them. Dopsch resolutely rejects the view that during the Carolingian period agriculture attained a completely predominant position in western economy. It was not true that almost everywhere each separate farmstead primarily produced to supply its own needs; nor was the economic importance of the commercial and market towns reduced to a minimum. On the contrary, trade was not only active throughout the Carolingian period but was even on the increase.

On point after point, Pirenne maintained completely different opinions, exactly the opposite to those of Dopsch. The Merovingian age was a prelongation of the ancient world; the Carolingian period the true beginning of the Middle Ages. It was in Carolingian times that the transition occurred from the mercantile economy of the preceding epoch to the largely agrarian economy of the true medieval world. Internal trade declined within the Frankish empire and, except for a few isolated cases, the international exchange of goods ceased. The fundamental reason for this, says Pirenne, lay in the transformation which the map of Eurasia underwent in the seventh and eighth centuries. The Arab conquest of the eastern and southern coasts of the Mediterranean in the course of these centuries shattered the

unity of the civilization that had existed until that time. Thereafter the
Mediterranean no longer bound together the different parts of the
same culture; instead it separated two alien and hostile civilizations,
the Arab-Mohammedan world and the European-Christian world.
There were very few connections between these two spheres of culture. Peaceable trading ships no longer sailed the Mediterranean as
before; the Sea was now dominated by the pirate fleets of the Arab
Saracens. The Carolingians accepted the implications of the changed
geopolitical structure of the world and moved the center of their
empire away from the Mediterranean coast to the region of the Rhine
estuary. Charlemagne's palace at Aachen became a new political and
cultural center. The expansion of Charlemagne's empire was directed
towards the east and the north; its economy was agricultural, its
culture purely Germanic. The foundation of this new empire was,
according to Pirenne, Charlemagne's most important contribution to
world history. But the reorganization which he accomplished was
made possible in the first place by the shattering of the Mediterranean world and thus indirectly by the developments which began
with Mohammed. Pirenne epitomized his point of view in a striking
paradox: without Mohammed, no Charlemagne.

The writings of Dopsch and Pirenne provide a clear statement of
the different interpretations of the Carolingian period and reveal the
difficulties of the problem. Both writers are specialists in early
medieval studies and they are the two leading authorities on the
period. Nevertheless, their opinions on this fundamental question are
as far apart as east and west.

That this can be so is due, of course, to the nature of the original
sources on which medieval historians have to rely. For the early
Middle Ages there is no documentary source material to make statistical comparisons possible. The widely scattered references in chronicles, legends, decrees and other sources, to trade, merchandise or
economic conditions, can be used on either side of the argument. It
can be shown for instance that papyrus ceased to be used in western
Europe in the eighth century; on the one hand, this may be taken to
indicate that the connections with the Orient were much fewer; on
the other hand, it can be held that this merely reflects changed
governmental practices in the Frankish empire, since the conserva-
tive papal Chancery continued to use quantities of papyrus until the
eleventh century. If one party quotes the many markets and fairs of
the Carolingian period as evidence of a flourishing and growing

trade, the other can interpret them as indicating that normal trade, conducted by a class of professional tradesmen, had declined. Circumstance after circumstance, source after source, may be interpreted in either of the two opposing ways.

There are two facts, however, in the mercantile history of the early Middle Ages which are so familiar and generally accepted that they need no further substantiation; they are so well known that it may seem banal to mention them. Firstly, whether or not trade ceased between Western Europe and the Arab world during the Carolingian period, it is quite certain that, within the Caliphate, trade, industry and a town economy flourished as never before. Secondly, whether the internal trade of Western Europe increased or decreased during this epoch, the ancient connections between Europe and the northern and Baltic countries became very much more important, especially in the first part of the Carolingian age.

If these two accepted facts are set in juxtaposition, however, the main problem again thrusts itself forward. One is led to ask whether the communications between the Frankish empire and the North became more lively in consequence of reduced communications between the West and the Orient, or whether the same factors were responsible for the prosperity of trade both in the Caliphate and around the North Sea.

Faced with this dilemma, we are obliged to look for some kind of original sources which permit comparisons to be made as directly as possible between different periods of time and different spheres of culture.

There is in this case only one type of study which can really provide the basis for direct comparison between economic conditions at different ages and in different countries, namely numismatics. The history of coinage is abundantly rich in source material—coins and coin hoards by the thousand. The coins run in unbroken series from the beginning of the period to the end of the Dark Ages; their date of minting can be ascertained to the year or at least within rather limited periods. They originate from every part of the civilized world of that time. It is always possible to determine the country in which they were minted, very often the exact place. If the basic problem which confronts us, of discovering the main commercial developments during the Carolingian period, can be solved at all, then it is through a study of the coins which have been discovered.

Coin hoards play an important part in discussions on commercial relationships in early times. Discoveries of Roman and Byzantine coins in Germanic territories and in India from the first six centuries A.D., of Arab and western coins in northern and eastern Europe from the period 800–1100, of Bohemian coins in Russia from the last centuries of the Middle Ages, of Portuguese and Dutch coins in India from more recent times, all bear witness to the changing pattern of international trading connections. It may therefore appear that an examination of the hoards of coins from Carolingian times will show fairly directly how close the connections were between the Frankish and Arab worlds and whether trade within the Frankish empire increased or declined. It could be assumed that, if connections between East and West were close, many Arab coins would have been discovered in western Europe or many western coins inside the Caliphate. The absence of such discoveries might indicate that there were no close connections between the two spheres of culture. In the same way, by studying the composition of the coin hoards found in western Europe and the radius of circulation of the coins, it would seem possible to determine the main lines of the development of internal trade; if the radius of circulation tends to become smaller and smaller—that is to say, if the hoards in course of time tend to be dominated by coins minted in towns near to the place of discovery while coins from distant places become rare—it might be taken as a sign of reduced trade; if the opposite is shown to be the case—that the treasures contain greater numbers of coins from distant mint-cities—it might be assumed that trade had expanded.

No information is available from this era concerning discoveries of western European coins in the East, but there is some evidence regarding discoveries of Arab coins in the West. These are not, however, so frequent that they can be considered to prove that close connections existed between the two cultures. On the contrary, they are so few that, if we were compelled to draw a conclusion only from this evidence, we would have to infer that trans-Mediterranean intercourse had practically ceased.

An inspection of the radius of circulation of the coins from the Frankish treasures reveals that this radius was wide during Merovingian times: the hoards from this period consist of coins originating from the most distant parts of the Frankish kingdom. The same applies to the hoards from the reigns of Charlemagne and Louis the Pious. But in the later Carolingian treasures, from about the middle of the ninth century onwards, the coins often have a limited radius of circulation; in some cases all the coins discovered in one place originate from a single mint not far away. Certainly, the main trend is a contraction of the area of circulation, and this might be taken as a sign of diminished trade; there have been pronouncements to that effect from students of the age.

This would, however, be an oversimplified reading of the coin hoards. The two facts that Arab coins in western Europe are so few and that the coins of the later Carolingian hoards show a contracted radius of circulation cannot in themselves give much information about the state of trade. These phenomena must first be regarded in the light of the prevailing currency arrangements.

Certain fundamental currency principles were applied from the outset in the Carolingian kingdom. They persisted into the High Middle Ages and are called the principles of feudal coinage. One was that precious metal was worth more when minted than unminted. Another—and this has greater relevance to our present study—was to the effect that any type of coins was valid only within a limited area and that, within the area, only one type of coin could be used. Thus, within the Frankish empire, currency was limited by national boundaries as early as Merovingian times and by the beginning of the Carolingian period. The limitation was rigid: for the purposes of internal trade only the national coinage might be used and the area of validity of the coins thereafter became still more restricted. From the middle of the ninth century, coins only had territorial validity. This implied that, from the beginning of the Carolingian period, no foreign coins at all could be used within the boundaries of the Frankish empire; all foreign coins had to be reminted as Frankish coins—that is, they were melted down and the metal was used to make Frankish deniers. As, then, coins came to have this merely territorial validity, the deniers from one area of circulation in the Empire had to be melted and reminted in exactly the same way whenever they crossed a territorial frontier. These principles were strictly observed, as may be seen from various hoards discovered near the Loire. During the later part of the ninth century the southern boundary of one area of circulation ran just south of the river, the area reaching to the north as far as the Channel. Some hoards of this period have been found near the Loire, both south and north of the river. These hoards contain coins from all parts of northern

France but none at all from the southern currency areas which were outside the boundaries of the territory, although geographically much nearer to the places where the hoards were buried.

It is thus obvious that, no matter how close the trade connections may have been between the Caliphate and western Europe, they could not have left behind any more than the slightest trace in the evidence found in the coin discoveries. Furthermore, it is obvious that the limitation of the area of validity of the coins must result in a contraction of their radius of circulation. We may thus conclude that the coin hoards from western Europe can be of no direct assistance in helping to unravel the complex problems in dispute.

It will, therefore, be necessary to examine and compare the Frankish and the Arab coins themselves. . . .

[Pp. 12–24 of the original article are omitted. In this section Professor Bolin concludes that shortly before the middle of the eighth century, increased production of silver in the Caliphate influenced the coinage of both the Caliphate and the Frankish Empire, which now assumed some important characteristics in common. Carolingian coins reveal a fundamental Arabic influence. It is thus impossible to agree with Pirenne that Western Europe was cut off from the East during the Carolingian period. These points are summarized in the first two paragraphs which follow.]

Let us return at this point to Pirenne's epigram on Mohammed and Charlemagne. The facts we have just described certainly speak for the existence of a bond uniting the two, but not in the sense intended by Pirenne. His view was that the Arab conquests led to a break-up of the world culture as it was known until then and to an end of trade across the Mediterranean.

Instead we may summarize the position as follows: through the wars of conquest begun by Mohammed the unity of world culture was shattered and civilization was divided into separate spheres; but it was also enlarged, for, far to the east, new countries, the lands of Khurâsân and Transoxania, both rich in silver, were brought into the Mohammedan orbit. Silver production increased to very large proportions. So began a new era, the age of oriental silver. From this newly-won territory there issued a mighty flood of silver over the whole world fructifying trade and economic life—just as 700 years later a similar flood issued from other recently discovered lands. The flood did not stop at the boundaries of the Caliphate but penetrated into western Europe, where also it led to changes in economic life: we observe that maximum prices had to be fixed and the currency system modified. Commercial life flourished within the Frankish empire as well as internationally.

In other words, the Carolingian renaissance had not merely its intellectual but also its material prerequisites in the Caliphate. In this sense one may reiterate Pirenne's paradox, without Mohammed, no Charlemagne, but in disagreement, not in accord, with his views.

In order to assess completely the connections between the Frankish empire and the Caliphate we must establish what goods were the basis of trade between the two territories.

An Arab source which has little reliability as evidence says that silver was imported by the Franks from the Mohammedan world; for the rest, historical writings contain no more than occasional surmises. The foregoing exposition should establish beyond any doubt that silver was exported from the Mohammedan world to western Europe. Moreover, spices and oriental luxury goods of various kinds were imported into western Europe just as during an earlier period.

The question therefore arises of what the Franks gave in exchange. It has not been possible for writers who have relied solely on western sources of information to supply a complete answer. The Monk of St. Gall relates that Charlemagne sent to Hârûn-ar-Rashîd red fabrics which were very highly valued in the Arab world. This has been quoted as proof that textiles were exported from western Europe to the Orient. It is clear from western European sources that France and Italy exported slaves to the Caliphate; this fact has already been stressed by scholars whose conclusions derive from those sources: slaves certainly were an item of import into the eastern countries as early as Merovingian times.

Far more detailed information about the imports of the Caliphate from western Europe is to be found in Arab writings. The ninth-century geographer Ibn Khurdâdbih states that the Franks exported to the Mohammedans eunuchs, male and female slaves, brocade, beaver-skins, marten-skins, other furs, swords, the perfume of the styrax and the mastic drug. Other statements, from tenth-century writers, are worth noting. Istakhrî writes that from Maghrib came white eunuchs, brought thither from Spain, and valuable girls. Ibn Hawkal, whose work is closely allied to that of Istakhrî but contains more detailed and more useful information, relates that beaver-furs were brought to Spain from the Slav territories; among the articles of trade which came from Spain to Maghrib and Egypt were male and female slaves of Frankish and Galician nationality and Slav eunuchs. Mukaddasî was aware of the export from Spain of Slav eunuchs. An eleventh-century geographer describes how the Franks took Slav prisoners of war and had them castrated by Jews living within the country or in neighboring Mohammedan lands after which they were sold to Spain. The Italian writer Liutprand confirms this in the tenth century: according to him, merchants from Verdun made incalculable profits out of making men into eunuchs and then selling them to Spain.

These Arab sources show that the Frankish exports were, except for occasional examples of less important goods, weapons, brocade (the account of the Monk of St. Gall does not seem to have been entirely invented out of thin air), furs and slaves. There can be no doubt that, of these, the last two were the most important.

But, as far as is known, furs were never produced in the Frankish empire on any significant scale; on the other hand many sources indicate that northern Europe and the territory inhabited by the Slavs were the principal fur-producing regions. Nor did the slaves, the other leading article of export from the Frankish empire to the Caliphate, originate in the empire. We have seen already from the passages quoted from Arab writings, that the slaves sold by the Franks to the Caliphate were Slav. A decision of the Council of Meaux in 845 is of interest in this connection: Jewish and other merchants traveled with heathen slaves across Christian lands and sold them to infidels; this practice should be prohibited in the future. It is true that cases are known of Christian slaves also being sold to Spain—the anti-Semitic letter-writer Agobard lays the blame for this upon the Jewish merchants. But as a general rule Christian slaves were not sold to infidels. Thus, after the conversion of the Saxons to Christianity, the slaves sold to the Caliphate from the Frankish empire must have come largely from the same regions as the furs, the Slavic territory east of the Elbe, or northern Europe.

Once the fact is established that the chief articles of export of the Franks to the Caliphate were furs and heathen slaves, the part played by the Frankish empire in the international trade of the time is set clearly into perspective. The main Frankish exports were primarily not its own products. Instead, the Frankish empire was a country of transit between the fur- and slave-producing territory in northern, central and eastern Europe and the Mohammedan world. This conclusion may be somewhat startling but it is incontestable. Indeed, it supplies us with the key to an understanding of many problems relating to the development of and changes in world trade during the early Middle Ages.

It now becomes possible to understand why there were such active connections in the early Carolingian period between the Frankish empire and the North. Ancient trading routes linked the East with the Frankish empire as well as the Frankish empire with the North and the Baltic lands. When the supply of silver greatly increased in the Caliphate, slaves and furs were imported in increasing quantities. Naturally, the routes used for this trade were the old line of communication between the Orient and western Europe. But the increased export of slaves and furs from the Frankish empire most certainly had its counterpart in the increased import of these two commodities into the Frankish empire from their countries of production. Consequently, trade increased and commerce became livelier along the old route between western Europe and the northern and Baltic lands at precisely the same time.

We have here an answer to the problem which confronted us at the beginning of this inquiry. The livelier trade on the North Sea and the commercial prosperity of the Mohammedan world were not isolated phenomena. They were intimately connected and were both symptomatic of the world-wide economic boom during the age of oriental silver.

There is indeed a great deal of evidence of the active connection between northern and western Europe in early Carolingian times. It was in the 790s that Nordic Vikings set out on their first raid on the west, when they went to England. The earliest Nordic coins minted at home follow the pattern of Frankish coins of precisely this epoch, the later part of the eighth century. The first treasures buried in Scandinavia and the immediately surrounding territory during the time of the Viking conquests consist exclusively of Frankish coins of the reigns of Charlemagne and Louis the Pious. Coins from western Europe are found to some extent up to the middle of the ninth century in graves and in other scattered places in the North. The ancient towns known to have been in existence around 800—Reric, Slesvig-Hedeby, Ribe and Birka—are unmistakable evidence of the importance of trade in the Baltic region. Visits to these towns by Frisian merchants, as well as journeys by Northmen to Duurstede, the trade metropolis of Frisia, are described in written documents. Archaeologists and philologists alike stress the importance of these links between the North and Frisia in their respective studies. Both the political intercourse between Franks and Danes in the first three decades of the ninth century and the attempt which started about this time to convert the Nordic peoples to Christianity show plainly how Frankish interests tried to assert themselves in the North.

Of course, the links between northern and western Europe were never broken, but hardly any western European coins are to be found in any Nordic discoveries from a very long period after 850. References in western European writings to conditions in the North become rare after 830. The Frankish intervention in the Danish wars of succession ceased; by the middle of the ninth century the Frankish missionary activity had ended. But after 830 the Viking excursions to the West increased in strength and number.

Thus, a change seems to have occurred in the relations between the North and western Europe and this change should be regarded against the background of developments in international trade.

It was natural, indeed essential, that when the age of oriental silver began, the trade in furs and slaves should follow the old paths which for centuries had linked the Orient with western Europe and western Europe with the North and the Baltic lands. But it was by no means essential, hardly even natural, for such a roundabout commerce to persist.

The Frankish empire was the *entrepôt* but the market was the Caliphate. In 750 the center of the Caliphate moved from Syria to Iraq. Economic life flourished in Persia in the Abbasid period; the silver was won still further to the east; there was a considerable development of industry.

The territory which offered the best opportunities for procuring slaves was the Slavic lands which at this time extended in the east as far as the Upper Volga. Furs were to be obtained in the North and the Baltic regions and in the countries to the east. The great eastern European rivers provided excellent means of transport. In other words, circumstances were more favorable for a more direct connection between producers and consumers than was provided by the circuitous method of using the old traditional routes by way of Frankish territory.

The Nordic expansion eastwards and the creation of "the great Svitjod," the area of Swedish dominance in eastern Europe, must be seen against this background. Later sources attribute the foundation of the Russian state to the Viking chieftain Ruric of the people of Rus and date it at 862. Ruric may be only a legendary figure but his name may remain as a symbol of a historical reality. The year 862, which was once regarded as a cornerstone in the chronology of the history of eastern Europe, is certainly the product of a late and hypothetical reconstruction of events on the basis of known sources; modern research attaches no value at all to it.

The Nordic expansion towards the east across the territory of the eastern Slavs had begun earlier. Swedish influence was strongly felt in the Baltic coastal areas before 800, although not further inland. But Swedish archaeological evidence from the early part of the ninth century bears witness to long-range connections between the North and the territory north of the Caspian Sea; it shows that the eastward expansion had progressed very far. From the same period there are questionable archaeological traces of Nordic settlement south of Lake Ladoga. It is certain that in 839 Swedes advanced along some of the rivers of eastern Europe as far as Constantinople; they pretended to be emissaries from the Khan of the Rus. In 860 the first Viking expedition took place in the direction of Constantinople. Perhaps as early as about 846, certainly before the end of the century, Ibn Khurdâdbih says that merchants of the Rus visited Constantinople and Bagdad. Modern historians have every reason to put the date of the Nordic penetration of East Slavia in the early part of the ninth century.

The nature of the Nordic expansion is fairly well known. The Norsemen in the east were typical equivalents of the Spanish conquistadors of the sixteenth century. They were conquerors in foreign lands, callously exploiting a subdued people.

They acted like marauding pirates—less, however, in the east than in the west: only two assaults on Constantinople and three or four on the Caliphate are definitely established as historic facts.

The Norsemen came as mercenary soldiers. The Varangian Guards of the Byzantine emperors in Constantinople are well known. The Arab author Mas'ûdî gives us to understand that men of the Rus—and Slavs—found employment as soldiers and servants to the Jewish khan of the Khazars in his realm north of the Caspian Sea.

The Norsemen settled inside the east Slavic territory and forced their subjects to support them and furnish them with commercial merchandise. The Arab Ibn Rustah relates that the Rus owned no

arable land but lived on what they took from the Slavs; they forced
them to surrender goods of all kinds. Constantin Porphyrogennetos
describes how the Rus passed the winter living among the conquered Slavs and then spent the spring and summer in Kiev and on
trading journeys.

They came to look for slaves. Ibn Rustah and Gardîzî say that the
Rus made war on the Slavs, carried them off as slaves and sold them.
In these comments describing conditions at the beginning of the
tenth century, there are accounts of actual slave-hunts made by the
Norsemen in the eastern parts.

The Norsemen were not only dealers in slaves; they appeared, in
the east more than in the west, as merchants in general. It has truly
been said that the ruler of Kiev himself was a great merchant who
traded in the goods he received in taxes from his subjects.

There are many references in Byzantine and Arab literature to the
activities of the Norsemen as merchants in eastern Europe. One of
their trading routes ended at Constantinople where, according to an
Arab source, they sold furs and swords. A fact of a greater interest in
this investigation is that the trading journeys of the Norsemen regularly took them to the capital city of the Khazars on the Lower Volga
as well as to the town of Bulgar situated in the lands of the Volga
Bulgars near the junction of the River Kama with the Volga. Mohammedan influence was strong in both these places; it is true that in the
Khazar empire the khan and the nobility had been won over to the
Jewish faith but there were also many Mohammedans in the country;
the Emir of the Volga-Bulgars went over to Islam before 922. Both
places were termini of Arab routes, one of which came from the
north of Persia across the Caspian Sea to Khazaria, the other from
Transoxania across Khwarizm to Bulgar. The tenth century writer
Mas'ûdî describes the ceaseless passage of caravans along this latter
route; they were provided with military escort as a protection against
the nomadic tribes wandering on the Steppes.

It is easy to ascertain what the Arabs bought in Khazaria and
Bulgar. Mukaddasî baldly enumerates all the merchandise which
came from Bulgar by Khwarizm: sable, miniver, ermine, marten, fox,
beaver, the many-colored hare, goatskin, wax, arrows, birch-bark,
caps, fish-glue, fish-teeth, castor, amber, granular leather, honey,
hazelnuts, hawks (falcons?), swords, armor, maple, Slavic slaves,
sheep, goats, pigs and cattle. Several of these items were produced
by the Volga-Bulgars themselves. This was certainly true of birch-

bark, caps, maple, nuts, sheep, etc., goatskin and fish-glue, and probably of wax and honey. On the other hand, the other items which were not produced locally, were more important. They were principally of three types: furs, slaves and weapons. According to several authorities, including Ibn Rustah and Ibn Hawkal, the Rus in Khazaria and Bulgar supplied the first two of these articles. Ibn Fadlân, who personally met merchants of the Rus on the Volga in 922, describes how, on arrival in a market town, they used to invoke the assistance of their God: "I have brought with me so-and-so many sableskins and so-and-so many bondwomen. Give me a buyer, rich in dinars and dirhems." His comment that the Russians carried Frankish swords should not pass unnoticed.

The principal exports from the Rus to the Mohammedan countries were obviously slaves and furs. As we have already seen, these had been imported into the Caliphate by way of the Frankish empire.

The evidence about the Frankish transit trade is, however, commonest and most important in the early Carolingian period. The Arab influence on the Frankish coinage made itself felt particularly strongly around the middle of the eighth century. The most reliable evidence of the transport of slaves across the Frankish empire is from the years before 850; after 900 no export of slaves to the Caliphate is spoken of, other than of eunuchs. These were luxury slaves from which Frankish merchants, as we are told, certainly made great fortunes, but they obviously could not have had the same importance in world trade as the virile slaves and bondwomen.

The situation concerning the sources for the direct Nordic-Arab trade is entirely different. Not until after 800 can the connections along the eastern route be traced in literary and archaeological sources but they appear with increasing frequency as the century progresses.

In the tenth century the Arab geographer Ibn Hawkal compares the importance of the two routes in the fur- and slave-trades. He says that the beaver-hides which were brought to Spain from the rivers of Slavia were only a very small proportion of the total quantity produced. The majority of beaver-hides—almost all—came direct from the territory of the Rus, from Yâjûj and Mâjûj, and were sold from there to Bulgar, Khwarizm and Khazaria. Ibn Hawkal further states that the Slavic slaves which were taken via Spain were usually eunuchs, while those taken by the eastern route were not so; the majority of Slavic and Khazar slaves came by way of Khwarizm.

The sources make it clear, therefore, that in due time the Frankish transit trade between the fur- and slave-producing regions in northern and eastern Europe was out-flanked by a direct Nordic-Arab trade along easterly routes.

As lords of the great Svitjod, the Norsemen controlled a region with a very great productive potential. It produced slaves and furs in greater quantities than any other European country. Slaves provided labor force; furs were the only raw materials of clothing which the Mohammedan world could not itself produce in any appreciable measure. These two commodities were imported in mass into the Caliphate. In addition the Norsemen controlled the best routes to the Orient, to the economic and cultural center of the age; and the Norsemen were the nearest European neighbors to the country from which sprang the source of oriental silver.

It is fairly clear that under these circumstances the stream of silver was bound to spread all over eastern and northern Europe. It was a stream of no small dimensions. Ibn Rustah and Gardîzî state that the Norsemen refused to accept payment for their goods in anything but silver coins. Ibn Fadlân gives us another description of the situation: when a Rus merchant had made a profit of 10,000 dirhems, he usually gave his wife a necklace and there were many Rus ladies who owned several. The numismatic material bears out the truth of this and other information in Arab literature. The discoveries of Cufic coins show that the stream of silver had already penetrated into eastern Europe in 825 and that not long afterwards, certainly before the middle of the ninth century, it was pouring into the northern countries. An examination of the composition of the coin hoards establishes beyond doubt that silver was entering eastern Europe across the Caspian Sea and by the caravan route across Khwarizm as early as the beginning of the ninth century. The point which is of greatest interest to us is that the coin hoards from northern and eastern Europe reveal the intensity of the flow of silver. Their geographic distribution extends from Norway and northern Sweden in the north as far as Silesia and the Ukraine in the south, from Schleswig-Holstein and Mecklenburg in the west to the Urals in the east. The hoards of Arab coins here can be counted in hundreds; they often contain very large numbers of coins. There are reports of treasure troves as rich as Aladdin's cave. The largest find known with certainty is imposing enough: it consisted of more than 11,000 dirhems, in addition to an indeterminate number of fragments, and weighed more than 65 lbs. Hoards containing many hundreds or a few thousands of dirhems are common.

The great reorientation of international trade meant that the North became its center. It is significant that Ibn Khurdâdbih mentions the Rus of the North along with the Radanite Jews as the leading carriers of international trade; after the description we quoted earlier of the journeys of the Jews on and around the Mediterranean, he continues: "the Rus come from the most distant parts of the Slav lands, cross the Roman Sea to Constantinople where they sell their wares, furs of beaver and black fox as well as swords. Or, they sail up the Don (?), the river of the Slavs, and make for the capital of the Khazars. There they embark in boats and cross the Jurjân Sea to various points on its coastline. Sometimes they carry their merchandise on camels from Jurjân to Baghdad where Slavic eunuchs act as interpreters for them."

The politico-commercial position in which the Norsemen found themselves is without parallel in their history. Conditions at this time were the direct opposite of normal conditions at all other times. At other times the Baltic region has always imported precious metals from the west and exported to the west the lion's share of their own produce. But during the age of oriental silver its most important products went east and the flow of silver came from the east.

It now remains to investigate the nature of the trade connections between northern and western Europe during this period.

The archaeological evidence from Sweden shows that several commodities such as swords, glass and ceramics were imported from the Frankish empire. Discoveries in eastern Europe show that Frankish swords even went so far. The references in Arab literature to Rus exports of swords to Byzantium and of Arab imports of swords from Bulgar should establish beyond doubt that the Norsemen in eastern Europe carried on not only an important trade in slaves and furs but also a transit trade in Frankish swords.

It is more difficult to discover what the Norsemen gave the west in exchange. Probably it was still furs, but hardly on the same scale as in early Carolingian times. The main question now becomes whether the flow of silver from the east stopped at the western boundaries of northern and central Europe or whether it crossed these boundaries, with the result that silver became part of the exports from the North to western Europe.

It was remarked earlier that, in consequence of the currency principles which prevailed, the coin hoards found in western countries cannot reflect the importation of foreign coins, no matter how large, to any appreciable extent. This still holds good. The western European hoards from the time after about 850 to the beginning of the tenth century are not particularly plentiful but there are undoubtedly some which include dirhems which have come by way of the northern countries. There are not many of these coins, but certainly many times more than the number of western deniers in the abundant treasures from the same period found in the North.

It is not to be expected that evidence could be found in literary sources either for or against the existence of a heavy drain of dirhems into western Europe across its eastern border. It would indeed be remarkable if documentary evidence relevant to this investigation could be found. Nevertheless, this is the case: towards the end of the reign of Otto I, a Jew from Spain was staying at Mainz and he was shown some dirhems which he recognized. They were exactly of the type and from exactly the same period as those which are the most common in Scandinavian coin hoards. There can be no doubt that they came to Mainz by way of eastern Europe, perhaps also via the North.

A final answer to the question whether the flow of silver from northern and central Europe went further west can only be found from a thorough comparison of the eastern and the western European coin hoards. Such an examination shows the following. Throughout the ninth century the composition of the eastern and northern treasures was the same at all points of time. It can be seen in the discoveries from this century that coins which were predominant in the earlier treasures have completely disappeared in the later. This position changed in the course of the tenth century and two essentially different types of hoard are found, one in the North, the other in eastern Europe. Northern treasures are now characterized by the dominance of older coins—a Nordic hoard, for instance, from the 950s consists mostly of dirhems from the first two decades of the tenth century. But the hoards from the same time in eastern Europe contain considerably fewer coins from earlier times but many from the decades immediately preceding the year, when the latest coins in the hoards were minted. Shortly after the middle of the tenth century, a further differentiation took place within the eastern European region. The treasures found in Volga-Bulgaria with the last coins from the period after 970 are still consisting to a large extent of dirhems from the most recent decades. The treasures in the eastern Slav territory now take on a different structure: the dirhems from the period immediately preceding the minting year of the last coin are here no longer the commonest; coins of the 950s and 960s predominate. As the hoards from northern Europe still are dominated by coins from the beginning of the century, we thus have from this time onwards three types of treasures: the northern type, characterized by the predominance of dirhems from the beginning of the 900s, the eastern Slav type in which the dirhems are mostly from the middle of the century, and the Volga-Bulgarian type characterized by the predominance of dirhems from the decades immediately preceding the minting year of the last coin of the collection.

It is not difficult to explain the differentiation between the east Slav and the Volga-Bulgarian treasures. It occurred just at the time when, according to the evidence from Northern coin hoards, the import into the North of dirhems from eastern Slav territory ceased.[1] Formerly, the coins had passed beyond the latter territory further towards the northwest and, as long as this was the case, the number of older coins in eastern Slavia declined in relation to the coins newly arrived from the east, from Volga-Bulgaria. After the export of coins from eastern Slavia to the North had come to an end, the older coins, the dirhems of the 950s and 960s, remained in East Slavia; the movement of dirhems from Volga-Bulgaria largely brought with it newly minted dirhems but also—although to a steadily decreasing extent—older dirhems from the middle of the tenth century, but this flow was neither strong enough nor of sufficiently long duration to counterbalance the excess of the older coins. In that way there arose about that time an important difference between the East Slavic and the Volga-Bulgarian treasures.

It now also becomes easy to find an explanation for the difference between the treasures of eastern and northern Europe which arose in the first part of the tenth century. As long as the dirhems were exported from eastern Europe to the North, the older coins became increasingly rare in the former territory compared with the new dirhems arriving from the east. On the other hand, from the beginning of the tenth century, the coins were not re-exported from the

---

[1] Also after the middle of the tenth century Arab coins were brought to Scandinavia. These late Arab coins, however, cannot have been brought there from eastern Europe, as they were minted further to the west than contemporary Arab coins found in eastern Europe.

North and so the old coins accumulated there. The flow of coins from the East continued to bring dirhems to the North, mostly including recent coins, but with older coins as well. The flow was not strong enough nor lasting enough, however, to deprive the coins minted at the beginning of the century of their preponderance among the coins in the treasures. On the basis of material which is certainly imperfect, and assuming undiminished imports from the east and the complete cessation of exports from the north, it can be calculated that the dirhems from the first two decades of the tenth century should account for 86 percent of the coins in the treasures of the 930s and 56 percent of those of the 960s. In the extensive discoveries of coins in Gotland it is found that in fact the proportions were 84 percent during the 930s and 54 percent towards the 960s.

It would, therefore, seem that the continued recurrence in the hoards of the older coins, taken in conjunction with the appearance of other coins, is a phenomenon of very great significance; the territories where the older coins accumulated—the North up to the 970s and East Slavia thereafter—formed the territorial limits to the flow of oriental silver.

But why, in the ninth century, are no such differences to be found between the variously located treasures as they are in the tenth? Why, in the ninth century, is there no visible boundary line to the flow of oriental silver, marked by the accumulation of older coins? The simplest explanation must be that there was no such boundary line in the ninth century, but that the dirhems moved uninterruptedly across the whole territory of the discoveries, without running up against an impassable barrier anywhere—not even on the western frontier. Thus the flow of silver during the ninth and early tenth centuries must have, in fact, moved into western Europe.

Of course, no decisive proof of this can be presented, but there are strong arguments that, in the period immediately after the Nordic expansion across eastern Europe, Scandinavia held in yet another respect a position in relation to western Europe which was unique in its history; precious metals were apparently flowing across its territory from the East towards the West.

Whether the North exported silver to western Europe or not, the changed relationship between these two regions in the ninth century should certainly not be regarded in isolation from the new world situation.

After 830 and particularly after 850, western Europe became less influential in the North: the missions were withdrawn, the flow of coins from the west ended, the Frankish kings ceased to intervene in Danish domestic struggles. All this was natural if we remember how greatly conditions were changed by the growth of the direct Nordic-Arab trade in comparison with the situation at the time when slaves and furs from the Baltic region were transported to the Caliphate by way of the Frankish empire.

But, in reverse, Nordic incursions to the west became much more common and much more vigorous. At the same time as the Saracens were masters of the Mediterranean after the 830s, the Nordic Viking expeditions developed into great waves of conquest, reaching a climax after 850. The great Viking fleets captured London and beleaguered Paris. Kings and emperors made considerable cessions of territory to the Vikings and paid them tribute. The Norsemen founded kingdoms and principalities in Germany, France, England, Scotland and Ireland. They peopled large regions in those parts and colonized the expanses of Iceland and, later, Greenland.

Enterprises on such a scale have set out from the North at no other time before or since. To this period in the history of the North, there is neither economic nor political parallel. And these two aspects cannot be isolated. The two are closely interconnected: the Vikings who terrorized the Western world came from a country where oriental silver was common.

This then is the background of the Viking expeditions to the west which culminated in large-scale enterprises and conquests. The background is not at all that of an impoverished northern land extended to bursting point by overpopulation, but rather of the region further east which, according to the legend, had been conquered by Ruric and his men. The conquistadors of the North exploited the Slavic population tyrannously and ruthlessly and conducted a large trade with the principal centers of civilization in the commodities they thus acquired. The Nordic vessels brought up towards the Baltic and the North by the rivers of eastern Europe from Khazar and Bulgar precious metal from as far away as the most important silver producing regions of Central Asia. They formed—if this article may be concluded with yet another comparison between Viking times and the next great period of great discoveries, increased silver supply and expanding trade—a miniature of the treasure fleets of the Spaniards bringing silver from the New World in the sixteenth and seventeenth centuries.

Robert Latouche

THE SO-CALLED "GRAND COMMERCE" OF THE MEROVINGIAN PERIOD

Professor Robert Latouche, born in 1881 and recently deceased, was a distinguished French historian long associated with the University of Grenoble as professor of medieval history, as dean of the Faculty of Letters, and finally as honorary dean. An "ancien membre de la Commission Histoire Moderne *au Centre National de la Recherche scientifique," his publications included* Histoire de Comté du Maine pendant le Xᵉ et le XIᵉ siècle *(Paris, 1910), and* Les grandes invasions et la crise de l'occident au Vᵉ siècle *(Paris, 1946). The work from which this selection is taken was originally published as* Les origines de l'économie occidentale, IVᵉ–XIᵉ siècle *(Paris, 1956).*

Henri Pirenne infused new life into the economic history of the Early Middle Ages by giving the Moslem conquest pride of the place amongst the factors which transformed the structure of the ancient world. There is no need to summarize afresh a "thesis" which was first presented to several historical congresses, which in 1922 and 1923 he condensed into two brilliant articles in the *Revue belge de philologie et d'histoire,* and which was fully and finally developed in a posthumously published work, *Mahomet et Charlemagne.* In actual fact, however, as one of his disciples has written, it is perhaps doing Pirenne an injustice to apply the word "thesis" to a vast body of original ideas on the whole evolution of Europe from the third to the tenth century. It would be more accurate to say that new horizons have been opened up to those who are attempting to find out just how the transition from the ancient world to the Middle Ages was effected. . . .

One of Pirenne's main theories is that in spite of the barbarian invasions the movement of trade through the Mediterranean continued throughout Merovingian times right up to the Moslem conquest, and that the Mediterranean way of life which was one of the characteristic features of the Late Empire persisted. Under the rule of the Ostrogoths Italy continued to get supplies of grain and oil from the opposite shore of the Mediterranean, and trade relations with

From Robert Latouche, *The Birth of Western Economy: Economic Aspects of the Dark Ages* (London, 1961), pp. 117–25. Translated from the French by E. M. Wilkinson. By permission of Methuen & Co., Ltd., Documentation is omitted.

Byzantium were maintained, as may be seen from many references in the correspondence of Theodoric edited by Cassiodorus. A first essential was the construction of light ships which Italy needed for the importation of foodstuffs, particularly of corn. The ships bringing food to Rome landed at the port of Ostia, where they were welcomed by the "Count of the port of the city of Rome." The orders given by the King to this high-ranking official show how anxious Theodoric was to maintain the volume of this traffic:

It is a pleasant, rather than a heavy responsibility to hold the office of Count of the port of Rome. He supervises the arrival of innumerable ships. The sea, covered with sails, brings foreign peoples with merchandise from many different provinces. The task entrusted to you is therefore a privileged one; but it must be carried out with tact and good judgment. You are in a position to create prosperity by dealing fairly and justly with those who land there. An avaricious hand could close down the harbor altogether.

For a time, however, the occupation of North Africa by the Vandals was a threat to Mediterranean sea traffic, and Sidonius Apollinaris, who shortly before the fall of the Western Empire had assumed the grave responsibility of ensuring Rome's food supplies, has told in one of his letters how difficult his task was and with what breathless joy he sighted the ships bringing the *annona*.

This regime based on imports suited the indolent Romans to perfection, and Justinian's chief aim in reconquering North Africa from the Vandals was probably to regain for Italy a source of grain which had been partially lost to her for almost a century; yet in spite of the efficiency of the Byzantine merchant fleet, it is by no means certain that trade relations were fully restored. The Lombard invasion brought disorder, as well as poverty, to the peninsula. When Gregory the Great was elected Pope (590), an epidemic of the plague was raging in Rome, and when eventually it died down, famine threatened to descend upon the city. The letters written by the new Pontiff to the Praetor of Sicily urging him to speed up deliveries of corn seem to indicate that from the close of the sixth century Africa was no longer the great grain-provider.

Further concrete facts about the Mediterranean economy during the Merovingian period have also come to light, for instance the use of olive oil for food and lighting, replaced only at a later date by that of butter and wax, and the use of Egyptian papyrus for writing which persisted in Gaul until the middle of the eighth century. Coastal traffic along the shores of the Mediterranean was still relatively brisk in the sixth century in spite of the dangers involved. Pilgrims traveling from Central Gaul to Rome in the time of Gregory of Tours embarked at Marseilles and sailed along the coast of Provence and Italy. The island of Lérins was connected with the continent by a fairly regular service of boats. A hermit like St. Hospice, who lived near Nice, fed on dates and herbs brought him by merchants from Egypt. The port of Marseilles was sufficiently busy for the Merovingian kings to quarrel for possession of it. At Fos, where the Rhone river-boats took over from seagoing ships, there was a warehouse belonging to the Treasury. A scholar who is also a skilled chemist[1] has discovered that the glass factories in the Rhineland needed imports of Mediterranean natron, and that the garnet used in cloisonné enameling up to the sixth century, but not later, came from markets in Asia Minor. Pirenne has listed other examples of this trade with the East which continued up to the Saracen invasion: ivory, silk, Syrian wines, spices such as pepper, cummin, cinnamon.

Such an accumulation of facts proves the existence of relations, uneasy perhaps but continuous, with the countries around the Mediterranean. We should not be deceived by their number. After the Germanic invasions the economy of Western Europe underwent a profound change, but without disputing the repercussions which followed the Moslem conquest it has to be admitted that it did not bring about the complete rupture, the clean-cut break, which has been attributed to it, since it was preceded by a long period of decay. The European economy was already in decline when the victorious Saracens closed, or tried to close, the Mediterranean to Christians. Pirenne never questioned, nor even minimized, the influence of the Germanic invasions, in describing which he coined the happy phrase "barbarization." Applied to economic life, it admirably epitomizes the muddled, spineless Merovingian world of the sixth century. There was, it was true, no definitive break between East and West, and Gregory of Tours in his *History of the Franks,* so rich in informative anecdote, gives facts which prove this, but the continuance of these relations simply means that the easy-going Merovingians left things as they were, the more willingly since it was in their own interests to maintain the *status quo.* The miserly Chilperic I found *laissez-faire*

[1] E. Salin, *La civilisation mérovingienne,* Pt. I, p. 136.

the best policy when the Emperor Tiberius made a point of present-
ing him with beautiful gold medallions each one pound in weight.
Childebert II was no less devoted to the Byzantine alliance, since it
brought him 50,000 gold *solidi,* the price of his army's support for the
Empire against the Lombards. Yet no effort was made to revitalize
trade with the East. The administration simply let things slide. The
native nobility, the Gallo-Romans, who lived in the country, with
certain very rare exceptions did not engage in trade, and the majority
of Germans also seem to have been allergic to this calling, so that
commerce passed almost wholly into the hands of foreigners.

It was chiefly the Syrians, whom St. Jerome called the most avaricious of mortals, who seized upon it and acquired a monopoly.
Large numbers made their way into Gaul, and in some cities such as
Orleans they formed veritable colonies. They succeeded in infiltrating
into the Rhineland, into Germany and even into Great Britain. They
had other eastern competitors: Greeks and Jews. One of the latter
named Priscus had put himself at the service of King Chilperic I, who
entrusted him with the purchase of goods. At the beginning of the
seventh century Dagobert also had his Jewish *negociator,* a certain
Solomon. They were commission agents, who filled the gap left by
the lack or scarcity of merchants owning permanent shops. Shops
were very rare, and the few allusions which might conceivably refer
to them are not very convincing. When Gregory of Tours speaks of
domus negociatorum, it is not certain that he means shops; they are
more likely to be the merchants' actual homes. This lack forced
people of means to resort, as the Emperors and high officials of the
Late Empire were already doing, to agents whom they sent to make
purchases on the spot. They royal example was followed by the
abbots of monasteries who, responsible for the food supplies of their
communities, also had their abbey merchants, veritable quartermas-
ters. Thus the Abbot of Saint-Pierre de la Couture at Le Mans com-
missioned his agents to go periodically to buy fish in Bordeaux,
where a house which had belonged to Bishop Bertrand was put at
their disposal during their stay.

It would give quite a false impression of the merchants and their
many-sided activities, which have been recorded for us in Merovingian documents, to equate them to merchants of our own day. These
men were adventurers, whether they were Orientals come to the West
to sell the produce of their native countries or inversely, a few rare
inhabitants of Gaul who were genuine pirates, like Samo of Senon, a

contemporary of Dagobert. He had set out for Esclavonia, in other words Bohemia, to engage in trade, and imposing himself on the inhabitants of the country, had eventually become King of the Wends. Amongst the Germanic barbarians one nation alone seems to have had a flair for trading—the Frisians. Inhabiting the strip of coast in the Low Countries between the mouth of the Scheldt and that of the Eider, they engaged in trade in the Merovingian period. The poverty of a country very little of which had been cleared for cultivation, and which was exposed to frequent inroads from the sea, doubtless impelled them to leave their own land to trade as hawkers abroad. Their chief stock-in-trade was cloth (*pallia frisonica*) and it is tempting to think of them as ancestors of the Flemish cloth-merchants, but the connection remains problematical.

Trading, carried on in these various ways, was frequently a dangerous undertaking and the men engaged in it banded themselves together for protection. In the sixth century the merchants of Verdun formed an association, and it was probably their influence which enabled the bishop to obtain from King Theodebert a loan of 7,000 gold *solidi* for his town. Samo himself did not set out for Esclavonia alone, but in the company of other merchants. It is recorded that one merchant armed six ships in order to undertake a certain expedition.

After a study of the various documents (most of which tell us very little, and which in any case are few in number) dealing with the Merovingian merchants, it is singularly difficult to define their activities. It is an exaggeration to speak in terms of big business, "*grand commerce*," international trade, import and export trade. Such phrases are far too grandiose to describe the modest activities in which most of these traders engaged. On the other hand we should not yield to the temptation, great though it may be, and not altogether wide of the mark, to compare them to the North Africans of our own day who hawk carpets and other native products, pester passers-by in the streets and haunt the cafés of our modern cities. They too form colonies in our cities, exactly as did the Syrians in Merovingian times, and who as we have seen did not live by themselves when they were in Gaul. Such a comparison would, however, rate the medieval merchants too low, since they did at least fill a gap in the contemporary economy by selling eastern products, such as spices, which were both useful and valued.

We cannot quite agree with those who have interpreted the presence in Gaul of foreign, and particularly of eastern merchants, as proof that large-scale trade continued to flourish in the West. We regard it, on the contrary, as evidence of the inertia of the western peoples and of the stagnation of their economic life. It was the deterioration of commercial activity resulting from the Great Invasions which spread over Gaul and Italy industrious eastern traders who hoped to make a substantial profit from the bundle of wares they had brought with them. Their advent in such large numbers was not the mark of a sound economy. Moreover, the goods in which they dealt were not always respectable. Slaves were the most profitable of their wares, and the money to be made from them attracted the Gallo-Romans also, who, following their example, went into business on their own account. The Frank Samo was a slave trader, of that there can be no doubt, since Esclavonia fed the slave-markets from the Early Middle Ages. The Great Invasions, by pushing the Germanic peoples westward, created east of the Elbe a vacuum which was filled by the Slavs. Certain of these peoples became human merchandise and traffic in them became so widespread that in the Roman languages the word slave, originally a man of Slav nationality, supplanted the Latin words *mancipium* and *servus,* which had been used to denote a human being in a state of slavery. But these dealers in human flesh sought their merchandise from many other countries as well. They made frequent expeditions to Great Britain whence many slaves were drawn, since, as Ferdinant Lot wrote: "The Anglo-Saxons used to sell their fellow-countrymen." The Frisians, who traded on other side of the Channel, certainly engaged in this traffic. Though it was so widespread and though slavery was not officially condemned by the Church, it shocked religious people, and the buying back of captives, wretched creatures who though endowed with a soul were herded about like cattle to be sold and dispersed, they regarded as a charitable duty. St. Eloi, Dagobert's minister, who was very rich, practiced this on a large scale, buying back in batches of fifty or even one hundred souls the very moment they set foot on Gallic soil the Britains and Saxons being brought in as slaves. The slave trade increased in volume after the Saracen conquest; large numbers were imported into Spain which became an important market for the traders. It has even been asserted that this export trade brought in a little Moslem gold, that first dinars then Abbasid dirhams, flowed into the West, but its importance has probably been over-exaggerated. A black-market—and the slave trade was in fact a kind of black market—rarely benefits the community and brings its monetary gains into general circulation.

One serious defect in the Merovingian economy prevented trade from establishing itself on solid foundations, namely the poor quality of the coinage. . . . The points already discussed may perhaps serve to justify a skeptical approach to this so-called Merovingian economic activity which, so the theory runs, was inherited from the ancient world, continued to flourish until it was blocked by the Moslem conquest, went into rapid decline from the middle of the seventh century and finally petered out under the Carolingians. We believe the opposite to be the case, and shall endeavor to prove that the dawn of the Carolingian era marks a restoration or in any case a serious attempt to put the economy on a sound footing.

Howard L. Adelson

EARLY MEDIEVAL TRADE ROUTES

Howard L. Adelson is professor of history at the City College and City University of New York. Born in 1925, he received his B.A. degree from New York University and his Ph.D. from Princeton. One of his special interests has been the history of numismatics and the topics developed in the article from which this excerpt is taken are treated at length in his Light Weight Solidi and Byzantine Trade during the Sixth and Seventh Centuries *(1957). For some years he was director of studies at the Summer Seminar in Numismatics; in 1958 was published his* The American Numismatic Society: 1858–1958. *From 1969 to 1972 he was the editor of* Studies in Medieval and Renaissance History.

The techniques and methodology of numismatics as an ancillary science were developed through the study of the ancient world. The application of numismatics to the study of the medieval world is of much more recent origin. This, of course, is not to say that some great medievalists such as Henri Pirenne and art historians of the stature of André Grabar have not utilized numismatic data in their

From Howard L. Adelson, "Early Medieval Trade Routes," *American Historical Review* 65 (January 1960): 271–73, 276–79, 285–87. For documentation the reader is referred to the original article. Reprinted by permission of the author.

own researches. By and large, however, scholars of the Middle Ages have neglected the vast mine of material available to them in the form of thousands of monetiform objects which have resisted the onslaught of time.

Perhaps the study of a single limited problem in which a new synthesis is reached can serve to demonstrate the utility of numismatic research. The problem we shall attack had its origins in a simple numismatic oddity that escaped mention by most numismatists and virtually all historians. Its solution appears to have vital implications and ramifications for the interpretation of the history of the early Middle Ages. Historians and numismatists have been struck by the longevity of the Byzantine solidus from the time of Constantine to the siege of Constantinople by the Turks and by the persistence of the Byzantines in maintaining that coin at a given weight and fineness for the entire early Middle Ages. There are, however, three generally ignored series of Byzantine solidi that were issued in the sixth and seventh centuries which deviated from this legal weight and standard, though both the weight and fineness were expressly stipulated in the Theodosian and Justinian recensions of Roman law. This variation from the norm in the case of coins obviously marked to indicate excessive lightness and a lesser degree of fineness cannot be the result of anything but a manifestation of an imperial policy which was deliberately carried out. Coinage in gold was a jealously guarded prerogative of the Byzantine emperor, as we know from statements by Ammianus Marcellinus, Procopius, Zonaras, and other late Roman authors as well as from the numerous laws regarding the striking of gold. In one instance the Byzantines fought a war against the rising power of Islam because the tribute payments had been made in a new variety of gold coin which was not of imperial origin. Still there are three series of gold solidi of twenty siliquae, twenty-two siliquae, and twenty-three siliquae respectively which are clearly of Byzantine origin and noticeably different from the normal solidus of twenty-four siliquae.

On the bases of two passages in Procopius referring to the issuance of light-weight solidi in terms of disapproval, the introduction of these coins can be dated to A.D. 547–548. They continued to be issued until about A.D. 670. Thus they cover a crucial period for the understanding of the Pirenne thesis.

What was the purpose of these coins and why was their issue stopped about A.D. 670? A survey of the finds of these solidi shows a distinct concentration of them along a route from northern Italy over the Alps and down the Rhine to Frisia and Britain. Another concentration, but one of later date, occurs in the Ukraine along the Dnieper. Three scattered specimens were found in the upper Balkans, one in North Africa, and some few in a single hoard from near Antioch in Syria. Only the single coin from North Africa and those from the Syrian hoard were found on territory that was at the time under Byzantine domination. From this distribution of the finds it is evident that these light-weight solidi were not intended for use within the boundaries of the Empire. In fact, a great deal of literary and legal evidence can be cited to prove that their circulation within the Empire was forbidden. . . .

The first signs of economic recovery appeared during the reign of Anastasius. His coinage was imitated in some quantity in the West. It occurs in the hoard of Bresin in Germany and in a number of Scandinavian hoards. His coinage and imitations of it also form an important segment of the hoards of Gourdon and Chinon, which were actually buried during the reign of Justin I. But the largest increase in number of Byzantine coins and imitations found in the West occurs for the period from Justinian through Heraclius (610–641). P. C. J. A. Boeles lists 208 coins, mostly gold, found in Frisia. Ninety-five of these are clearly imperial gold or imitations, and better than half are of the above-mentioned period. After Heraclius, the Frankish currency seems to have held sway in Frisia. Since many of the early imitations probably come from Italy, it is clear that a route existed in the early years of the sixth century which brought a steady stream of coinage over the Alps northward. This same situation is noted from a survey of the coins in Austrasia. By far the greatest number are from the period from the reign of Anastasius through that of Heraclius.

One naturally associates this rather startling growth in Byzantine interest in the West with the Persian difficulties which became acute during the reign of Anastasius and continued to afflict the Romans until A.D. 639. During that period war between these two peoples was as much the order of the day as peace. Justinian comprehended fully the immense task facing him. His attempt to reconstruct the Roman Empire around the Mediterranean necessitated the adoption of a defensive attitude toward the Persians. The interest of the Emperor had turned toward the western portions of the old Roman Empire, and his conquests must have stimulated the activities of the oriental merchants in that region. These merchants, however, had begun to play a more vital role in the economic life of Western Europe as early as the reign of Anastasius and the beginning of the Persian troubles. The rebuilt Byzantine fleet certainly controlled the entire Mediterranean in the period preceding the death of Heraclius, and, as a direct result, trade in the West became safer than it had been at any time since the Vandals reached Carthage. It should be noted that in Procopius's description of the Emperor's actions regarding the two customs houses on the straits on either side of Constantinople, he specifically speaks of merchants traveling between the capital and Italy or Libya. Even the trade of Alexandria, the greatest of all the Mediterranean ports, with Western Europe and particularly with Italy seems to have been more active after the reconquest of the West by the Byzantines. The fact that the communities of merchants in Western Europe were composed primarily of Syrians, Jews, and Greeks, however, must have given Antioch and Constantinople a predominance that Alexandria could not challenge successfully even during the late sixth and early seventh centuries, when trade relations between the patriarch and the pope seem to have reached a peak.

It is pointless to repeat all of the evidence collected by Pirenne and others for the existence of very significant sea trade between the two halves of the Mediterranean. The case is very clear-cut for a great expansion of that trade during the sixth and seventh centuries after a period of decline during the preceding epoch. It is, however, necessary to return to the subject of the trade route from Italy by land to the Frisian coast. The route actually never seems to have been entirely closed. Miss Joan Fagerlie, a graduate student at a recent seminar of the American Numismatic Society, has shown that it is most likely that the Byzantine gold found in Scandinavia traveled over this same route. Archaeology provides a certain basis for the use of this trade route in pre-Carolingian times. Theodoric's conquest of Italy and his preeminence among the Germanic kings provided a long period of peaceful relations with the more northerly peoples. The concentration of finds of Ostrogothic silver coins and those of the Exarchate of Ravenna in the middle Rhine region seems to be conclusive proof of a continuous use of that trade route during the pre-Carolingian era.

The route followed must have been one that crossed the Alps in the neighborhood of Lake Constance. Archaeological evidence gathered by Joachim Werner, based on finds of specific articles such as "Coptic" bronze vessels, ornamental gold crosses, and fibulae of

a close-cell type, shows a concentration of these items in the region
north of Lake Constance along the headwaters of the Danube. The
coins seem to have followed a more westerly route. Within the limits
of southern and western Germany nineteen siliquae of Justinian
struck in Ravenna and forty Ostrogothic siliquae have been found.
The evidence provided by these finds as well as the coins struck in
the area suggests that the route in question along the Rhine was of
greater importance for the area to the east of the river than for the
lands to the west of it. If the number of recovered pieces that may
possibly have been in southern and western Germany can be
used as indicative of the whole, the amount of coinage struck in that
area during the sixth century must have been very small. Only a very
few coins can be attributed to Rhenish mints, and even these are
from sites such as Trier, which are located on the Gallic side of the
river. In the seventh century, Frankish mints seem to have been in
operation at Windisch, Basel, Strassburg, Speyer, Worms, Alsheim,
Mainz, Boppard, Andernach, Bonn, Cologne, Zülpich, Julich (?),
Trier, and Pfalzel near Trier, all sites on the left bank of the Rhine.
Basel, Strassburg, Mainz, and Trier were the outstanding mints while
the others only struck coins intermittently. Only occasionally are
coins from these Rhenish mints found on the right bank of the river.

In the sixth century, the mass of currency in southern and western
Germany on the right bank of the Rhine must have been composed
principally of Italic coinage such as Ostrogothic silver and the later
silver currency of Justinian. In addition, Ostrogothic and Byzantine
gold, which must have crossed the Alps in the same body of commercial transactions that brought the silver, played a significant role.
The coinages of the Rhenish and more distant Gallic mints did not
occupy a significant position in the sites on the right bank. It can
only be concluded that the commercial ties in this area on the right
bank were much stronger with Italy than with the Gallic lands.

If anything, the seventh century shows an even more perceptible
distinction between the regions to the right and to the left of the
Rhine. It is true that since the importation of silver coinage had come
to an end, the total number of coins found is much smaller. But the
same phenomenon of a commercial connection with Italy rather than
the Frankish realm on the left bank is noticeable. The occurrence of
Anglo-Saxon sceattas and Frisian trientes in the middle Rhine region,
however, marks even further the economic unity of the river valley at
the later period. Merovingian coins at the same time are only occa-

sionally found among the Alemanni, Franks, and Thuringians on the right bank and are totally lacking among the Bavarians.

At the extreme continental end of this trade lay Frisia—the area from which the trade about the North Sea radiated. Boeles lists only twenty-six gold coins from Frisia struck before the reign of Anastasius. After that time the expansion in the area's use of gold is easily traced by the great increase in the number of coins of the later period that have been found there. Evidence indicating the importance of the light-weight solidi is probably best shown by the fact that of the four coins of Heraclius and Heraclius Constantine listed by Boeles three are of the light-weight series.

The finds of twenty-seven coins from Cologne, Mainz, Alsheim, and Worms as well as related currencies that have been made within Frisia easily establish the commercial bonds between that area and the Rhenish regions. In addition there are five coins from the mints on the Moselle and ten from those on the Meuse, including imitations. Thus of the 208 coins listed by Boeles, forty-two pieces come from the trade area formed by these river basins. At the same time it should be noted that a few Frisian and Anglo-Saxon sceattas, probably of a later date, are also found in the Rhineland. It is to be expected, however, that the direction of the currency's flow would be northward in this region. Frisia must be considered one of the more primitive western areas in Merovingian times, and it would therefore import rather than export currency. . . .

The Pirenne thesis laid stress upon an extensive oriental commerce in the Merovingian age. This picture of intense Mediterranean trade has been questioned. A careful examination of the light-weight solidi has shown that not only is there excellent evidence that this trade was important enough to merit consideration and action by the imperial government, but that its nature was quite different from what Pirenne and later scholars have envisioned. Virtually all historians agree that the Germanic invasions did not mark a turning point in the economic history of Europe though they may well have accelerated the decline and disintegration of the Roman Empire. Nevertheless, as soon as the first waves of these invaders had settled down in the new successor states, the Byzantine merchants revived western trade. A large portion of the evidence cited to support the persistence of the Roman pattern of Mediterranean trade after the *Völkerwanderung* actually reflects this revival of commerce in the sixth and seventh centuries after the decline in the fifth. The causal nexus for this commercial renaissance is to be found in the increasing Persian pressures along the eastern frontier which began in the reign of Anastasius and continued through that of Heraclius. The Persian difficulties, which we know affected the eastern silk trade, were coeval with the growth of western commerce. Expansion of trade with Western Europe was possible because there were colonies of oriental merchants in Gaul and Italy who jealously guarded and preserved their identity apart from the common populace and maintained their connections with the Byzantine Empire. It is even probable that the number of such oriental merchants in the West increased with the relative growth of their prosperity as the native mercantile class was eliminated. The rise of these communities in the late fifth and early sixth centuries and their disappearance after the reign of Chlotar II in the early seventh century when the independence of the cities of southern Gaul was extinguished are obviously connected with the expansion of Mediterranean trade. In Gaul the resident oriental merchants were responsible for the largest part of the overseas trade.

If we shift our view momentarily from the question of the quantity of the trade to its character, we must also revise Pirenne's thesis. Pirenne laid great stress upon Byzantine exports to the West and upon the supposed four great disappearances: papyrus, spice, gold, and textiles. Robert Lopez has shown that the connection between changes in the trade in these articles and the advance of Islam is not quite as close as Pirenne had proposed. In addition, though the evidence is by no means definitive, it would seem that the Byzantines had an unfavorable balance of trade with Western Europe during the very early Middle Ages. This phenomenon of a net loss of precious gold coinage from the Roman Empire to the underdeveloped lands surrounding it can easily be demonstrated in much earlier times with respect to the free Germans. Western Europe in the sixth and seventh centuries was at a low economic and cultural level, without the taste and desire for exotic and refined luxury items and products of industry in great quantities, but with an excess of raw materials available for export. Perhaps the most valuable of these exports from the West was human—slaves. Evidence of slave trading in Western Europe is quite extensive, and more important still is the fact that their movement was from the northern frontier districts to the seaports on the Mediterranean for transshipment overseas. The slaves themselves were recruited from all Central and Western European races, primarily as a result of the persistent warfare of that period. Charles Verlinden has collected all the evidence relating to slavery in the Frankish state. It seems clear that after the reign of Dagobert, who was a contemporary of Heraclius, the sources of the slave trade diminished appreciably. Dagobert was the last of the Merovingian rulers who displayed any energy along the frontiers of his kingdom to increase its size. Without successful campaigns against other peoples of the West, the sole sources of new slaves were the natural increase of those already enslaved or the additional few who might suffer reduction to servitude for offenses against the law or who might sell themselves. Thus, as Verlinden points out, the slave trade must have declined sharply before the mid-seventh century. If the price for individual slaves was as high as twelve or fifteen solidi and the trade was very brisk, both of which seem likely from a study of the texts, this would account fully for the vast quantities of Byzantine gold found in the West prior to A.D. 650 and its virtually complete absence in the following years.

There is one further factor to be taken into account. The effects of the Islamic conquests on the Byzantine Empire were not treated by Pirenne as causative factors save for the exclusion of the Byzantine fleets from the western Mediterranean. In effect, this is to deny any importance to the economic history of Byzantium as an element in the story. Quite the reverse, however, appears to be the case. The Moslem conquests and migrations had cut the Byzantines off from the supplies of gold ore, and only by the most rigid controls was Byzantine currency maintained after the mid-seventh century. Byzantine trade had to readjust itself to the new conditions, which required that trading in the West be favorably balanced. Steps in this direction must have been taken as early as the last years of Heraclius. Thus by A.D. 650, over fifty years before the completion of the Moslem conquest of the Mediterranean, events in Gaul and a changed Byzantine trade policy resulting from the loss of direct contact with the sources of gold had effected the sharp reduction in trade that Pirenne attributed to the closing of the western Mediterranean by Moslem pirates. There can be no doubt that the concerted effort at building up the trade of Byzantium with the West, which began in the closing years of the fifth century and which is reflected in the issuance of the light-weight solidi, was over by the reign of Constantine IV Pogonatus. It was indeed declining sharply as early as Heraclius's reign. Of course it did not cease abruptly and completely, and some articles necessary for maintaining the prestige of the chancelleries of the western monarchs or the Church continued to be imported, but the fact that Byzantine hoards and coins no longer occur with any frequency cannot be denied. Byzantine policy, as has been recognized by all Byzantine historians, was different in the eighth and ninth centuries from what it had been in the period from Justinian through Constantine IV Pogonatus.

Philip Grierson

COMMERCE IN THE DARK AGES: A CRITIQUE OF THE EVIDENCE

Philip Grierson is a leading numismatist, and has numerous publications in the field. Born in 1910, he has been associated with Gonville and Caius College, Cambridge University, from the time of his matriculation. In 1966 he was elected president of the college and in 1971 his readership was converted into a professorship of Numismatics. He was a Ford lecturer at Oxford University, 1956–1957, and president of the Royal Numismatics Society, 1961–1966. He is a Fellow of the Royal Historical Society, London. Much of his scholarly work is directed at specialists in the field, but the undergraduate and laymen in general will be greatly interested in his Numismatics, *scheduled for publication in 1975 by the Oxford University Press in the OPUS series in England and Galaxy Books in the United States.*

When Pirenne contributed an article entitled "Mahomet et Charlemagne" to the first issue of the *Revue Belge de Philologie et d'Histoire* in 1922, he can have little realized how the ideas he there put forward were to be developed. His paper was designed as a protest against the traditional and deep-rooted conviction of western scholars that Latin Christendom was the direct and almost the sole heir of classical antiquity. Its argument was the now familiar one that Greco-Roman society survived with little change the shock of the Germanic invasions, and that it was only the appearance of Islam upon the scene that pushed the center of Latin Christendom away

Philip Grierson, "Commerce in the Dark Ages: A Critique of the Evidence," *Transactions of the Royal Historical Society,* Fifth Series, IX (1959), pp. 123–40. By permission of the author and the Royal Historical Society, London. Documentation is omitted, save for a few references which identify authorities cited in the text.

from the Mediterranean and made possible the emergence of a new cultural unit based upon the land mass of western Europe. Medieval Christendom was not a continuation of the Roman world but something new, and Muhammed was a necessary precursor of Charlemagne.

In his first formulation of this point of view, Pirenne was not particularly concerned with economic issues, but he did argue that even after the invasions the west remained under the economic dominance of the east. Jewish and Syrian merchants continued to provide it with luxury goods, and it was through their intermediacy that it received the papyrus used in its chancelleries and the gold necessary for its coinage. Economic emancipation did not occur until the end of the Merovingian period, and when it did occur, it was almost synonymous with economic collapse.

Such opinions were not likely to pass unchallenged, and as discussion of Pirenne's views developed, economic and social considerations came more and more to the fore. Statistical evidence could not be hoped for: for the centuries in question there was a total absence of commercial documents, of customs and taxation records, of gild regulations, of detailed trade agreements, of the innumerable sources from which we can piece together something like a credible picture of the nature, direction and volume of commerce during the last four centuries of the Middle Ages. The west provided one with nothing comparable even to such Byzantine sources as the *Book of the Prefect* or the *Rhodian Sea Law,* unless the *Capitulare de Villis* could be regarded as coming into such a category. In the absence of quantitative evidence, such scraps of qualitative evidence as were available had to do. Chronicles, ecclesiastical biographies, *Miracula* and *Translationes* of relics, royal and episcopal correspondence, monastic privileges and concessions, Carolingian capitularies and Anglo-Saxon law codes were ransacked for references to traders and trade. Archaeology and in particular numismatics were brought in to help, since they provided much information on the distribution of coin and of certain other types of manufactured articles. The net result by now, thirty-five years after the opening of the great debate, is the very wide-spread impression that Pirenne and his critics were almost equally wrong. Commerce In the Dark Ages was much more considerable in volume than has been generally allowed, even if less highly organized than it was to be in later centuries.

This view I believe to be largely incorrect. It results in the main from the failure to distinguish between three different types of evidence: (1) evidence of the existence of traders, i.e., of persons making their living by commerce; (2) evidence of trade, in the narrow sense of the sale of specialized or surplus goods directly by producer to consumer without the intervention of any third party; and (3) evidence for the distribution by unspecified means of goods, particularly luxury goods, and money. The confusion between the first two categories is not perhaps very important, but that between trade and distribution, and still more the habit of treating evidence for the distribution of luxury goods and coin as if it were nothing more than supplementary evidence of the existence and activity of traders, is of a serious character. It involves the error of reading history backwards—or in this case also forwards, of assuming that because material goods were later, as they had been in Roman times, distributed largely by the agency of trade, the same was necessarily the case in the Dark Ages. Even the briefest reflection must show that this is scarcely likely to have been the case. The whole approach, that of accumulating evidence for the existence of trade instead of trying to form an overall picture of how and to what extent material goods changed ownership, is in itself profoundly misleading and can only result in conclusions that are far from the truth.

II

The confusion between "traders" and "trade" need not delay us for long. *Mercator* and *negotiator* were elastic terms. They could cover a *quidam pauperculus* hawking a mule-load of salt between Paris and Orléans, or two petty traders in the Saturday market at Fleury quarreling over a shilling, just as effectively as rich Syrian or Jewish traders who dealt in slaves and spices or wealthy merchants at Mainz who bought corn in the upper Main valley and sold it in the Rhineland. The merchants of Verdun who are found specializing in the slave trade in the ninth and tenth centuries, shipping their unhappy merchandise from eastern Europe or Britain as far afield as Spain and Constantinople, may well have vied in wealth with some of their counterparts in the Islamic or Byzantine worlds. Merchants of these various types, ranging from pedlars to rich traders but alike in the fact that commerce was their profession and means of livelihood, existed throughout the Dark Ages. Only their numbers and character, and to some extent the regions in which they operated, altered with the passage of time.

The *mercatores* dealt mainly, though not exclusively, in goods that were to some degree luxuries; only exceptionally did they deal in corn or clothing. The ordinary surplus of a great estate, the eggs and chickens and the fish from the fish ponds which the lord's household did not need and which the steward in the *Capitulare de Villis* is told to use his discretion over selling, would go to the local market; only when an estate was of a specialized character, possessing vineyards or salt deposits or minerals, were professional *mercatores* likely to be interested in its produce. The development of this local buying and selling can probably be related to the transition from gold to silver as a medium of exchange in the last quarter of the seventh century. The spread of a silver coinage in regions where no coin had previously circulated—Mercia and Wessex in the ninth century, Germany and east central Europe in the tenth—is intimately connected with its further extension.

The development of markets—and grants of *moneta* are closely associated with those of *mercatum publicum* and *teloneum*—is one of the most noticeable features of the economic history of the ninth and tenth centuries, but while recognizing the importance of the mutual buying and selling of surplus farm produce or peasant handicrafts, we must be careful to distinguish its economic consequences from those of the activities of the *mercatores*. Such exchanges might in varying degrees raise the standard of life of those participating in them, but they would only rarely serve as a stimulus to increasing output and to saving and investment. It is here that the activities of the *mercatores* left their mark: they injected the element of a profit motive into a society so organized as to exclude it from many aspects of its daily life. Mr. Southern has with characteristic felicity described the far-reaching consequences of "the taste for spices and the charm of luxuries":

> It was to satisfy this taste that merchants traveled, sailors perished, bankers created credit and peasants raised the numbers of their sheep. As so often happens, the secondary effects are more interesting than the primary ones: . . . the activities and organization which existed to satisfy the demands of the relatively few colored the whole history of the Middle Ages, and are the foundations of modern commerce and industry.[1]

[1] R. W. Southern, *The Making of the Middle Ages* (London, 1953), p. 42.

One of my colleagues, a specialist on the economy of underdeveloped countries, has commented to me on the insight displayed in this passage, since in regions as far apart as west Africa and Malaya he had again and again seen the same process at work at the present day.

In dealing with the economic life of the Dark Ages, therefore, there are good reasons for keeping these two types of trade separate from one another. The undoubted importance of the Vikings in the economic development of Europe has often been attributed to their interest in trade and supported by somewhat unconvincing parallels between their activities and those of Elizabethan buccaneers in whose enterprises no hard and fast line between piracy and commerce can be drawn. The situation of the two was in fact very different. The background in the one case was a society with a money economy in which the profit motive, if not dominant, played at least a leading role; in the other it was a society in which coined money did not even exist and money and the concept of mercantile profit were alike in an embryonic stage. The reputation of the Vikings as traders depends very largely on archaeological evidence, which is ambiguous, or on the misinterpretation of such texts as that which describes their first landing at Dorchester, when they were taken for peaceful merchants instead of pirates. It is true that Franks had to be prohibited from selling them arms and horses and that Danegeld sometimes included a demand for wine as well as gold and silver, but these objects were obviously required for use, not for sale. This was trade, if you like, but it scarcely proves that the Vikings were traders. Their importance in the history of European commerce resulted, it seems to me, from quite different considerations: by their accumulation of treasure they naturally encouraged enterprising merchants to attempt to relieve them of it by offering them goods in exchange. These hopes were sometimes disappointed, as in the case of the luckless merchants who made their way into Asselt in 882 hoping to trade with the victors and were massacred for their pains. Even in the case of such acknowledged trading centers as Hedeby and Birka we do not know how far the "trade" was in Viking hands or how far their influence extended.

Furthermore, in recognizing the existence of traders and of trade, we must also remember that purchase was not the "natural" way in which a household in the Dark Ages strove to satisfy its needs. Its ambition was to become as self-sufficient as possible. Lesser households could not hope to match the range of produce envisaged in the *Capitulare de Villis,* but the desire to do so was a universal one. The efforts made by monasteries to acquire "propriétés excentriques" which would supply them with wine or salt or wax was not characteristic of the Carolingian era and a contracting economy, as Van Werveke argued;[2] it was natural and reasonable in itself and examples of it can be found in any of the centuries for which a reasonable documentation exists. Buying was only resorted to when all else failed. Einhard might resign himself to paying £50 for the lead required to cover the roof of his church at Seligenstadt, but Servatus Lupus preferred to write directly to the king of Wessex and a court official named Felix and beg for the metal he wanted as a gift. Merchants would thus be excluded from the transaction; the lead would be paid for not in material wealth but in the promise of prayers, and the abbot arranged to send his serfs to the mouth of the Canche to collect the lead and bring it by barge to the abbey. Similarly, when Pope Adrian I was promised a thousand pounds of lead for the repair of the roof of St. Peter's, he requested Charlemagne to have it sent in hundred-pound packages in the baggage of court officials who happened to be visiting Rome, instead of arranging its transport by the care of traders. In both these transactions we are in the presence not of commerce but of a form of gift-exchange to which we will return in a moment.

III

Distortion of the picture arises less from the confusion of traders with trade than from the assumption that goods and money necessarily passed from one hand to another only by means of trade. Here we come up squarely against the archaeological evidence, which in its very nature substitutes inference for explanation. It has been said that the spade cannot lie, but it owes this merit in part to the fact that it cannot speak. There is of course some written evidence, such as references to silks, spices, ivories and similar objects in the inventories of monastic possessions or in the correspondence of the time. But the evidence is mainly archaeological: the finding of Byzantine coins and silver plate in such hoards as Pereshschepino and

[2] H. Van Werveke, "Comment les établissements religieux belges se procuraient-ils du vin au haut moyen âge," *RBPH,* ii (1923), 643–62; "Les propriétés excentriques des églises au haut moyen-âge," *ibid.,* iv (1925), 136–41.

Sutton Hoo, of "Coptic" bronze bowls and Frankish brooches in England, of Islamic silver coins in gigantic quantities in eastern Europe and Scandinavia. The importance of this type of evidence has grown enormously in recent years, since archaeological advances in the last half-century now enable us to speak with greater assurance than was previously possible on the dates and places of origin of many of the objects that have been found. Almost all scholars who have written about them have assumed that they reached their destination through the medium of trade. This is particularly true of numismatists, whose approach to the whole subject is sometimes one of singular naivety. Walter Hävernick, perhaps the most distinguished living German numismatist, virtually assumes that even coins of an exceptional character, like the gold solidi of Louis the Pious, were produced for commercial reasons and that since they were distributed in the normal course of trade it is possible to draw valid conclusions regarding trade routes from studying the localities in which they have been found. One of the best of English numismatists[3] can write, of a silver coin of Athalaric found at Brighton, that "this piece can have journeyed hither only by the slow process of trade. In this way it might have taken upwards of a century to reach Britain"—and this despite the fact that the coin was quite fresh and in good condition when it was found. The most recent work on the economic life of the Dark Ages, Professor A. R. Lewis's *The Northern Seas,* takes it for granted that trade, and trade alone, was responsible for the distribution of goods and coins in the centuries with which he deals.

IV

Such a view is altogether too narrow, and prejudges too many issues. There are other means whereby goods can pass from hand to hand, means which must have played a more conspicuous part in the society of the Dark Ages than they would in more settled and advanced periods. They can be characterized most briefly as "theft" and "gift," using "theft" to include all unilateral transfers of property which take place involuntarily—plunder in war would be the commonest type—and "gift" to cover all those which take place with the free consent of the donor. Somewhere between the two would be a

[3] C. H. V. Sutherland, "Post-Roman Coins Found at Brighton," *Numismatic Chronicle,* 6th ser., 1 (1941), 87.

varied series of payments, such as ransoms, compensations, and fines, while such payments as dowries, the wages of mercenaries, property carried to and fro by political exiles, would all form part of the picture. Our difficulty lies in trying to estimate their relative importance.

We need not linger long over the category of "theft." Life in the early Middle Ages was insecure in the extreme, and plundering raids, highway robbery and theft in the narrow sense were everywhere of frequent occurrence. There is a curious clause in the laws of Ine of Wessex which seeks to define the various types of forcible attack to which a householder and his property might be subjected: if less than seven men are involved, they are thieves; if between seven and thirty-five, they form a gang; if above thirty-five, they are a military expedition. Such phrases as *cum preda* or *captis thesauris* form a regular accompaniment to the accounts of wars in Gregory of Tours and Fredegarius. Plunder and robbery must be accounted factors of major importance in the distribution of valuables in the Dark Ages, and would sometimes be effective over a considerable area. Gifts from the plundered Avar treasure were sent to English kings and bishops as well as to favored recipients throughout the Frankish kingdom, and much of the plate and many of the silks and oriental embroideries which occur in ninth-century ecclesiastical inventories had probably passed through Avar hands.

Almost equally important, and in their total bulk far overshadowing transfers of bullion for commercial purposes, were payments of a purely political character. These might be war indemnities, annual tributes, *ex gratia* payments intended to keep a potentially troublesome neighbor in a good humor, or the purchase of services under specific circumstances and on carefully defined conditions. The distribution of gold, in particular, must have been largely influenced by the political payments which bulk so large in the history of Byzantine foreign relations from the fifth century onwards. Theodosius II, for example, was compelled in c. 430 to promise an annual tribute of 350 pounds of gold a year to the Huns, a figure which was doubled in 435 and sextupled—with a lump payment of 6000 pounds—in 443, the consequent payment of 2,100 pounds a year continuing down to the accession of Marcian. His successors were only to a slight degree more fortunate, and if Germans and Avars were normally less well placed to bring pressure on the empire than the Huns had been, the tradition of tribute continued throughout the sixth and well into the seventh century. We find Maurice paying 50,000 solidi to Childebert II in the hopes of enlisting his aid against the Lombards, while the exarch of Ravenna had to buy off the attacks of the latter by an annual tribute of 300 pounds of gold. Similar payments, sometimes in one direction and sometimes in the other, played a major part in Byzantine-Arab relations, and the huge sums involved in such transactions—the 6000 pounds of gold paid to the Huns in 443 would have amounted to nearly half a million solidi—must have largely determined the distribution of bullion between the Byzantine empire and its neighbors.

Political payments of a similar character were also effective within the barbarian world itself. Witigis paid the Franks 2000 pounds of gold in the hope of securing their neutrality in the Gothic war. At one moment, in the late sixth century, the Lombards were paying the Franks an annual tribute of 12,000 gold solidi. It was probably a Beneventan tribute paid in gold that made possible the scanty gold coinage of Louis the Pious. The payments of Danegeld by the Franks and Anglo-Saxons were at a later time responsible for the transfer of comparable sums in silver from one part of western Europe to another. Works of art, as well as coin or metal in ingot form, sometimes passed to and fro in a similar fashion. It is notorious that many of the surviving gold medallions of the later empire have been found in Germanic territory and probably reached it by way of gift, like the gold medallions of Tiberius II which Chilperic I showed with pride to Gregory of Tours. When the Visigothic king Sisenand revolted against Swinthila and asked help from Dagobert, he promised in return an immense gold *missorium,* part of the royal treasure of the Goths, which weighed 500 pounds and had been given by Aetius to King Thorismund two hundred years before. In the end, the Gothic nobles vetoed its alienation, and Dagobert had to content himself with 200,000 gold solidi instead.

Two further facets of diplomatic intercourse, the exchange of gifts between rulers and the expenses of embassies, must not be overlooked. The interchange of gifts can be regarded as a survival of gift-exchange, and will be referred to later. The payment of the expenses of envoys was an extension of the custom of hospitality, but served the not unimportant functions of gratifying and impressing potentially friendly individuals and allowing suspicious governments to exercise some control over their activities. The sums involved were often enormous. Procopius estimated the total lavished by Justinian

on a Persian ambassador, including his expenses within the empire
and what he was able to take home with him, at 1000 pounds of gold,
and Constantine Porphyrogenitus gives the precise reckoning of the
payments in silver, amounting to over a million *miliaresia,* which
were made to the Russian princess Olga on the occasion of her visit
to Constantinople in 957. A substantial proportion of these sums
would no doubt be recovered in the form of gratuities before the
envoys departed, but much of it would normally leave the empire in
the form of either bullion or luxury goods. In the case of Olga's
embassy, the *miliaresia* brought back to Russia must have exceeded
the total number of Byzantine silver coins found in that country many
times over.

Sums paid in ransoming captives formed likewise an element of
great importance in the life of the early Middle Ages. A successful
raid into the Byzantine empire would be followed by complex negotiations regarding the fate of those who had been carried off, while
towns and cities might have to buy immunity during the actual campaign. Enormous sums of money might change hands in this way.
Procopius has recorded the levies of Chosroes on the cities of Syria
during the Persian wars of Justinian: 2000 pounds of silver on
Hierapolis and Beroea, 1000 pounds of gold on Antioch, 1000 pounds
of silver on Apamea, 200 pounds of gold on Chalcis, 200 pounds
of gold and later a further 500 pounds on Edessa. Such huge figures
were no doubt exceptional, and it is probable that in the relations
between Byzantium and the west, and within Latin Christendom itself, personal ransoms were as a whole of rather greater significance.
A solidus per head was the common reckoning at Constantinople,
though it might be higher or lower on occasion: when Maurice broke
off negotiations with the khagan of the Avars for the ransom of over
12,000 captured soldiers, they were priced at only 4 *keratia*—a sixth
of a solidus—apiece. Individuals of any importance were naturally
worth a great deal more. When Isaac Comnenus, duke of Antioch and
brother of the future emperor Alexius, was captured by the Seljuqs in
the reign of Michael VII, a sum of 20,000 nomismata had to be paid
for his release, and the ransom of Romanus IV after the battle of
Manzikert was reputed to be a million or even a million and a half
nomismata. At Byzantium, amid a mass of legislation forbidding the
alienation of church property, an exception is always made *causa
redemptionis captivorum; cum non absurdum est,* in the words of the
Code of Justinian, *animas hominum quibuscumque causis vel ves-*

timentis praeferri.[4] Probably many of the articles of silverware which
left the empire in the sixth and seventh centuries did so for the
ransom of prisoners; one remembers that a silver dish in the
Pereshschepino hoard had previously belonged to a bishop of Tomi,
and Priscus tells us how a far-sighted bishop of Sirmium set aside
the sacred vessels of his church to ransom him in the event of his
capture during the campaigns of Attila.

The payment of mercenaries must also not be forgotten. In the
later Roman period we hear mainly of the services rendered by
neighboring tribes, or on occasion by the Huns, to such leaders as
Stilicho and Aetius, but we are ignorant of the precise figures for
which they were hired. Individuals—adventurers or exiles—may have
come from even further afield; it is reasonable to conjecture that the
gold coins of the fifth and early sixth centuries which have been
found in considerable numbers in the Baltic region reached there as
payment to mercenaries instead of by trade, as they are frequently
assumed to have done. One of the clearest examples of such payments to mercenaries dates from the mid-eleventh century. In the late
1040s there was a sudden spread of Byzantine types in Danish coinage, which up to then had been mainly English in inspiration. It was
quite short-lived, starting under Sven Estrithsson (1047–75) during
the civil war between him and his predecessor Magnus (1042–47) and
ending under St. Cnut (1080–86). But it was intense while it lasted:
almost half of the 77 monetary types attributed to Sven Estrithsson
are of recognizably Byzantine origin. The explanation is not a sudden
expansion of Byzantine trade with Scandinavia, but the return of
Harold Hardrada from Constantinople in 1046 with an immense treasure which, if a gloss in Adam of Bremen can be believed, twelve
men could scarcely lift. Its dissemination during the twenty years
between his return and his death at Stamfordbridge provided the
models for this whole remarkable series of coins.

The compensations and fines of Germanic law would normally
result in dissemination of wealth only within relatively restricted
areas, but there would be exceptions, as for example when the men
of Kent paid "thirty thousands" to Ine of Wessex in compensation for
the death of Mul and his companions or when Theodore of Tarsus
induced Aethelbald of Mercia to pay compensation to Ecgfrid of

---

[4] For the reason of ransoming captives; since it is not absurd, in the words of the Code
of Justinian, that the lives of men should be preferred to any reason or garments
whatsoever.—Ed.

Northumbia after the death of the latter's brother at the battle of the Trent. Dowries might be important: a Frankish princess took with her fifty wagon-loads of treasure in gold, silver and other valuables when she set out to marry Reccared of Spain. The constant movement of exiles to and fro must also not be forgotten. Lombard exiles in Bavaria, Frankish exiles in Ireland, Northumbrian exiles at the court of Charlemagne would rarely be entirely penniless, and the feuds of the Germanic world must have frequently contributed to the transfer of jewelry and personal valuables from one country to another.

Last but not least, though perhaps the most likely to be overlooked, is the survival in early medieval society of the phenomenon known to anthropologists as gift-exchange. The custom of present-giving is only vestigial in modern society, confined to such occasions as Christmas and Easter and to birthdays and other anniversaries, but in earlier times it was a major form of social activity, serving a function analogous to that of commerce in securing the distribution of goods and services. Such gifts would not be one-sided, for social custom required that every gift had to be compensated sooner or later by a counter-gift, or by equivalent services if persons of different social status were involved. This mutual exchange of gifts at first sight resembles commerce, but its objects and ethos are entirely different. Its object is not that of material and tangible "profit," derived from the difference between the value of what one parts with and what one receives in exchange; rather it is the social prestige attached to generosity, to one's ability and readiness to lavish one's wealth on one's neighbors and dependents. The "profit" consists in placing other people morally in one's debt, for a counter-gift—or services in lieu of one—is necessary if the recipient is to retain his self-respect. From this point of view, indeed, the relationship between the Church and its benefactors can be regarded as involving no more than a particular form of gift-exchange, the counter-gift taking the form of prayers for the souls of the donor and his family.

The practice of gift-giving is naturally most strongly found in the period of the invasions and the barbarian kingdoms, where society had altered less from its primitive Germanic pattern. Tacitus had long before recorded the peculiar pleasure which Germanic chieftains took in the receiving of presents from neighboring states, such objects as fine horses and armor, or metal discs and collars, and there is a striking passage in Beowulf in which Hrothgar bids farewell to the hero, praising him for the peace he has brought about between the Danes and the Geats, so that in the future gift and counter-gift can be freely exchanged between the two peoples:

> *There shall be, while I rule this spacious kingdom*
> *Interchange of treasure: many with good things*
> *Shall greet one another across the gannet's bath;*
> *And over the deep the ringed ship shall carry*
> *Gifts and love-tokens.*

Again and again, in Anglo-Saxon literature and in northern sagas, the giving of gifts and the generosity of a ruler is singled out for the highest praise. In the preface to Wulfsige's copy of the Old English translation of Gregory's *Dialogues* the bishop describes Alfred as "the best ring-giver" he has ever heard of amongst earthly kings, and in such poems as the *Battle of Maldon* the relationship of mutual obligation created by gift-giving is one to which appeal is made again and again. Meanness vies with cowardice as the most shameful of human defects; the miserliness of the Scylding Prince Hrethric, son of the generous Hrothgar, earns him the nickname Hnauggvanbaugi, "the niggard with rings," in the Old Norse royal list (*Langfedgatal*). The wealth amassed with insatiable cupidity by Merovingian kings was not intended to defray the expenses of an elaborate system of government, as was the heavy taxation of Roman times, but was designed to maintain the social prestige of the kings by being lavished on their followers.

The custom of gift-giving survived the heroic age, and the correspondence of such men as St. Boniface and Alcuin, as later of Einhard and Servatus Lupus, is full of the passage of gifts to and fro. Often these are objects which would be produced in the household of the donor, or in his monastery if he happened to be an abbot, but they might be luxuries or manufactured goods of some special type. Spices being both valuable and easy to transport were in constant demand, and a number of Boniface's correspondents at Rome accompanied their letters with such gifts. These are constantly referred to in the letters which accompanied them as being of a most trifling character—"small indeed, but given out of heartfelt affection"—but such depreciatory terms should not delude us into believing their values were as slight as the donors pretended. The hawk, two falcons, two shields and two spears which Boniface sent to King Aethelbald of Mercia cannot really have merited the description of them as "those trifling gifts" (*munuscula*), and the presents of spices must always have been costly. No doubt they represent a development in the direction of the modern custom of gift-giving, where the gifts are of the nature of tokens, but they have not yet reached that point. Nor were men reluctant to ask for what they wanted, however curious or unusual their demands might be. When King Aethelbert of Kent sent Boniface a silver cup weighing 3½ pounds and two woollen cloaks—*nonnulla munuscula*—he asked the bishop to procure him in return a pair of falcons of a breed, rare in Kent but common in Germany, which would attack cranes. We have seen already how such a raw material as lead might form an acceptable gift, and in any picture which we make of exchange in the early Middle Ages, the phenomenon of gift and counter-gift must be allowed a conspicuous place.

V

In attempting to assess the importance of trade in the Dark Ages, then, we have a body of "positive" evidence for the existence of traders and trade, another body of "positive" evidence for the existence of various alternatives to trade, and a third body of "neutral" evidence—mainly archaeological—for the distribution of wealth—goods or coin—by unspecified means. All that we know of the social conditions of the time suggests that the alternatives to trade were more important than trade itself: the *onus probandi* rests on those who believe the contrary to have been the case. In a few instances we can say definitely that trade was *not* involved: for example, Dr. Adelson's[5] view that Byzantine lightweight solidi were struck for the convenience of merchants trading with the Germanic world is contradicted by reiterated imperial legislation forbidding merchants on pain of death to export gold from the empire. This case, however, is exceptional; in general, we do not know how coins or jewelry or similar objects reached their destinations, and with so many possibilities from which to choose any conclusions that we draw can only be of the most tentative description. Much evidence alleged to "prove" the existence of trade proves nothing of the kind, and in dealing with the Dark Ages, in cases where we cannot prove, we are not entitled without a careful weighing of the evidence to assume.

[5] Howard L. Adelson, *Light Weight Solidi and Byzantine Trade during the Sixth and Seventh Centuries.*

Paul Craig Roberts

THE PIRENNE THESIS: TOWARDS REFORMULATION

Paul Craig Roberts, born in 1939, is a professor of economics at West Georgia College. He is also a Research Fellow at the Hoover Institution of Stanford University. The article from which this excerpt is taken originated as a paper in a graduate seminar at the University of California at Berkeley, and was prepared for publication in its present form while Professor Roberts was Relm Fellow at Merton College, Oxford. Since then he has ranged widely as a scholar and has made important contributions to a reinterpretation of Soviet economic organization and Soviet economic history.

In this paper the Pirenne Thesis will be examined in a novel way. Out of this examination will come a strong case for the general validity of Pirenne's thesis that Islam was the most significant of the causative factors in the transition of Roman Gaul to Medieval Europe. This examination will also give us a glimpse of why Pirenne is not guilty of a purely economic interpretation of history as his critics have claimed. And yet at the same time we will see that Pirenne did not fail "for the simple reason that economic factors play a subsidiary role," but because he emphasized the wrong economic factor. . . .

There are two questions to examine. One is whether the advance of Islam is a better causative factor by which to explain the break with Antiquity that gave rise to Medieval Europe than is the German invasions, the pirate fleet of Vandal Carthage, the decadence succeeding the Antonines, or the Atlantic Civilization of the Scandinavians. The other question is whether the economic medium is a better one through which to trace the effectuation of the "barbarization" of Gaul and the rise of medieval civilization (and the revival of trade) than is the political, social or ideological. It is a matter of *finality* in causative factors. It is a matter of the medium through which this conclusiveness was effected.

The validity of the Pirenne Thesis rests upon the answers to the above two questions. It is a matter of qualitative analysis. It has nothing to do with the question of the volume of trade carried on

Excerpted from Paul Craig Roberts, "The Pirenne Thesis, Economies or Civilizations; Towards Reformulation," *Classica et Mediaevalia* 25 (1964): 297–315. By permission of the author and of the editor of *Classioa et Mediaevalia*. Documentation is omitted.

under the Merovingians; it has nothing to do with the question of the presence of professional merchants in Gaul during the Carolingian period; it has nothing to do with the relative availabilities of oriental cloths, spices, papyrus, or quantity of gold in circulation in Gaul under the Romans, Merovingians, Carolingians, or during the eleventh century, the twelfth century, or at any time.

The validity of the Pirenne Thesis does not turn on any quantitative measures. It turns on the qualitative analysis of a factor that has been ignored. It is the purpose of this paper to introduce this factor.

The growth of great cities gives rise to demands inflated beyond the possibility of their being locally satisfied. Rome's growth and provisioning was effected only by enlarging the dimensions of the tributary hinterland. Also a required factor for the growth of a city is an efficient means of mass transport. The lack of transport or ease of its disruption constitute a check to a city's growth and a threat to its very existence.

The Roman Empire was the product of a single expanding power center striving (among other things, of course) to extend and protect its claim on resources. It was a vast city-building enterprise which left the imprint of Rome on every part of Europe, Northern Africa, and Asia Minor, altering the way of life in the old cities and establishing by *purposeful design* hundreds of new cities, always following a deliberate policy of dispersal, in subordination to Rome. The conquered towns were often altered, but the new towns were founded in accord with the economic and military needs of the empire.

Economic control was the basis of the Roman Empire, and the widened province of transportation and communication given by the control of the Mediterranean allowed Rome to exercise its command over men and resources in distant areas. By its organization of cities the Roman Empire united the lands of the eastern Mediterranean, from which it drew its chief wealth, with the less developed lands of the western Mediterranean and northern Gaul. The unifying medium was the economic. All economic trade was purposely orientated by Rome towards Rome. Thus, Rome was the concentration into a few square miles of the resources of a whole empire.

Despite the unity, there was a profound difference between Roman civilization in the East and in the West. Roman Gaul was created by Rome and out of Rome. The towns of Gaul were *new* towns; they were Rome's towns; their commerce was Rome's commerce. They received their culture from Rome, the life-line of the connection being the economic orientation. Cicero called Narbonne in southern Gaul "a colony of Roman citizens, a watch tower of the Roman people, a bulwark against the wild tribes of Gaul." These towns were founded for military and economic reasons—to mobilize the resources of Gaul for Rome. The institutions and systems of administration reflect this.

Before Rome, Gaul had known only wild tribes. Italy had known the Etruscan and Hellenic cultures. The East had been blessed richly.

In normal times in Gaul or Aquitaine, these "new towns" could draw their food from the surrounding region, so they maintained the urban-rural balance that larger cities of the other provinces, by their very growth, upset. Thus, they usually did not need to be provisioned with essentials (and when they did, they usually needed the legions as well). Consequently, Gaul's commerce was significantly different from that of the other provinces. Gaul was economically self-sufficient. Its surpluses were largely exported to Rome and to the East. This "trade" was one way. Commodities of trade produced in Gaul were either heavy, bulky, or fragile objects, requiring an efficient system of transportation. There was little interregional trade in Gaul of its own products.

The records we have of the earliest cities tell us that in them the functions of the market were undertaken by the temple, though, as in the Soviet Union, a portion of the peasant's production might be privately exchanged, once the collective demand was satisfied. Thus, trade characterized by spontaneous mutual interaction grew up around the periphery of a hierarchically organized economic order. Should one above substitute "Gaul" for "earliest cities" and "Rome" for "temple," the analogy would not be altogether uninteresting. Gaul's prosperity was based on the exploitation of its own natural resources under the protection of Rome. Its imports of oriental cloths and spices had little significance for its economic organization and well-being or for its civilization.

The cities of the East present a different picture in more ways than one. In the East there was civilization before Rome and civilization after Rome and its independent foundations were retained under Rome. The Romans had an empirical respect for any established order, even when it contradicted their own—a trait that served them well. The commerce of the East was bilateral and extensive; it went in many directions. . . .

The Vindication of the Pirenne Thesis

Under Rome there was economic unity of the Mediterranean, and the general direction of commerce was towards the coasts of the sea—was towards Rome. This had very real significance for the Roman Empire. It was the factor that allowed life to be breathed into its institutions; it made possible its existence. And it was what allowed Gaul to be Roman.

With the founding of Constantinople as the eastern capital, the whole center of gravity in the Empire shifted to the eastern provinces. Yet "Rome" was the Mediterranean and the Mediterranean was "Rome." "A city of the far-flung earth you made."

In Gaul the effect of the Germanic invasions was on the *volume* of trade. They hastened the process of passage from the uniform imperial economic organization to an economy of local production and barter. Hand in hand with this process went the deterioration of Roman society in Gaul. Yet the process was not one of unbroken regression, and it was *not irreversible*.

The effect of the Islamic encirclement of the Mediterranean was on the *orientation* of trade. From the beginning of the eighth century, the whole economic movement of the western Mediterranean was directed towards Bagdad, or that of Gaul confined within itself, later to be directed northward. From this fundamental fact, Roman Gaul *necessarily* breathed its last breath.

Pirenne is wrong when he says commercial activity did not survive the Saracen mastery of the western Mediterranean. The Mediterranean had long been the great artery of commerce, and it remained so. However, the orientation of Gaulish trade toward the Empire did not survive the Saracens.

Perhaps now we can see why Pirenne's thesis might be true, as well as why he failed to prove it so. He chose to emphasize the role of international trade rather than the qualitative differences in the organization and economic orientation of markets and the significance of this for Roman Gaul. It was not the amount of trade, but the type of trade; not the quality of markets, but the method of organization of markets; not the existence of trade, but the orientation of trade. The Muslim conquest in itself did not transform the money economy of the Merovingians to the natural economy of the Middle Ages. However, it ended forever the orientation of Gaulish trade toward the Empire.

Pirenne recognized the connection between Rome, trade, and the cities of Gaul. However, he misinterpreted the meaning of the connection. Gaul was orientated towards Rome, not towards international trade. When trade revived in Gaul, it was not orientated toward the provisioning of regal cities. It did not gravitate towards empire. Thus, it did not serve the purpose of empire. Formative economic forces were no longer "Roman." Thus, in what had been Gaul, economic activity, and thereby society, could take a new turn.

The medieval town was born out of local protection. There was no central power. Regionally, the protection offered by the bishops rivalled that of the feudal nobility. In no sense were medieval towns agents of a far-flung institution. Trade could begin to grow to be more and more the result of spontaneous mutual interaction, to be promoted, organized, directed, coordinated, and orientated mainly by the prospect of gain—the means to dignity for those outside the titles of church and nobility. With the Roman power center, which had functionalized things in its interest, passed from the scene, a mostly custom-bound economic system could be modified by continuous stages towards a market system, *with the various intermediate forms offering different combinations of functional and commercial rationality.* For this reason it is justified to study economic history with a view to the presence of different combinations of the functional and commercial methods of organization in order to assess the dominating influence arising out of the conflict between the convivial existence of custom and impersonal commercialism upon social and economic organization (and on intellectual history, i.e., Socialism).

The new trading economy based on individual enterprise and mobile capital was almost from the beginning outside the authority of the domain of both feudal and guild systems. Mobile capital proved to be a powerful force. It tore away the shielding that had protected the medieval town and the powers of the Church and feudal nobility and reached through to break the chains on human action of ritualistic prescription, proving itself to be even more ruthless in the destruction of historic institutions than the most reckless of authoritarian rulers. These institutions were destroyed because their rationality was given to them by their being based on a functional economy. Thus, the administrative and coordinative limitations of this custom-bound system did not permit its institutions to stand in the face of a rising level and rate of change in economic activity. The power of privilege as an organizing and coordinating force was replaced by the power of contract. The functional economy gave way to the commercial economy. The concrete marketplace of the medieval town was made dynamic by the advent of the abstract market. But this came later. Yet even in the eleventh century Alain of Lille could say "Not Caesar now, but money, is all."

Summary

This paper contains the following main points:

1. The Pirenne Thesis has been sidetracked into irrelevancies.
2. Pirenne justifiably used the economic medium to struggle with a thesis about civilizations which he never clearly presented. I suggest Pirenne can be vindicated by showing that what is now western Europe of what was the Western Empire had no independent social, economic, political, or cultural foundations. Its life-line was its economic orientation to Rome which was functionally organized by Rome to serve Rome. When the West was cut off from the Empire by the Moslems and infested with the Germans, Roman civilization simply died. Pirenne was concerned with civilizations, not economies.

Lynn White, Jr.

THE NORTHWARD SHIFT OF EUROPE'S FOCUS

Lynn White has had a varied career as teacher, scholar and administrator. Educated at Stanford and Harvard, he taught history at Princeton and Stanford before becoming president of Mills College in 1943. Fifteen years later he returned to the classroom as a professor of history at the University of California at Los Angeles; from 1964–1970 he was director of the Center for Medieval and Renaissance Studies. His administrative duties continued as president of the History of Science Society, as president of the Society for the History of Technology, and as president of the American Historical Association. As a scholar he has been a leader in opening up the fields of medieval science, technology and invention. Medieval Technology and Social Change *(1962) brought together many of his ideas; the same theme also dominated his collected essays,* Machina ex Deo: Essays in the Dynamics of Western Culture *(1968).*

In 1937 there appeared posthumously the masterpiece of the Belgian historian Henri Pirenne, *Mahomet et Charlemagne.* Since then it has dominated discussion of the economic history of the Mediterranean from the fifth through the tenth centuries. According to Pirenne, the Western Roman world did not "fall": it slowly disintegrated. Until *c.* 700 the essential unity of the Mediterranean was preserved despite political chaos. Levantine traders continued to do business as far west as the Merovingian kingdom, and indeed this commerce may have remained as active as in earlier and happier times. But the upsurge of Islam in the seventh century tore apart the seamless robe of the Middle Sea. Commercial connections with the East were severed, and the conquest of Visigothic Spain by the Muslims in the eighth century left the Frankish king as the only considerable power in what was left of the Latin West. Cut off from the great currents of the continuing life of the Mediterranean, the Frankish realm turned inward upon itself and became the nucleus of a new kind of civilization. . . .

No other historical work of our century has provoked such an outburst of research, mostly in opposition. His critics have now destroyed Pirenne's thesis in the greatest detail. Mediterranean commerce suffered a long and steady decline; the Islamic conquest did not close the Mediterranean to the meager trade still existing between the Orient and the West; economic historians can draw no sharp line between Merovingian and Carolingian times as regards contacts with the East.

But this controversy has been misleading. Pirenne's explanations have been cut to bits, but what he was trying to explain has not yet been clarified by other means. The observable fact from which he started was a shift of the focus of Europe, in Carolingian times, from south to north, from the classic lands of the Mediterranean to the great plains drained by the Loire, the Seine, the Rhine, the Elbe, the Upper Danube, and the Thames. The lands of the olive and vine remained vigorous and creative, but who can doubt that, save for brief periods, the core of European culture has been north of the Alps and the Loire from the ninth century to our own day? If Pirenne's answer has been refuted, his question remains.

A more durable solution of the historical problem of the change of the gravitational center of Europe from south to north is to be found in the agricultural revolution of the early Middle Ages. By the early ninth century all the major interlocking elements of this revolution had been developed: the heavy plow, the open fields, the modern harness, the triennial rotation—everything except the nailed horseshoe which appears a hundred years later. To be sure, the transition to the three-field system made such an assault on existing peasant properties that its diffusion beyond the Frankish heartland was slow; but Charlemagne's renaming of the months indicates how large the new agricultural cycle loomed in his thinking. We may assume safely that its increased productivity was a major stimulus to the north even in his day.

The agricultural revolution of the early Middle Ages was limited to the northern plains where the heavy plow was appropriate to the rich soils, where the summer rains permitted a large spring planting, and where the oats of the summer crop supported the horses to pull the heavy plow. It was on those plains that the distinctive feature both of the late medieval and of the modern worlds developed. The increased returns from the labor of the northern peasant raised his standard of living and consequently his ability to buy manufactured goods. It provided surplus food which, from the tenth century on, permitted rapid urbanization. In the new cities there arose a class of skilled artisans and merchants, the burghers who speedily got control of their communities and created a novel and characteristic way of life, democratic capitalism. And in this new environment germinated the dominant feature of the modern world: power technology.

William Carroll Bark

THE PROBLEM OF MEDIEVAL BEGINNINGS

William Carroll Bark, now professor emeritus of history at Stanford University, was born in 1908. Himself a graduate of Stanford, he received his doctorate at Cornell where he studied with M. L. W. Laistner and Carl Stephenson. A member of the history faculty at Lawrence College and then at the University of Chicago, he joined the Stanford faculty in 1947, with a professorship in 1957. In 1969 he became a Senior Fellow of the Hoover Institution at Stanford. His scholarly interests in recent years have turned to the philosophy of history—more specifically, to a study of how Western man came to take the course he did. This will be the theme of his next publication.

More than thirty-five years have passed since Pirenne first advanced the thesis which was finally presented in his posthumously published book, *Mahomet et Charlemagne,* namely, that the beginning of the Middle Ages is inseparably connected with the westward expansion of Islam and the destruction of the Mediterranean unity long preserved by Rome. Mohammed and Charlemagne share the title for the reason that, in Pirenne's words, "it is strictly true that without Mohammed Charlemagne is inconceivable." It was not the Germanic invasions that effected the great rupture between antiquity and the Middle Ages, not the Visigoths, certainly not the Ostrogoths, and not even the Merovingian Franks. It was the Saracens who made the difference. Their conquest of North Africa and Spain meant that after the eighth century the Franks held a dominant position in the West.

Reprinted from *Origins of the Medieval World* by William Carroll Bark, with the permission of the publishers, Stanford University Press. Copyright © 1958 by the Board of Trustees of the Leland Stanford Junior University. The selection reprinted is from pp. 7–9, 11–13, 15–20, and 24–28. Documentation is omitted.

The Moslems also aggravated the separation of East and West; since their clash with the Byzantine power in the East prevented the Eastern emperor from going to the aid of the papacy against the Lombards, the popes had perforce to turn to the only real power in Western Europe, that of the Frankish king, soon to become emperor.

It was thus, in Pirenne's view, that Mohammed prepared the way for Charlemagne and set in motion a whole train of momentous events. Government, the relationship of Church and State, the place of the Church in society, all changed. Feudalism superseded the centralized State, and the ecclesiastical institution took over the leadership of a once secular society. The Mediterranean became a Moslem lake, and the center of Western European life was pushed back from the Mediterranean toward the North. A long evolutionary process culminated at length in A.D. 800 with the coronation of Charlemagne at Rome and the establishment of a new Empire.

What has appeared to some students to denote a decisive alteration in the status quo, namely, the Germanic invasions of the fourth and fifth centuries, long before the birth of the Prophet, Pirenne considered only a superficial political novelty. Nothing was really changed by the Germans, who admired Roman institutions and wished to preserve what they had fallen heir to. They did not introduce a new form of government. Politically, they did no worse than to replace the old unified Roman state with a plurality of states. In this analysis Pirenne seems to have proceeded on the assumption that if the Germans wrought no change, then no change took place. The proviso is fundamental; on it depends the validity of his thesis. If further examination should reveal that even though the Germans themselves did not introduce basic changes, nevertheless such changes occurred, and had occurred *before* the Germans came in, the Mohammed-Charlemagne relationship would be seriously shaken. The westward movement of the Saracens and their domination of the Western Mediterranean would then be only part of a process which had begun long before Mohammed, Clovis, or even Alaric. It was after all Gothic, not Roman, rule that the Saracens displaced in Spain, and to the north it was not Gallo-Romans who opposed the new invaders but the cavalry forces of their Frankish masters. Gaul was continuing a change long in process; it was becoming France.

Somewhat similar doubts and questions are raised by Pirenne's contention that there was no fundamental change in the economic situation of the Roman West before the Saracens. The old commercial life continued, allegedly, suffering only a shrinkage due to the "barbarization" of customs. The same was true of agriculture, finance, taxation, and other aspects of economic organization. Even as late as the seventh century Pirenne would have it that nothing announced the passing of the community of civilization established by the Roman Empire. "The new world" did not lose the Mediterranean character of "the ancient world."

Others have seen the course of developments differently, however. Norman Baynes suggested some years ago that perhaps the Vandal pirate fleet had shattered the unity of the Mediterranean world in the fifth century, long before the rise of Islam. François Ganshof and Robert S. Lopez have questioned Pirenne's assumption that commerce came to an end in the West after the Saracenic expansion. Of the two assaults, one on Pirenne's treatment of the period before his crucial century, A.D. 650–750, and the other on his interpretation of the era just after it, namely, the Carolingian, the latter has so far been the more vigorously pressed. Trade did continue, and Lopez draws attention to important aspects of the problem wholly neglected by Pirenne. Thus one notes that fluctuations in the use of papyrus, Oriental luxury cloths, gold currency, and spices were due to internal changes not only in the West but also in the East, depending upon the efficiency of state control of monopolies by the Byzantines and Arabs and upon the system of alliances between the two Eastern governments. Lopez makes the further interesting point, suggested earlier in a much more general way by Rostovtzeff, that possible alterations in taste should also be taken into account; it may be that the Western barbarians did not care for the shimmering cloth and pungent spices of the Orient so much as their more refined predecessors and successors.

There may, in short, have been relevant changes in both West and East, which had nothing to do with the openness of the Mediterranean to travel and commerce. For example, Pirenne's belief that the irruption of Islam into the Western Mediterranean had an immediate repercussion in the Netherlands may be a distortion of considerable proportions. That none but linen or woolen garments were worn in the West after the beginning of the Carolingian period and that it was Frisian cloth Charlemagne chose to offer the Caliph Harun al Rashid may quite conceivably mean that many of the active, fighting Franks of Charlemagne's time had come to have a high opinion of linen and woolen clothing, not only because it was cheaper or more easily available but also because it was in certain pertinent respects superior to Oriental luxury cloths. In sum, the curtailment of exports to the Franks was not simply a matter of obstruction by the Saracens of Spain. The refusal of the Byzantine and to a lesser extent of the Eastern Moslem rulers to permit their products to be sent West was also a factor, and perhaps a more important one. Presumably the Franks had little that the Oriental world wanted and, as noted, there is at least the possibility that the Western demand for Oriental luxuries had decreased.

Still another weak point, economically, in the Pirenne front is to be found in the short shrift given fundamental economic changes in Gaul in the period before the Franks ruled there, above all to the widespread destruction of the market for the natural products of the region. It must be added in passing, that Pirenne again and again, just as in this instance, had difficulty with the paucity of available information. An examination of the "evidence" he garnered from Gregory of Tours is likely to leave the reader with the feeling that not only was Pirenne able to make bricks without straw; he on occasion did not even require clay, . . .

Pirenne further weakened his case by virtually dissociating affairs in the economic sphere from those in the political, although the two are inseparable in this series of developments. Again, though Fustel de Coulanges long ago called attention to the role of the Church in the granting of immunities and the weakening of royal power, Pirenne failed to give due consideration to the bearing of this fact upon the course of events. It is evident that the character of Frankish society was changing—witness the weakening of absolute, centralized power, the greater importance of local, landed proprietors, and the increasing influence of the Church in this social change— well before the appearance of the Saracens. Pirenne saw that the granting of immunities was a result of the king's weakness, but he did not realize that this weakness had been demonstrated early in the Merovingian era with the disappearance of public services. Nor does he appear to have given due credit to the testimony of Gregory of Tours, otherwise ransacked so exhaustively, that even in the sixth century the Church had stepped in to defend those whom the monarchy no longer attempted to serve, thereby early becoming an immensely powerful agent in the political and economic life of Merovingian France.

To those who approach the Merovingian period by way of Roman history, one of the most disturbing aspects of Pirenne's explanation of medieval beginnings must be the scant consideration he gave to changing conditions within the Empire. This rather too brisk treatment may have led him to oversimplify and sometimes to take a distorted view of the later situation by passing too quickly over the earlier. The major question in the present context is whether Roman civilization underwent a serious and meaningful alteration between the second and fifth centuries of the Christian era. Pirenne seems hardly to have been aware even of the possibility, as he writes of the continuance of *Romania,* of a Roman type of absolute government, and of the Roman community of civilization.

Yet it must be allowed that one's understanding of medieval beginnings depends on how one looks at the early Middle Ages. Considered from the point of view of the later Middle Ages alone, they look one way; if the earlier period of Roman grandeur is also considered, they have a different appearance. Accordingly Rostovtzeff, well aware of the crucial nature of the changes going on in the Later Empire, warned against speaking carelessly of the "decay" of Roman civilization, for he saw what happened as a "slow and gradual change, a shifting of values in the consciousness of men." Nevertheless he held that "*ancient* civilization in its Greco-Roman form" disappeared, and he underlined "*ancient.*" This disappearance coincided chronologically with the "political disintegration of the Roman Empire and with a great change in its economic and social life." It was indeed "a great change" laden with the greatest and most extensive meaning for later ages. Virtually to ignore it would be a fatal flaw in any attempt to explain the problem as a whole. Merely to refer to the continuation of trade, largely by Syrians and Jews resident in Frankish Gaul, and to the continued existence of seaports and cities, could do little to account for a complex development. For so many-sided a situation Pirenne's "Saracenic" explanation was entirely too simple.

Other questions arise in quick succession. The hastiest comparison of East and West, for example, must inevitably suggest certain lines of thought. Was not much more to be made of the contrast between East and West than Pirenne was willing to allow? It is a matter of very great moment that the economic and social backgrounds of the Eastern and Western parts of the Roman Empire were so different. The way they responded to the rigid stabilization effected by the fourth-century emperors alone serves to underline the point. The East had a long history of Hellenistic monopoly and control behind it, and it enjoyed conditions of relative prosperity. The East was more urban, the West more rural, and commerce and industry were much more strongly based in the one than in the other. . . .

Yet another aspect of the case touches upon the much-touted "unity of the Mediterranean." According to the Pirenne argument, Byzantium prevented the Saracens, after they had made the Western Mediterranean a Moslem lake, from taking over the whole area. Thus the old Roman sea became the frontier between Islam and Christianity and the Occident was separated from the Orient. In this way Islam broke the unity which the Germanic invaders had left intact. This rupture, "the most essential action" to take place in European history since the Punic Wars, in Pirenne's eyes marked the end of the ancient tradition and the beginning of the Middle Ages at the precise moment when Europe was being Byzantinized.

It has already been suggested, chiefly through the illuminating remarks of Robert Lopez on Western trade or lack of trade with the East, that this "Byzantinization" was not a foregone conclusion. Moreover, Pirenne himself observed that somewhat later the commercial interests of Naples, Gaeta, and Amalfi led those towns to abandon Byzantium and enter into negotiations with the Moslems, a defection which permitted the Saracens finally to take Sicily. This action reveals on the one hand that the Saracens were not wholly intractable, on the other that a conflict of interests between Western and Byzantine traders was not impossible. In the Pirenne construction, however, things appear quite otherwise. Charlemagne is portrayed as incapable of making the Franks a maritime power, despite the great profit to be derived thereby; Venice is shown to be entering the Byzantine orbit; and the Saracens lurk always as the dire danger.

In this piece of detective work Pirenne did not charge the real culprit. Western Europe had access to a good avenue of commerce, and this access was denied it not by the Moslems but by the Byzantines. It is true that the Moslems held the Western part of the sea, but after their initial hostility to the West and Western trade, they clearly had no aversion to dealing with the Franks and Italians. The reality was that Byzantium opposed the intrusion of the Carolingian Franks, who in turn were scarcely more energetic than the Merovingians had been in improving trading conditions. As for the Venetians, they would trade with anyone, provided there was sufficient profit to be made. They gladly sold Christian slaves and eunuchs to the Moslems, and they formed alliances as expediency dictated. It should be added that in this eagerness to trade, the Venetians were not essentially different from their Italian, Moslem, and Byzantine counterparts. And the Moslems were no more free of internal dissension than the Eastern and Western Christians.

It becomes ever clearer that Europe's political and economic center of gravity began to shift northward well before the Saracens took Spain, and one may even dare to suggest that strong spiritual forces also began to move in that direction at a very early date. This shifting of power may be detected, or at least suspected, from a careful reading of the *Mahomet et Charlemagne,* even though Pirenne, enchanted by his Saracenic theory, did not so interpret the evidence he marshaled. His views on early medieval, that is, Anglo-Saxon, Britain provide an excellent illustration of this preoccupation.

Britain, after its Germanic invasions, differed decidedly from the rest of Europe, according to Pirenne, for there a new type of civilization, Nordic or Germanic in character, began to come into existence. The Roman State vanished completely and with it its legislative ideal, its civil population, and its Christian religion. It was replaced by "a society which preserved among its members the blood tie, the family-centered community with all its consequences in law, morality, and economy, a paganism related to that of the heroic lays." Thus a new age was beginning in Britain, Northern rather than Southern in outlook and having nothing to do with *Romania.* On this view the Anglo-Saxon invaders of Roman Britain remained quite untouched by Roman civilization, and the historian had to conclude that "the Germanic, Nordic, barbarian soul, the soul of peoples whose state of advancement was, so to speak, Homeric, has been in this land the essential historical factor."

This description is poetic, even romantic, but regrettably it is not historical. Though Pirenne caught a glimpse of the North-centered society to come, it was fleeting and he drew no important conclusions from the changing state of affairs. He continued to rely on his old assumption that the Merovingian Frankish society was vastly superior, because it was Roman, to that of Britain after the Anglo-Saxon invasions. The cruelty and viciousness of the Merovingian brood of princes counted for nothing. One must also wonder, though in vain, if Pirenne found the Anglo-Saxon soul more "Germanic, Nordic, and barbarian" than, say, the Lombard soul. As for the

"Northern" character of the new civilization of Britain, here again one must insist on a comparison with other invaded areas of the Western half of the Empire and remember that, in some respects at least, the northerly movement was begun by the Franks as early as, or before, the sixth century. Nor may it be forgotten, with reference to that strong Anglo-Saxon paganism, that the movement to bring the northerners into the Church was initiated by Pope Gregory the Great also in the sixth century.

Another oversimplification involves the Celts of the North, who are whisked out of sight somewhat too briskly. Unfortunately for the fixed interpretation, there were Celts in Britain as well as in the isles and on the Continent, and though not Nordic, they made history in this crucial period. By way of example, Pelagius, a Celtic monk probably of British origin, stirred St. Augustine of Hippo to the formulation of some of his strongest and most influential dogmatic views. It is equally indefensible to overlook the activities of other Celtic monks, notably Columba and Columban, in the sixth century, or to minimize the continuation of their work by Anglo-Saxon scholars, teachers, and missionaries in the seventh and eighth centuries, culminating in the outstanding labors of Bede, Boniface, and Alcuin. The isolated, "pagan," Homeric North could and did have an effect upon Frankland and even upon Mediterranean Italy before, during, and after the Saracenic expansion.

Here, as in several other cases, the most surprising point about Pirenne's argument is that he was aware of the close connection between Rome and the British isles after the time of Gregory the Great. In spite of this awareness, he could conclude that "by the most curious reversal" the North replaced the South as the literary as well as the political center of Europe, and that this event provided the "most striking confirmation of the break caused by Islam." The inescapable realities are that in Britain and Ireland the new civilization in process of growth owed much to the combination of Anglo-Saxon and Celtic vigor and enthusiasm with Italian and Oriental skill and experience in organization and administration. It is reasonable to assume that the new civilization being molded by Celt and Saxon, by Frank, Syrian, and Roman, would have proceeded along much the same course if there had been no Saracenic expansion at all.

This contention may serve to introduce a further test of the validity of the Pirenne thesis. If Pirenne was correct, the culture and the cultural directions of Western Europe as a whole ought to be measurably different after the Saracenic expansion, and the difference ought to be clearly attributable to forces set in motion by the Saracenic eruption. Pirenne consistently took up the problem of cultural change, as he did that of social change, by absolving the Germanic barbarians of responsibility. Thus he maintained that "the Germanic invasions could not and did not in any respect alter" the ancient tradition, i.e., the old unity of intellectual life. In support of this view he could point to an occasional prominent layman, such as Cassiodorus or Boethius, declare that a simple Latin was written by Eugippius, Caesarius of Arles, and Gregory the Great only so that the people could understand, and argue that the Church absorbed the Empire, thus becoming a powerful agency of Romanization. He conceded that the intellectual life and the ancient culture were decadent after the third century, the "decadence of a decadence"; all he insisted on was that the Germans made no break with the classical tradition, that the break came later with the Saracens.

Here the problem is much the same as it was in a smaller way in the case of Anglo-Saxon Britain. The essential question is whether the intellectual transition to the Middle Ages was far advanced even before the great Germanic inroads of the fourth and fifth centuries, not to mention the later era of the Saracenic expansion.

Unhappily Pirenne did not take up this basic question fairly and directly. Consequently the impression one receives from reading his chapter on intellectual life after the invasions in the *Mahomet et Charlemagne* is chiefly one of incompleteness. After referring to the general decay in science, art, and letters from the end of the third century, Pirenne proceeds with a brief sketch of intellectual conditions. Some, though not all, of the subjects that ought to be mentioned are mentioned; reference is made, for example, to the increasing Christian influence, to the growth of monasticism, to the continuing process of Orientalization, and to the deterioration of classical learning and literature. It is primarily the conclusions drawn from this survey that give the impression of distorted vision and unfinished work.

A few examples will suffice to clarify the objection. In the Ostrogothic kingdom, according to Pirenne, "everything continued as under the Empire" and "it is enough to recall the names of two of Theodoric's ministers: Cassiodorus and Boethius." Two short, barren paragraphs are then given to these extraordinarily influential men, and even these brief references are so presented as to give a false impression in support of the thesis. For it is misleading to say nothing at all of Boethius's Christianity and his interest in the great theological controversies of his time, controversies which had a shattering impact upon the dogmatic unity of the Byzantine East and contributed also to the estrangement of the Eastern and Western churches. No one would ever suspect from this little paragraph that Boethius has with reason been termed "the first of the scholastics" as well as "the last of the Romans." Cassiodorus is brushed aside just as brusquely. His devotion to the religious life at Vivarium and his patronage of monks are cited, but nothing is said of his extensive religious writings, or of his views on education, or indeed of the real temper of his mind. What is said is accurate, as in the case of Boethius, but since too much is omitted, here again the effect is misleading. Pirenne mentions, for example, that Cassiodorus wished his monks to bring together all the literary works of classical antiquity, a perfectly acceptable statement as far as it goes; but in referring to Ennodius, he gives the impression that ancient rhetoric was flourishing as strongly as ever, among Christians as well as pagans. Obviously, it is implied, the classical tradition was still in full swing, with no essential change in mood or values. In reality, however, it was quite otherwise. Pirenne's construction ignores the moribund state of pagan rhetoric and literature in general and the bitter struggle, both long before and even after the time of Cassiodorus, against the profane tradition in literature, in which Jerome, Augustine, and Gregory the Great figured so largely. To try to use Boethius and Cassiodorus as props for the view that society was still secular and essentially unchanged, to fail to bring out the very close contact of both men with the growth of Christian ideas and institutions in a crucial time, was a major error.

Similarly, Pirenne argued vigorously to show that the use of a simple Latin by such Church writers as Caesarius of Arles, Gregory I, and Eugippius did not denote any significant departure from the old tradition, but rather that the Church was deliberately debasing the language in an effort to make literature an instrument of culture, or rather of edification for the people. This adaptation could then be described as nothing more than a continuation of the old Mediterranean culture. By this ingenious but unacceptable reconstruction Pirenne would actually have made the most powerful single institution engaged in the formation of a new Western society, the Christian Church, only an agent for the preservation of *Romania,* with all its classical and pagan tradition. The facts, however, demand a far different interpretation. The simplification of Latin was another indication of the cultural decline that had long been going on; Caesarius and the others wrote in simple language, because of the great increase in the illiteracy of the people they served. . . .

Finally, Pirenne's method leads to difficulties in his account of Italo-Byzantine relations, chiefly in the age of Justinian. According to Pirenne, the separation of East and West and the alliance of pope and northern peoples were also products of the Moslem expansion. There was unquestionably some connection, but here again an extremely complex series of developments and relationships is oversimplified and, in the process, distorted. As elsewhere, Pirenne tends to slight the theological history of a time when theology not only affected matters of economics, education, ecclesiastical organization, and even art, but often played a decisive role in the making of domestic and foreign policy. It has already been pointed out that Gregory the Great, rather than the popes of the eighth century, began the work of attaching the northern peoples to the Roman Church, and that the Lombards as well as the Moslems may have had something to do with separating East and West. As for the secular character of the Germanic rulers before the Islamic expansion, a matter Pirenne made much of, it is true that the early Germanic kings, like the Byzantine emperors, interfered in ecclesiastical affairs. So, however, did later medieval rulers, and Philip the Fair was far from the earliest of them.

Too little has been made in Pirenne's pages of Justinian's careful negotiations with the papacy for the settlement of the Acacian Schism and his failure to placate the Monophysites. Again, Justinian's later intervention and theological failure to win over the fiercely dissident elements of Syria and Egypt contributed to the rapid success of Islam in those regions; surely the theological background of Eastern hostility to Byzantium deserved some study.

It is also highly doubtful that the "Byzantinization" of the West would have gone ahead on schedule, as anticipated by Pirenne, save for the rude interruption of the Saracens. In this connection the historical meaning of Justinian's Reconquest is a matter of the first consequence. Pirenne granted that it cost the emperor dear in his struggles against the Persians and Slavs, but nevertheless judged it a policy corresponding to "the Mediterranean spirit of all European civilization from the fifth to the seventh century." It would be more aptly described as shortsighted. Not only did it cost heavily in men and money, and also in the commercial sources of money, but it also contributed to Eastern resentment against Greco-Roman rule from Constantinople. Did the emperor act in response to Pirenne's "Mediterranean spirit" or to a fantastic dream of empire? Whatever the answer, at that time the Slavs, Bulgars, Huns, Avars, and Persians profited most heavily from the ill-conceived venture. Justinian has been described as "a colossal Janus bestriding the way of passage between the ancient and medieval worlds," one face turned toward the past and the other toward the future. This is an excellent description, though it is unfortunate for the emperor's reputation that he erred so often, both as a worshiper of the past in what he tried to preserve or restore and as an innovator in what he misprized and blighted.

In West as well as East the Reconquest had consequences of vast moment, though not what Justinian envisioned or Pirenne believed them to be. In Africa the decadent Vandal power was replaced by a Byzantine rule too feeble to stem the Saracenic advance. In Spain only a strip of coast was won, but the Visigoths were weakened enough to make them easy victims of the oncoming Moslems. The Franks were affected too, though indirectly; they were enabled to take over Provence from the Ostrogoths. In Italy the Byzantine armies finally succeeded in destroying the Ostrogothic kingdom, but at high cost; the peninsula was devastated, the population still further reduced, and the way prepared for the Lombard invasion. In short, the Reconquest backfired. Justinian succeeded in destroying the Ostrogoths and Vandals and weakening the Visigoths, but only to make the way easier for other and more dangerous enemies, the Arabs and Lombards and, to a degree, the Franks.

It must be granted also that the emperor seriously undermined his position by his concessions to the Persians, Slavs, and Mongols, by his vast expenditures, and by the antagonism he stirred among his Oriental subjects. The Reconquest, together with the emperor's religious policy, left both East and West much weaker than in the time of Anastasius I and Justin I. It might be suggested that if Charlemagne is inconceivable without Mohammed, Mohammed is inconceivable without Justinian. Such formulas are often more striking than useful, however, and it would be preferable merely to say that there was a great deal of history involved in making Mohammed, just as there was in making Charlemagne. In the period under observation the history of the West was closely connected with that of the East; and to be understood, the two have to be examined together. That the Byzantinization of the West would have continued, had it not been for the Saracenic interruption, is unlikely. Not even Justinian could bring back to life what was dead. He could not conquer the Western half of the Roman Empire, for it no longer existed; he could not restore, by Byzantinization or any other means, a civilization that was gone. East and West were no longer what they had been, either in themselves or in their relationship to each other. With reference to this point, it is significant that a Latin-speaking emperor of Illyrian peasant origin, ruling in the East, could dispute possession of Italy with its barbarian masters. That his own armies were composed of "barbarians more savage than the Goths" makes the point indelibly clear.

Perhaps Pirenne's worst blind spot in examining the five centuries before Charlemagne was his inability to discern in that difficult time the beginnings of a new civilization. Gibbon's famous remark that he had described the "triumph of Barbarism and Religion" made a strong dramatic appeal, as the tough old age it has now reached clearly demonstrates. Pope's uncharitable line that "the monks finished what the Goths begun" makes the same point. The familiar terms "Spätantike," "Bas-Empire," and "Later Roman Empire" clearly imply that civilization was coming to an end and night was soon to fall. In essence, Pirenne followed the traditional path, adding only the new twist of his "Mediterranean unity" theory and his insistence upon an economic cause for the end of *Romania,* and with it the end of absolute, secular, financially independent government.

It remained to account somehow for the far-reaching changes in Roman society, the persistent and successful invasions of the West by small bands of barbarians, and the tremendous upsurge in the Church's prestige and power after Constantine. Pirenne disposed of the Germans as noted above, by contending that they effected no change, with the implication that consequently no change occurred. He admitted decadence in the old Roman rule but maintained that it was still Roman and in the old secular way still dominated the Church. More will be said later about all three of these subjects, but particular attention must be called here to Pirenne's astonishing failure to recognize the immense historical significance of the Christian religion in the conditions prevailing in Western Europe in this period. The history of Western Europe from about A.D. 300 to 600 can only be understood as a whole composed of two parts, each essential to the other: (a) Christianity, and (b) the more or less gradual breakdown of the Roman local government and economy, the increasing self-sufficiency of an agrarian society, the oft-renewed disorder created by repeated invasions. The new society was not the product of invasion, experiment, and readjustment alone, nor was it the creation of Christianity alone; the two had to work together to produce it.

Pirenne failed to perceive plainly and to assess realistically the newly rising society for the same basic reason as Gibbon and most of his successors: he was blinded by the magic of the Roman name. Historical writing on the Later Roman Empire, even the most recent, is full of such terms as "a breathing space was granted," "a respite was gained," "the foundations of civilization were shored up," "the disaster [of invasion] was postponed." Only too rarely is it suggested that, possibly, what was crumbling away was beyond repair, indeed was not worth repairing and had never been all that these laments imply. Contrary to the traditional view that the collapse of Roman civilization in the West was a catastrophe, and that the fourth and later centuries were admirable primarily to the extent that they retained Roman influences, very nearly the opposite is true. The breakdown here simply betokened the collapse of machinery which could no longer perform even the modest functions imposed upon it. It was the end of an experiment that failed, and this failure left the way open for a new experiment with new creative forces. True, certain bequests of classical antiquity served the new world well; they were valuable, however, not in themselves as survivals of a civilization that had ceased to civilize, but as useful adjuncts to a new culture. The best of the noble Greco-Roman accomplishment was not lost. "If it die, it bringeth forth much fruit" would not be an inappropriate epitaph for the doomed civilization.

It must be conceded that the circumstances in which the new civilization began its rise were far from imposing. Compared with the poverty and disorder of the post-invasion period, Roman or perhaps even Babylonian society might seem advanced. The comparison would be unfair to the oncoming civilization, however, if it did not go on to consider the possibilities latent in the new West. In a strange, indirect way the backward conditions of its origin proved useful to the Western Europe to come. If it had not been divided, inefficiently governed, and poor, the influence of Christianity could not have been exerted freely and extensively. As will be brought out later, the early medieval society was a pioneer society living on a frontier, both geographical and intellectual, and engaged in advancing it. It is remarkable that historians of the West should so long have failed to apprehend this absolutely vital truth about the origins of their own tradition.

Perhaps the objection to Pirenne's slighting of the place of Christianity in this constructive process may be best expressed in this way: that there is more than one kind of economic causation, and that religious and economic vitality are not mutually exclusive. To say that the medieval Church occupied a leading position, in part because of the social backwardness of the time, is not to say that its influence was always and everywhere overwhelming and that there were no motives, interests, or activities except those inspired by religion; then, as in other times, men, even churchmen, were not always true to their principles, and the Church did not always win out in its struggles with secular forces. What is important, and what Pirenne failed to acknowledge, is that the Church was powerful enough to win most of its battles and to play a part in many events that were not, strictly speaking, its concern; and above all, that in the fourth and fifth centuries, when the classical spirit was almost dead in the West, along with the Roman form of political administration and much of the rest of the old social system, the Christian spirit that was to create a new civilization was full of life and hope and confidence.

Bryce Lyon

HISTORICAL REALITY

The "biographical and intellectual study" from which this excerpt is taken is the most recent and most significant of the many contributions of Professor Bryce Lyon to the study of Pirenne. In the second edition of The Pirenne Thesis *was included a selection from his important article "L'oeuvre of Henri Pirenne aprés vint-cinq ans,"* Le Moyen Age 66 (1960): 473–91. *Other studies are referred to in the Suggestions for Additional Reading at the end of this book. He now has in press Pirenne's war diary, written while Pirenne was a German prisoner, 1916–1918; this will appear as Pirenne's* Journal de Guerre *and will be published by La Commission Royale d'Histoire de Belgique.*

Active in other areas of medieval history as well, Professor Lyon has in progress a revision of his A Constitutional and Legal History of Medieval England. *Since 1965 he has been Keeney Professor of Medieval History at Brown University.*

Pirenne's theory is provocative. It postpones the end of the ancient world in the West until the eighth century and hinges imperial survival and, with it, Graeco-Roman civilization upon control of the Mediterranean. If valid, it nullifies most previous explanations or debilitates their strongest arguments. Controversial and dramatic, it stunned, provoked, or excited historians and refocused the attention of numerous medievalists on this important period of transition. Pirenne forced historians to reexamine the whole problem and to question the conceptual framework that had dominated historical thinking since the Renaissance. Spurred to research and writing by this unorthodox theory, historians ever since have been busily appraising it; few historical theories of the nineteenth and twentieth centuries have aroused more interest or caused more debate.

What is the present status of this last celebrated theory of Pirenne? Most historians are now convinced that the German conquests were not a sudden catastrophe for western Europe, abruptly ending classical civilization, and introducing centuries of "Gothic barbarism," but many have refused to change their chronology, holding firmly to the fourth and fifth centuries as the beginning of the Middle Ages, even though conceding that fragments of classical civilization survived the Germans' entry into the empire, and labeling

From Bryce Lyon, *Henri Pirenne: A Biographical and Intellectual Study* (Ghent, 1974), pp. 446–456. By permission of E. Story-Scientia P.V.B.A. and the author.

these and the following two centuries a sort of *Uebergangszone* (transitional period) that saw the Germans introduce new concepts which transformed political institutions, the law, classical thought, and the Christian church, and which wrought fundamental cultural and psychological changes. Other historians, especially classical, still defend the traditional explanation, with one insisting that the sack of Rome in 410 by Alaric "spelt the fall of the Empire; it even meant the end of the world." Another group of historians continues to discount the impact of the Germans, arguing that from the second through the fourth century social, economic, political, and cultural decline was so serious that by the fifth century the empire in the West and its civilization had virtually disappeared and the Germans, therefore, merely occupied a hulk. One scholar has concluded in respect to the early medieval agrarian economy that "the rural bases of the western economy were the product of a very ancient history."

Because Pirenne rested his theory upon the unity of the Mediterranean, a unity that sustained the economy of the ancient world, he was less concerned with cultural and religious history, thereby becoming vulnerable to the charge of neglecting vital cultural and spiritual change as a reason for decline. Those critical of Pirenne on this score paint a decline of classical literature and art, an abandonment of pagan gods and philosophy, and an aridity of creative endeavor that combined to make the fourth and fifth centuries a watershed and produced a mentality and spiritual outlook which nurtured those qualities associated with the medieval mind. Perhaps Pirenne was not enough attentive to cultural and religious history, but in seeing a progressive cultural and intellectual decline from the late imperial period to the ninth century he was more correct than some intellectual historians who attribute a dynamic and creative character to this period.

Economic and institutional historians, in agreement with Pirenne on the continuity of Roman institutions, differ with him over the degree and chronology of continuity. Some, like Dopsch, see a thread of continuity from the late imperial period to the economic revival of the eleventh century, while Pirenne believed that continuity ended with the Arab conquests around the Mediterranean during the seventh and eighth centuries. Whereas Pirenne considered the Carolingian period as the lowest point in the western economy prior to the revival in the eleventh century, Dopsch and others saw in it signs of economic improvement, especially during the reign of Charlemagne when there was virtually an economic renaissance. Other adherents of continuity such as Latouche differ with both Pirenne and Dopsch in regarding the Merovingian period as a time when continuity came closest to being snapped and as an indication of the serious consequences of the German conquests, "of the inertia of the western peoples and of the stagnation of their economic life."[1] Differing with Pirenne in arguing that the Carolingian period saw a temporary restoration of the western economy, Latouche, however, agreed with Pirenne that the Viking raids and invasions of the ninth century were a severe but temporary disruption because the Vikings soon ceased their raids and piracy and used their exceptional seafaring ability to stimulate the northern economy.

But why in general have the interpretations of Pirenne, Dopsch, and Latouche so sharply differed? Why should Pirenne, a moderate Romanist, disagree in many respects with the more committed Romanists Dopsch and Latouche when all three studied the same evidence? Why are their views of the Merovingian and Carolingian economies so widely divergent? Some historians, as we have seen, convinced that the economy of the empire in the West had so disastrously declined that an agrarian economy prevailed before the Merovingian period, would consider this question superfluous. But many others, while convinced of its validity, believe it cannot be answered without intensive, almost minute study of the economic evidence of the Merovingian and Carolingian periods to see how much trade there actually was in the two periods.

Some historians have concluded that in the Merovingian period trade relations did not continue, that Pirenne exaggerated what little evidence there is. Others, ignoring the Merovingian period and concentrating upon the Carolingian, have also concluded that Pirenne exaggerated, this time painting too dreary a picture of the consequences of the Arab conquests for western Europe. What emerges from the bulk of their research is that trade did indeed continue on the Mediterranean between East and West, that it existed on the North and Baltic seas and northern inland waterways, and that it reached east into Russia where it linked up with routes going to Constantinople. There is also the conviction among some of these historians that Arab domination of the Mediterranean was never as complete as Pirenne thought, that Byzantium, retaining control of the

[1] *Birth of Western Economy* (London, 1961), p. 123.

eastern Mediterranean, was able to implement an economic policy aimed at a monopoly over trade with both the Arab lands and with Italy where she still had some possessions. She was, in a sense, the middleman of the Mediterranean determining what goods flowed from the East to the West and she did not favor trade that drained her gold reserves outside her monetary zone located in the eastern Mediterranean. This explains, so the argument runs, why the flow of eastern goods to the West was reduced to a trickle, why Pirenne found so few eastern goods coming immediately from the Arabs or western products going directly to them. Some Arabic specialists, however, have examined the evidence and concluded that there is no reason why Arabs and Christians should not have traded while others believe that the Arab conquests even stimulated the western economy. In either case Pirenne, they affirm, was wrong to see a barrier between western Christendom and Islam. Countering this opinion, the research of a considerable number of historians substantially corroborates Pirenne's conclusions. If the results of research on this problem are not conclusive, it is because the evidence is meager and cryptic. As one historian declares, "All that we know of the social conditions of the time suggests that the alternatives to trade were more important than trade itself: the *onus probandi* rests on those who believe the contrary to have been the case."[2]

The effort of numismatists to obtain a fuller picture of economic relations between western Europe and Arab lands by scrupulously examining various coin hoards have also been inconclusive. Some believe that from the vast quantities of crude gold which they controlled, the Arabs struck their famous gold dinars and then poured them into the West in return for slaves and raw materials such as wood and furs with the result that this influx of gold into western Europe abetted the recovery and resurgence of the western economy. Others believe to have found a correlation between Carolingian silver coinage and the silver and gold coinage of the Arabs which, they contend, proves that regular trade relations existed, while still others see little evidence of trade relations. Some numismatists have concluded that a long-term adverse balance of trade between East and West caused a hemorrhage of gold eastward during the last centuries of the Roman Empire which continued for the next two or three centuries, and that therefore the agrarian economy that pre-

[2] Philip Grierson, "Commerce in the Dark Ages: A Critique of the Evidence," *Transactions of the Royal Historical Society* 9 (1959): 140.

vailed in western Europe by the eighth century was not produced by the Arab conquests but was simply a consummation of a long trend. Such conflicting results should warn the economic historian to use numismatic evidence from the early Middle Ages with caution because it seldom tells him anything certain about trade routes or about the volume of trade. A recent study of Carolingian coinage emphasizes that there is "no numismatic evidence of extensive contact with peoples outside the Carolingian empire" and that written sources support this conclusion.[3] It is obvious that the evidence of coins, like the written evidence for this period, is extremely difficult to interpret.

Finally, in the view of some economic historians Pirenne and his critics have generalized too much from too little data. Economists see very little economic activity between the fifth and eleventh century. There was, some contend, no investment of capital in instruments of production, production of goods was low, consumption was limited, communications were hazardous and irregular, monetary circulation was weak, and the balance of trade with the East was so unfavorable as to cause a chronic deficit and descending demographic curve. These observations lend credence to the assertion that in this long interim the economy was inactive or severely depressed, that there was steady decline accelerated by the Arab conquests around the Mediterranean, and that the period between the fourth and eighth centuries saw the end of one world and the genesis of another.

Is there any validity, then, to Pirenne's theory? As we have seen, much of the subsequent research has weakened his thesis. He obviously overemphasized Merovingian economic activity and its continuity with the Roman, and may have underemphasized Carolingian economic activity. He seems also to have assigned to the Arabs too decisive a role in the destruction of Mediterranean economic unity and, consequently, in the emergence of the Middle Ages. His treatment of politics and institutions is victim to the same weaknesses as his interpretation of economic and social history—overemphasis regarding the continuity of Roman institutions in the Germanic kingdoms and some delusion in believing that the German chiefs took the Roman emperors as models. Although correct in stressing the exclusively secular bases of German political authority prior to Char-

---

[3] Karl F. Morrison, "Numismatics and Carolingian Trade: A Critique of the Evidence," *Speculum* 38 (1963): 432. See also his *Carolingian Coinage* (New York, 1967).

lemagne and his father Pepin, Pirenne perhaps attributed too much
to the spiritual sanction of secular authority given by the church. It is
true that his bent toward social and economic causation caused him
to slight the cultural and religious differences separating the ancient
from the medieval world or to place such differences out of focus as
in distorting Theodoric's love of classical culture and his patronage of
such as Boethius and Cassiodorus. Undoubtedly there was more
religious and educational reform and more cultural achievement in
the so-called Carolingian renaissance than Pirenne admits, but not in
the inflated proportion that many historians would have it. Like most
theories concerned with the explanation of vast historical transformations, Pirenne's suffers from over- and understatement, gen-
eralizes at times upon evidence too scant and cryptic, and explicates
too much from certain types of evidence. Later research suggests
that the Carolingian and post-Carolingian periods were not as dark
socially and economically as Pirenne portrayed.

But Pirenne's theory has by no means been completely dis-
credited. Scholars in cultural and religious history with their subjec-
tive evaluations continue to agree or disagree with Pirenne, continue
to under- and overemphasize the cultural vigor of the Merovingian
and Carolingian periods and to distort Christian influence on pagan
thought. Some see St. Augustine imbibing in classical thought.
Others see him at its fringes, sabotaging it and preparing the way for
a completely new view of man and his use of knowledge. Some see
Pope Gregory the Great as a competent continuator of good Latin
and an admirer of the classical tradition. Others point to his simple
Latin compositions, seeing him as epitomizing the difference between sophisticated, rational, classical thought and simple, mystical,
Christian thought. Christopher Dawson in his fine cultural and religious study of early medieval Europe has come to conclusions that
parallel those of Pirenne. He attached great significance to the Arab
conquests of the seventh century, asserting that "it is in the seventh
century, and not in the fifth, that we must place the end of the last
phase of ancient Mediterranean civilization—the age of the Christian
empire—and the beginnings of the Middle Ages."[4] Like Pirenne, he
interpreted the coronation of Charlemagne in 800 as inaugurating a
new age because it brought final fusion of the classical, the Christian, and the Germanic elements that were to become the base of

[4] *The Making of Europe* (London, 1932), p. 136.

medieval western civilization. Henceforth, Dawson contended, culture regarded as typically western and European was to arise in the north between the Loire and Rhine rivers. Pierre Riché's more recent study of education and culture in the barbarian West has also confirmed the main lines of Pirenne's interpretation of the cultural and religious transition from the ancient to the medieval world. Like Pirenne, Riché sees a transformation in education and thought during the late imperial period that was even given impetus with the advent of the Germans. In spite of the decline of classical culture and its conversion to serve Christian truth, he believes that the aristocratic contemporaries of the Merovingians Chilperic and Dagobert still lived in an antique atmosphere, that Merovingian Gaul remained a part of the Mediterranean cultural community into the first half of the seventh century, and that not until the second half of that century did cultured men become scarce and barbarism sweep over the West. By Charlemagne's time Roman education and thought were dead in western Europe.

Some historians have found Pirenne deficient in his analysis of the evidence but most, except perhaps classical historians, admit that his large picture or synthesis has credibility. He was, after all, not the first historian to perceive that after the empire in the West no longer existed politically some features of its civilization continued. He did not deny that during the third and fourth centuries political disintegration, social and economic misfortunes, cultural malaise, and a profound shift in religious values occurred, but he did not believe that they alone ended Graeco-Roman civilization. Despite the German conquests with their turmoil and new political arrangements, no new civilization arose because the Germans were generally willing to partake of the Mediterranean civilization and the unity upon which it depended. What impressed Pirenne was how much all this had changed in the West by the time of the Carolingians. He noticed that after 600 Italy lay prostrate with the Ostrogothic kingdom destroyed by Justinian's unfortunate attempt to reconquer the West; that all the lands ringing the Mediterranean, except for some in southern Europe, were under Arab dominion; and that the Carolingian state was oriented northward rather than southward to the Mediterranean with its center lying between the Loire and the Rhine. He sensed also that there was much less trade, especially on the Mediterranean, that few real towns existed, that the economy was much more agrarian, and that culturally Europe was relatively barren. But why had such change come after 600? For Pirenne the logical reason was the Arab conquest of the Mediterranean, which made it a barrier rather than a boulevard for East-West exchanges, causing the orbit of power in the East to shift to Bagdad and in the West, to the north. This transformation isolated western Europe and presaged seignorialism, feudalism, and the domination of the church, all of which were consecrated by the coronation of Charlemagne in 800.

Although giving the Arabs too decisive a part in this change, Pirenne was the first to understand that they had exercised a profound influence upon the Mediterranean and the West. In comparing the culture of the Arab lands with that of the West, he saw an impoverished and underdeveloped West facing in the East a thriving, creative culture rooted in a money economy. This picture was little changed until the West revived and pushed its way back into the Mediterranean during the eleventh century, a push climaxed by the First Crusade. For the first time in centuries the West again traded on the Mediterranean and established regular contacts with the East. Without this development the extraordinary achievements of the twelfth and thirteenth centuries would have been inconceivable. One may fault Pirenne for his details, but in terms of western history his synthesis is both credible and imaginative. Its hypotheses account for the relative darkness of the early Middle Ages and for the recovery and vigorous achievements of western Europe in the High Middle Ages. By placing in better perspective those centuries between 400 and 1000 that had been ignored by classical historians and slighted by medievalists, he dramatically reminded historians that in this period lie the answers to the uniqueness of western history. Historiographically he did even more. He delivered medievalists from Gibbon's spell by forcing them to acknowledge that they must repudiate much of what Gibbon had argued, and that this meant reexamination of a historiographical tradition dating back to the Renaissance. For this reason alone *Mahomet et Charlemagne* ranks among the historical classics. It compels every scholar of the Middle Ages to wrestle with its concepts because within their framework rests a truer understanding and appreciation of the Middle Ages. It may well be that what Gibbon referred to as the world's great debate will never end because we lack the evidence for a real solution. But as yet Pirenne's theory, though revised, has not been replaced by any other more credible or convincing on the enigma of the end of the ancient world and the beginning of the Middle Ages.

Suggestions for Additional Reading

In reaching beyond the selections in this volume to the extensive bibliography on Pirenne which has accumulated in the past half century one encounters two difficulties. In the first place, so wide are the ramifications of the Pirenne thesis that sooner or later all aspects of the Mediterranean world and of society in western Europe from 400 to 900 are encountered. In the second place much of the commentary is by historians of French, German, Belgian, or Scandinavian nationality, and is found only in specialized periodicals not available in the average college library. However, it is not difficult to single out representative books and articles, and the issues are so interrelated that any significant discussion is likely to cite a considerable portion of the bibliography, including contemporary source material, interpretation of which constitutes so much of the controversy. The sources may be readily studied because their number is limited, as recourse to a standard collection, Robert S. Lopez and Irving Raymond,* *Medieval Trade in the Mediterranean World* (New York, 1955) will reveal.

But any and all bibliographical problems will now be handled more quickly and more satisfactorily with the guidance in Bryce Lyon, *Henri Pirenne: A Biographical and Intellectual Study* (Ghent, 1974). Lyon's detailed examination of Pirenne's "life and intellectual achievements," the product of a dozen years of study and research, rests largely on archival collections in the possession of Pirenne's son, Count Jacques Pirenne. A considerable portion of this collection is in *Henri Pirenne, Hommages et souvenirs* (2 vols.; Brussels, 1938). A personal memoir is found in Jacques Pirenne, "Henri Pirenne, mon père," *Revue Générale Belge* (1962), pp. 21–35. Other short sketches, with interesting detail, are in James L. Cate, "Henri Pirenne, 1862–1935," in *Some 20th Century Historians,* ed. S. William Halperin (Chicago, 1961), pp. 1–29, and in Charles Verlinden, "Henri Pirenne," in *Architects and Craftsmen in History* (Tübingen, 1956), pp. 85–100.

Pirenne's own bibliography—his books and his articles—will be found, complete, in *Hommages et Souvenirs,* vol. I; but it will be much more readily accessible in Lyon's *Henri Pirenne* which contains references to nearly all of Pirenne's writing. For works on Pirenne see also Lyon's* *Origins of the Middle Ages* (New York, 1962), pp.

* Titles available in paperback are asterisked.

88–94. A short bibliography of the more important titles by Pirenne and items about him is provided in a useful brochure: Georges Gérardy,* *Henri Pirenne, sa vie et son oeuvre* (Belgian Ministry of National Education and Culture, Brussels, 1962), pp. 9–14. Of Pirenne's own writings, in addition to the titles excerpted in this volume, the most useful for studying the Pirenne thesis are: *Les anciennes démocraties des Pays-Bas* (Paris, 1910), first translated into English as *Belgian Democracy: Its Early History* (Manchester, 1915), available in paperback as *Early Democracies in the Low Countries** (Harper & Row Torchbook, New York, 1963); *Histoire économique et sociale du moyen âge . . . avec une annexe bibliographique et critique,* ed. Hans van Werveke (rev. ed.; Paris, 1969), in English as *Economic and Social History of Medieval Europe,** (London, 1936, and paperback, New York, 1937); *Histoire de l'Europe des invasions au XVIe siècle* (Paris, 1936), in English as *A History of Europe from the End of the Roman World to the Beginnings of the Western States** (London, 1939 and paperback, New York, 1958, 2 vols.)—a book written in German prison camps during World War I without benefit of notes or scholarly books. The last two titles incorporate in essence the Pirenne thesis, and together with a full reading of *Medieval Cities: Their Origin and the Revival of Trade** and *Mohammed and Charlemagne** will supply all that Pirenne had to say. *Medieval Cities* should be read in the translation by Frank D. Halsey, or, if possible, in the French edition, *Les villes du moyen âge: Essai d'histoire économique et sociale* (Brussels, 1927), which is more fully annotated. Likewise, *Mahomet et Charlemagne* (Brussels, 1937) provides a more exact text.

The student is advised to study the problem at the outset in conjunction with a standard text of the period to establish the status of Pirenne's ideas. Useful for this purpose is R. H. C. Davis, *A History of Medieval Europe* (2nd ed.; London, 1968); there is also Gerald A. J. Hodgett, *A Social and Economic History of Medieval Europe* (London, 1972), which is abreast of the latest scholarship. It is then interesting to examine a work published before *Mahomet et Charlemagne* appeared. H. St. L. B. Moss,* *The Birth of the Middle Ages, 395–814* (London, 1935) discusses at length the "Onslaught of Islam" without reference to *Medieval Cities*. Another interesting comparison is afforded by Ferdinand Lot,* *The End of the Ancient World and the Beginnings of the Middle Ages* (New York, 1931), first published in French in 1927. Pirenne and Lot influenced one another. If more detailed information on political and religious history is required the student will be rewarded by examining the somewhat forbidding-looking volumes of the *Cambridge Medieval History.*

The background of the Pirenne thesis is Roman, Germanic, Arabic. A brief but effective presentation of the barbarian invasions is found in J. M. Wallace-Hadrill,* *The Barbarian West, A.D. 400–1000* (New York, Harper & Row Torchbook, 1952). A massive treatment is in A. H. M. Jones, *The Later Roman Empire, 284–602: A Social, Economic and Administrative Survey* (3 vols.; Oxford, 1964), but with no reference whatsoever to the ideas of Pirenne—Jones assumes that the Roman world ended in the West in the fifth century.

For Islam and the Arabs the writings of Philip K. Hitti, long associated with Princeton University, provide ample material. His *The Arabs: A Short History** (5th ed.: New York, 1968) is a successful compression of a much longer work, *History of the Arabs: From the Earliest Times to the Present** (10th ed.; New York, 1970). A brief but excellent account of Arab expansion is found in Bernard Lewis,* *The Arabs in History* (London, 1950). For the Eastern Roman Empire, a good introduction is provided in J. M. Hussey,* *The Byzantine World* (London, 1958). Abreast of the latest scholarship is George Ostrogorsky, *History of the Byzantine State* (rev. ed.; New Brunswick, N.J., 1969). A meticulous presentation is in *Cambridge Medieval History*, vol. IV, *The Byzantine Empire* (new ed.; 2 parts; Cambridge, 1966–1967). Valuable and fascinating essays are in Norman H. Baynes and H. St. L. B. Moss, eds.,* *Byzantium: An Introduction to East Roman Civilization* (Oxford, 1948).

For further analysis, criticism and revision of the Pirenne thesis there is an abundance of scholarly and readable material. For competent examination of the issues, briefly examined, there is Sidney R. Packard,* *The Process of Historical Revision: New Viewpoints in Medieval European History* (Northampton, Mass., 1962), and Bryce Lyon,* *The Middle Ages in Recent Historical Thought* (2nd ed.; Washington, D.C., 1965). It is worthwhile comparing two earlier assessments—an effective defense of Pirenne in Pierre Lambrechts, "Les thèses de Henri Pirenne sur la fin du monde antique et les débuts du moyen âge," *Byzantion* 14 (1939): 513–36, and Anne Riising, "The Fate of Henri Pirenne's Theses on the Consequences of the Islamic Expansion," *Classica et Mediaevalia* 13 (1952): 87–130. By 1960 we have two important assessments representative of the controversy at that time. Bryce Lyon provides detail and complete documentation in his "L'oeuvre de Henri Pirenne après ving-cinq ans," *Le Moyen Age* 66 (1960): 437–93. William C. Bark,* *Origins of the Medieval World* (Stanford, Cal., 1958) in Chapter 2 examines point-by-point Pirenne's arguments in *Mahomet et Charlemagne,* and Bark's bibliographical notes are as valuable as his text. Lyon's latest judgments are in his *Henri Pirenne* (1974). Extensive extracts from both Bark and Lyon are reprinted above in this book. It would be highly profitable for the advanced student to make his own synthesis and then compare it with Lyon's analysis, tending to support Pirenne, and with Bark's, generally rejecting Pirenne.

On the recurring theme of the relation of the Merovingian era to the Carolingian, Pirenne, back in 1923, elaborated his theory in "Un contraste économique: Mérovingiens et Carolingiens," *Revue Belge de Philologie et d'Histoire* 2 (1923): 223–35. The celebrated Austrian historian, Alfons Dopsch (1868–1953) held to the notion of unbroken cultural continuity from the later Roman Empire through the Merovingian and Carolingian periods. His position, which should be studied with caution, will be found in his *The Economic and Social Foundations of his European Civilization* (London, 1937), originally published in German (2 vols.; Vienna, 1923–1924). The Dopsch interpretation, with modifications, was later elaborated by Robert Latouche in his *The Birth of Western Economy** (London, 1961).

On particular issues the student should consult at once the detailed bibliographies already indicated. On medieval trade—perhaps the most strongly contested issue—nearly every scholar has had his say. The selections in this book can be quickly augmented. There are the extraordinary articles of Maurice Lombard, particularly his "Mahomet et Charlemagne: Le probleme économique," *Les Annales d'Histoire Économique et Sociale* 2 (1948): 188–99. In his *Naval Power and Trade in the Mediterranean, A.D. 500–1100* (Princeton, 1951), Archibald R. Lewis develops the position that the Byzantine state destroyed Carolingian trade.

Lewis and other historians (notably Sture Bolin and Howard L. Adelson) have depended heavily on evidence from numismatics. For example, see A. R. Lewis, *The Northern Seas: Shipping and Commerce in Northern Europe, A.D. 300–1100* (Princeton, 1958). Bolin's important article, from which we have taken a substantial extract, was the basis for E. Perroy, "Encore Mahomet et Charlemagne," *Revue Historique* 212 (1954): 232–38. Adelson supports Pirenne's view that a basic unity remained in the Mediterranean until the mid-seventh century, after which the Arab expansion severely cut the Byzantine gold supply, thus reducing her trade in the West. See his *Light Weight Solidi and Byzantine Trade during the Sixth and Seventh Centuries* (New York, 1957). But these works should be read with some caution, for the use of coins and coin finds has in turn come in for criticism. Philip Grierson, in the selection in this volume, called for reexamination of the evidence. This Grierson himself has done in "The Monetary Reforms of Abd-Al-Malik," *Journal of Economic and Social History of the Orient* 3 (1960): 241–64. One should also consult an impressive article with an exhaustive bibliography: Karl F. Morrison, "Numismatics and Carolingian Trade: A Critique of the Evidence," *Speculum* 38 (July 1963): 403–32. He concludes: "Numismatic remains reveal much to the numismatic historian; but the economic historian must consult them critically and with great caution."

In the past few years there has been a lull in scholarship directly related to Pirenne. But, like Gibbon, Pirenne will be studied and restudied, as the presuppositions of historians change. Very likely Pirenne's influence in the future will in part be that of stimulating hypotheses that run counter to his own. Of this we already have examples. William C. Bark* (*Origins of the Medieval World*), after challenging Pirenne, developed his own position that the period 300–600 was a creative age, breaking decisively with pagan classical civilization. Likewise, Lynn White Jr.* in *Medieval Technology and Social Change* (Oxford, 1962) and in *The Transformation of the Roman World: Gibbon's Problem after Two Centuries* (Berkeley, 1966) put aside Pirenne's notion of stagnation in the Carolingian era and pursued his own thesis of an agricultural revolution that shifted Europe's focus from the Mediterranean to the northern plains. Both Bark and White merit reading beyond the selections reprinted in this book.

1 2 3 4 5 6 7 8 9